The growth of economic knowledge in the last two or three decades has not led to any greater agreement regarding its vital applications to public policy. Perhaps there is even less agreement on certain crucial questions of the relationship between economics and political values or ideologies. For example, flatly contradictory views are authoritatively expressed as to whether—to cite recent authoritative statements—economics 'is in principle independent of any particular ethical position', or whether, on the other hand, 'a disinterested social science never has existed', or whether 'hardly any economic theory can be considered ideologically neutral'.

How such questions are answered is of fundamental importance if economic knowledge is to play an authoritative part in shaping policy and if we are to reach such agreement as is possible on economic theories. The spirited defence of the principle of *Wertfreiheit* has recently been called for (by Professor Haberler) as 'more necessary than ever'; that is a restatement of what has been for more than a century more or less the orthodox view. It is not exactly such a defence which this book tries to supply, but rather a thorough examination of the question, including its history, the present conflict of attitudes regarding it, and the confusions in current policy discussions for which these conflicting attitudes are more or less responsible.

'POSITIVE' ECONOMICS AND POLICY OBJECTIVES

'Positive' Economics
and
Policy Objectives

BY

T. W. HUTCHISON
Professor of Economics, University of Birmingham

'*Political influences on economic
studies are not always wholesome*'
ALFRED MARSHALL
(*Industry and Trade*, 1919, p. v)

HARVARD UNIVERSITY PRESS
CAMBRIDGE, MASSACHUSETTS
1964

PRINTED IN GREAT BRITAIN

To My Wife

ACKNOWLEDGMENTS

This work first began to take on some kind of shape when in the spring of 1960 I delivered four lectures at the Thomas Jefferson Center for Political Economy at the University of Virginia. It was then suggested that these lectures might be written up for publication. I am deeply grateful to the officers of the Center, Professor J. M. Buchanan and Professor Warren Nutter, and to the members of the Economics Department of the University of Virginia, for their valuable criticism and generous hospitality. I am very grateful, also, to Professor Johan Åkerman for helpful suggestions on the occasion of a most enjoyable visit to his seminar at the University of Lund in September 1960, when I read a paper on some of the questions discussed in this book. My thanks are also due to Professor Giersch and Professor Serf for a very pleasant and profitable stay at the University of Saarbrücken in the spring of 1962, during which I attended a conference of the *Verein für Sozialpolitik*, the forum half-a-century previously of some of Max Weber's most challenging pronouncements on '*Wertfreiheit*', and again discussing problems of the application of social and economic knowledge to policy.

I am specially and deeply indebted to Mr Kurt Klappholz of the London School of Economics. He read the typescript with great care and made many penetrating and helpful criticisms. I know I have benefited immensely from discussions with him, and it is entirely my fault if it is not apparent that this book has also benefited. I am also very grateful to Mr I. M. D. Little for constructive comments, especially on Part II, Chapter 2. The research fund of the Faculty of Commerce and Social Science of the University of Birmingham has assisted with typing expenses.

T.W.H.

CONTENTS

INTRODUCTION

'Paradoxically, the soft sciences that are still akin to an art benefit more from an explicit awareness of the canons of scientific method . . . than do the hard sciences, where doing what comes naturally will protect even a fool from gross methodological error.'

P. A. SAMUELSON
(*Problems of the American Economy*,
Stamp Memorial Lecture 1961, 1962, p. 21)

'More than other scientists, social scientists need to be self-conscious about their methodology.'

M. FRIEDMAN
(*Essays in Positive Economics*,
1953, p. 40)

'When the foundations of the theory are discussed in print, one gets the impression that the author is impatient—impatient to get on with the job of reaching ambiguous conclusions. A serious economist hardly likes to be caught at the trivial occupation of discussing foundations.'

I. M. D. LITTLE
(*A Critique of Welfare Economics*,
Second Edition, 1957, p. 4)

The growth of economic knowledge in the last two or three decades has not led to any greater agreement regarding its applications to public policy, or, at any rate, regarding certain crucial questions thereof. The question, or complex of questions, as to how far 'objective' knowledge, free of 'subjective' ethical or political presuppositions, ideological bias, or 'value-judgments', is possible of the social and economic world, may seem to be one of those perennial philosophical chestnuts which never seem to reach, or likely to reach, anything like a settled or agreed solution. However, even perennial philosophical chestnuts should perhaps be turned over from time to time. And in the last decade, as we shall see, what had developed over about a hundred years into more or less the orthodox, or near-orthodox, view on this question, has been challenged by a wave of sceptical criticism. A distinguished authority has recently stated that 'the spirited defence of the principle of *Wertfreiheit* is unfortunately nowadays more needed than ever despite Cairnes, Max Weber, Pigou, etc. . . .'.[1] It is not a spirited defence that I am trying to supply, simply a reasonably thorough discussion of the question. Anyhow, disagreement on this question, far from declining, seems recently rather to have been increasing in scope and intensity. At any rate, flatly contradictory views are authoritatively expressed. For example, Friedman has stated that 'economics can be, and in part is, a positive science. . . . Positive economics is in principle independent of any particular ethical position or normative judgments.'[2] Myrdal, on the other hand, insists that 'a "disinterested social science" never has existed, and for logical reasons cannot exist . . . our very concepts are value-loaded . . . they cannot be defined except in terms of political valuations.'[3] Smithies holds that 'hardly any economic theory can be considered ideologically neutral',[4] while Stigler remarks that 'it does not seem necessary to retread familiar ground to show that economics as a positive science is ethically— and therefore politically—neutral'.[5]

Possibly, if a thorough elucidation of these statements was carried out, the apparent gulf between them *might* turn out to be simply a minor difference of assumption or terminology. But it is difficult to tell how far this might be so, because these sweeping categorical pronouncements are usually thrown off as *obiter dicta*, in a preliminary paragraph or so, with no recognition of any need to argue them out, or that diametrically contradictory views are authoritatively held.

Schumpeter said as regards this subject that 'the epistemological problem in itself is neither very difficult nor very interesting and can be disposed of in a few words'.[6] This may be so, if 'the epistemological problem' is defined sufficiently narrowly, and certainly it *is* usually dismissed in a *very* few words by contemporary economists. Unfortunately, as we have seen, their few words are apt to be flatly contradictory.[7]

[1] G. Haberler, *American Economic Review*, March 1963, p. 145.
[2] *Essays in Positive Economics*, 1953, pp. 3–4.
[3] *Value in Social Theory*, edited by P. Streeten, 1958, p. 1.
[4] *Economics and Public Policy*, Brookings Lectures, 1954, 1955, p. 2.
[5] *Quarterly Journal of Economics*, November 1959, p. 522.
[6] *History of Economic Analysis*, 1954, p. 805. I must admit that about a quarter of a century ago I wrote on this subject that 'for scientists at any rate the controversy must be very nearly played out'. *The Significance and Basic Postulates of Economic Theory*, 1938, p. 154.
[7] Another fundamental question of the application of economics to policies on which flatly contradictory views are current, which are never (or hardly ever) argued out, and which we touch upon later (see below, Part I, Chapter 2, Section 8), is that of prediction. Jewkes, for example, rejects 'prediction as an activity proper to economic science', holding that 'the economist's claim to predictive authority must be false', while Friedman maintains that prediction

Does this matter very much? It certainly does to the methodologist or philosopher interested in 'light' as much as, or more than, 'fruit'. Perhaps it also matters a great deal to those mainly interested in 'fruit'. For although the question of political and ethical value-judgments and biased subjectivity in economics is something of a perennial philosophical conundrum, it is one that bears very closely on the 'fruit-bearing' potential of economics, or on its practical applications to policies. If the applications to public policy of economic theorizing are not to consist to a large extent of arraying rival political points of view in impressively persuasive pseudo-technical jargon, or if the discussion of policies by economists is to amount to something other than a clash of rival brands of political propaganda dressed up in esoteric patter, then an area of consensus, in some sense, or to some extent, 'objective', must be reached. Surely it is likely to be much more difficult to attain to such a reasonable area or degree of consensus about policies if there is no agreement, or even clarity, not merely as to just what value-premises and political and ethical presuppositions, if any, are being made, and if so, at just what points, but as to whether or how far they are necessary or in fact being inserted; or as to whether they are being brought in unnecessarily or even 'illegitimately'; or as to how far the economic theories being applied are politically neutral or free of subjective bias.

The practical application of economic knowledge to some extent hinges on these questions, to which, as we have seen, apparently completely contradictory answers are being authoritatively given. But again this might not matter practically—though it seems rather disconcerting intellectually—if a reasonable degree of consensus, and hence of objective status or 'authority', on policy issues, was generally being attained, or if the nature of such disagreements as persisted was sufficiently clear and delimited. But it hardly seems that this is the case.

Economists' differences over problems of theory, and still more of policies, have been perennial and proverbial: 'The differences of opinion among political economists have of late been a frequent subject of complaint,' wrote Malthus in 1827.[1] The vastly increased flow of empirical and statistical material in recent decades, might perhaps have been expected, by reducing the purely speculative element, to mitigate disagreements or to reduce their area. But this

is 'the ultimate goal' of economics as 'a positive science', and that 'theory is to be judged by its predictive power'. Again, it is not easy to say whether this clash of views is as fundamental as it appears to be on the surface. See Jewkes's lecture in *Economics and Public Policy*, Brookings lectures 1954, 1955, pp. 82–3, and Friedman's *Essays in Positive Economics*, 1953, pp. 7–8.

[1] T. R. Malthus, *Definitions in Political Economy*, 1827, p. VII.

hardly seems to have happened. Sir Robert Hall was surely not indulging in exaggeration or alarmism when in his presidential address to the Royal Economic Society (1959) he described as 'disturbing . . . the fact of the very wide differences of opinion which appear to exist between economists on quite fundamental aspects of policy'.[1] What would be, and indeed is, particularly disturbing is lack of clarity as to the precise nature of the differences, or as to what kind of issues they precisely turn on.

It is usual to try to analyse economists' differences over policies by applying the dichotomy between 'positive' differences as to the predicted effects of policies, and 'normative' differences as to the *desiderata* or objectives of policies, the latter depending on differing political or ethical value-judgments. 'Even if philosophers are agreed as to facts,' wrote J. N. Keynes, 'they may still arrive at contrary solutions . . . because they differ as to the true ideal of human society.'[2] Differences as to policy recommendations, that is, may stem either from differences over preference-functions or from differences over possibility-functions, from differences in beliefs or from differences in attitudes (or, of course, from both).

Incidentally, it is perhaps of some interest to note—though we do not suggest that much importance should be attached to this—that generalizations in terms of this dichotomy, as to the nature of economists' differences over economic policies, themselves show the widest divergence, or pretty complete disagreement as to the nature of the disagreements. For example, Friedman (1953) ventured

'the judgment that currently in the Western world, and especially in the United States, differences about economic policy among disinterested citizens derive predominantly from different predictions about the economic consequences of taking action—differences that in principle can be eliminated by the progress of positive economics—rather than fundamental differences in basic values'.[3]

But one might perhaps have hoped that if differences simply related to 'positive' hypotheses, with no uncritically held political or other attitudes behind them, shaping and stiffening them, a patient agreement to differ, pending further empirical evidence and testing, might *rather* more often have emerged, instead of a persistent and apparently irreconcilable maintenance of conflicting positions.

---

[1] *Economic Journal*, December 1959, p. 647.

[2] *The Scope and Method of Political Economy*, 1890, p. 52.

[3] *Essays in Positive Economics*, 1953, p. 5. We assume that the concept of 'disinterested citizens', which might be very differently defined, is not simply to be taken to cover those citizens who share a particular set of values—which might render Friedman's generalization more or less tautological.

Devons, however (1961), views differences over policy quite otherwise:

'Arguments between economists advocating one policy rather than another, can usually be explained more significantly in terms of politics rather than economics. They develop into unedifying slanging matches, in which each faction picks out those particular elements or that particular formulation of the problem which lead to the conclusion it favours.'[1]

Differences in time and place may to some extent explain the contrast between Friedman's and Devons's generalizations. For reasons too speculative to go into here, Friedman may be broadly right regarding economists' policy disagreements in the United States, while Devons may be broadly right about Britain.[2] (Even the difference in time, between 1953 and 1961, may be relevant, for Devons seemed to be referring particularly to the new controversies between British economists in the 1950's over price-stability, employment and rates of growth.)

Anyhow, the dichotomy between normative and positive statements is not simply a matter of philosophy or logic. It has a considerable political significance in that it would widely be taken as dividing those questions on which it is the function of the technical expert to pronounce, in so far as he may be able to do so—that is, on predictions of the consequences of different policies—from the valuations and choices of different objectives which would widely be regarded as the prerogative of citizens and statesmen. Preference-functions—though they may need help in formulating them—are for the citizens and statesmen, while the technical experts have the function of setting out, with as much consensus as they can muster, the possibility-functions. In so far as one thinks it politically desirable to keep the role of the expert within limits, which, if not absolutely precise, are at least reasonably distinct, one must make an effort to keep the normative-positive distinction as clear-cut as possible, and this becomes increasingly important as economic advisers and economic councils and commissions play a more and more prominent part. To abandon the distinction altogether would leave hopelessly confused the role of the expert in policy decisions. The distinction, in so far as it can be drawn, has also a vital role in the public discussion of policies, essential in a healthy democratic process. Where, in a democracy, more ambitious economic policies

---

[1] *Essays in Economics*, 1961, p. 18.
[2] 'While opinions *on ends* may be more widely split in Britain, opinions on means are probably more widely split in the States.' P. A. Samuelson, *Problems of the American Economy*, Stamp Memorial Lecture 1961, 1962, p. 13n.

are being attempted, a basic minimum consensus as to shared, 'objective', historical and statistical 'facts'—for example, in respect of distributive shares—is essential for effective action.

However, the dichotomy between positive beliefs regarding the predicted effects of policies, and normative attitudes regarding alternative policy objectives, does not seem to have been applied very successfully to the rapid resolving of disagreements or to clarifying the points at issue. In fact, the dichotomy is not as easily and automatically applicable in the field of economic policy as some of the more facile expositions of it have seemed to assume.

This dichotomy between normative and positive propositions, and the assumption that it both could and should be clearly and cleanly applied, was almost a basic tenet of the 'orthodox' methodology of economics for about a hundred years from Nassau Senior and J. S. Mill, through Cairnes, J. N. Keynes, Pareto and Max Weber, down to Robbins and Friedman. It never acquired the exclusive acceptance and dominance of a completely orthodox dogma. There were always critics or dissenters who rejected either the possibility or the desirability of economists keeping to the positive side of the line, or even the possibility of drawing such a line at all, and there were numerous differences in application and interpretation. But recently there seems to have been a more massive wave of criticism or scepticism from leading writers than perhaps at any time since Senior and J. S. Mill first drew the distinction for economists. We shall attempt to survey the history of this development in the next chapter. For the moment let us simply insist that the general statement and advocacy of the distinction is no more than a possible starting-point, and that its application needs persistent analysis and discipline. Let us further very briefly note two reasons why the maintenance of the distinction is by no means as easy or automatic as its orthodox or semi-orthodox classical and neo-classical expositors seem to have assumed.

First, the neo-classical analysis of choice—whether of consumers' goods, producers' goods or government policies (in terms of 'welfare')—dealt almost entirely with choices between certainties, largely assuming away all uncertainty and uncertainty-attitudes. A simple clear-cut line with regard to the choice of policies, is considerably easier to draw between the positive functions of the predicter, and the normative, evaluative function of the chooser, in the simplified models which leave out all uncertainty. It is not, of course, necessarily *impossible* to draw the distinction when predictions are highly uncertain and choices and evaluations are between highly uncertain outcomes or objectives—though some authorities seem to urge this. But, as we shall discuss later, the distinction is by no means so automatically clear-cut with regard to highly uncertain real-world choices as it is in the simplified neo-classical 'certainty' model, and the frontier-line between the duties of the expert and the functions of the political authority responsible for policy, is more difficult to draw.

Secondly, the most important types, in economics, of 'value-judgments', political and ethical principles or presuppositions, ideological prejudices, and subjective bias, are concerned, explicitly or implicitly, with favouring or condemning policy objectives in the broadest sense. This is the connection between the two parts of this work. Especially in the last decade or so the range of policy objectives has become much more comprehensive, ambitious and quantitatively precise, and different objectives have obviously become much more liable to conflict, at least at the margin. It follows that in the discussion of economic policies, the value-judgments or preference-functions which logically require explicit statement, if confusion is to be avoided, are much more complex and elaborate than when the semi-orthodox distinction between normative and positive was expounded from Senior to Robbins, and when policies tended to be much more narrowly 'micro-economic' in scope. The explicit statement of value-judgments or preference-functions has thus become a considerably more elaborate and arduous task, and, when it is not adequately carried out, not merely disagreement but confusion results. Again, we shall attempt to survey historically this development of policy objectives or preference-functions.

I hope it may be useful to spend a little time and space on getting into historical perspective how the present position has been reached. At any rate, it is the history of unsettled or developing questions, not of settled questions, which we shall be looking at. As regards the kind of problem with which we are concerned in this book one can simply try to promote rather more clarity, not hope for some concise definitive solution, and the illumination of historical perspective, if one can achieve it, has its contribution to make to this clarification.

PART I

POSITIVE ECONOMICS?

CHAPTER 1

The Positive-Normative Distinction
in the
History of Economic Thought

'The history of the development, whether normal
or abnormal, of ideas is of all subjects that in
which we, as thinking men, take the deepest
interest.'

J. CLERK MAXWELL

(1) INTRODUCTION: STEUART, SMITH AND BENTHAM

Explicit, systematic and sustained attempts to distinguish and separate off the 'positive' propositions of 'the science of political economy' from policy recommendations and ethical and political postulates, or doctrines advocating policy objectives, can be traced back to the later classical writers of the second quarter of the nineteenth century. It is perhaps not too fanciful even to fix the actual year from which the distinction could be said to have taken root as 1836, when J. S. Mill's essay (written 1829–30) *'On the Definition of Political Economy and on the Method of Investigation proper to it'*, and Nassau Senior's *Outline of Political Economy*, first appeared. Not, of course, that the distinction was kept clear, or was faithfully maintained, from 1836 onwards—it never has been and perhaps never will be. Nor was this distinction generally agreed on as a methodological programme at which to aim. But it was then first set up as such in influential 'orthodox' writings. In this short survey we are primarily concerned with the history of a methodological programme rather than with how far this programme actually was, or could be, carried out by economists in practice.

Long before, in the seventeenth century, anticipatory groping attempts can be traced in the general direction of this distinction, as, for example, in the explicit programme of quantitative empiricism of Sir William Petty, when he claimed to 'have taken the course (as a specimen of the Political Arithmetic I have long aimed at) to express myself in terms of number, weight, or measure; to use only arguments of sense, and to consider only such causes, as have visible foundations in nature; leaving those that depend upon the mutable minds, opinions, appetites, and passions of particular men, to the consideration of others'.[1] Then that great original pioneer of economic analysis, Richard Cantillon, in his *Essai* (c. 1730), without any explicit mention of a deliberate methodological programme, 'brushes' — as Higgs vividly put it—'Ethics and Politics aside as imperiously as a referee orders the seconds out of the ring before a prize fight'.[2] Though the general philosophical technique of stressing the distinctness of statements involving 'is' from statements involving 'ought' derives very much from Hume, he does not seem to have furthered the distinction directly with contemporary political economists.

Sir James Steuart, however, on this point as on so many others, anticipated subsequent ideas in, for example, his discussion of the eighteenth-century controversy over luxury spending, in which moral issues and positive economic arguments as to the effects of policies, were apt to be thoroughly confused:

'As my subject is different from that of morals, I have no occasion to consider the term luxury in any other than a political sense, to wit, as a principle which produces employment, and gives bread to those who supply the demands of the rich. . . . My subject is too extensive of itself to admit of being confounded with the doctrine either of morals, or of government, however closely these may appear connected with it.'[3]

The systemization of modern political economy round its own corpus of theory by the Physiocrats and Adam Smith took place within the framework of the concept and philosophy of natural law, according to which positive and normative, what is and what ought to be, were thoroughly merged. In his exposition of 'the simple system of natural liberty' Smith was not much concerned to distinguish between positive analysis of actual tendencies, and normative prescription as to right and just policies—the great adjective 'natural'

---

[1] *The Economic Writings of Sir William Petty*, ed. by C. H. Hull, Vol. I, p. 244.
[2] R. Cantillon, *Essai sur la nature du commerce en général*, ed. by H. Higgs, 1931, p. 388.
[3] *An Inquiry into the Principles of Political Economy*, Dublin, 1770, Vol. I, p. 32n. Steuart, unlike many of his successors, also showed a cautious awareness of the problem of bias: 'Every writer values himself upon his impartiality because he is not sensible of his fetters'. He advised that 'the speculative person, who removed from the practice, extracts the principles of this science from observation and reflection, should divest himself, as far as possible, of every prejudice, in favour of established opinions, however reasonable, when examined relatively to particular nations: he must do his utmost to become a citizen of the world, comparing customs, examining minutely institutions which appear alike, when in different countries they are found to produce different effects'. *Op. cit.*, p. IX, and p. 3.

comprehended both. When Smith referred to political economy 'as a branch of the science of a statesman or legislator', the emphasis was on the function of policy prescription, as it had been with almost all his predecessors, whether natural law philosophers or practical topical pamphleteers. The term 'science' had for Smith little of its modern methodological significance. With the Physiocrats and Adam Smith, as Sidgwick put it:

'Political Economy became primarily a study of "what is" rather than of "what ought to be"; but this was because the two notions were, at least to a considerable extent, identified in the political economist's contemplation of the existing processes of the production and distribution of wealth. He described and analysed these processes, not only to show what they were, but also to show that they were not likely to be improved by human restraints and regulations. This is true not only of Adam Smith but of almost all his disciples and successors for more than half a century. It should be noted, however, that they have maintained this identity of the actual with the ideal in very different degrees and on very different grounds; and that a considerable amount of mutual misunderstanding and mistaken inference has resulted from not observing these differences. Such misunderstanding has been a good deal aided by the ambiguity of the term "Natural", applied by Adam Smith, Ricardo and others, to the shares of different producers as determined by the economic laws which these writers expound. For by the term "natural" as commonly used, the notion of "what generally is" or "what would be apart from human interference" is suggested in vague combination with that of "what ought to be" or "what is intended by a benevolent Providence": and it is not always easy to say in what proportions the two meanings are mixed by any particular writer:.'[1]

Though Malthus and Ricardo did little explicitly and deliberately, they did a considerable amount implicitly, to help forward the distinction and separation between normative and positive. The Malthusian theory of population and 'natural wages' helped to strip the adjective 'natural' of some of its optimistic penumbra of beneficence and justice. Ricardo's emphatic, if methodologically un-selfconscious abstractions did much to transform 'the simple system of natural liberty' into a set of simplificatory postulates or a neutral model. Though competitive conditions continued to be widely regarded as generally 'natural' and beneficent, there was now an opening for the methodological wedge which would prise apart 'positive' 'natural' assumptions from normative policy prescriptions. It was through the exploitation of this

[1] H. Sidgwick, *Principles of Political Economy*, 1883, p. 19.

opening afforded by the Ricardian method that Senior and J. S. Mill made their contributions.

In the nineteenth century much of the methodological discussion of the distinction between normative and positive was carried on in terms of the 'science' and 'art' of political economy, the precise significance of 'art' being somewhat indefinite and shifting. In eighteenth-century writers, this pair of terms 'science' and 'art' was used even more loosely. Sir James Steuart, for example, refers to political economy as an 'art' and as a 'science' without drawing any very clear line of distinction. As Sidgwick pointed out,

'No importance is to be attached to the fact that Steuart, Adam Smith and others, *call* Political Economy a Science while defining it as (what we should now call) an Art. The present general recognition of the distinction between the two terms, in its application to economic matters, is due, I think, to the combined influence of Senior and J. S. Mill, and cannot be traced further back. McCulloch, for instance, altogether ignores it.'[1]

Bentham, however, demanded and attempted more precision. We find him complaining of 'a cloud of perplexity raised by indistinct and erroneous conceptions' hanging over the terms 'art' and 'science'. He analyses the terms at length in *The Rationale of Reward*. An art is the practical application of science (though not of a single science corresponding to its art); and a science cannot be separated from its practical applications any more than an 'art' can be separated from the knowledge underlying it.[2] Bentham says specifically of political economy that 'in this instance, as in others, it is only as a guide to the art that the science is of use. . . . The only use of the science is the serving as a foundation to the art.'[3] But the point we wish to emphasize is that, according to Bentham, though

---

[1] *Principles of Political Economy*, 1883, p. 15n.

[2] Cf. J. Bentham, *Works*, ed. J. Bowring, 1843, Vol. II, pp. 252–3: 'As between *art* and *science*, in the whole field of *thought* and *action*, no one spot will be found belonging to either to the exclusion of the other. In whatsoever spot a portion of either is found, a portion of the other may be also seen; whatsoever spot is occupied by either, is occupied by both: is occupied by them in joint tenancy. . . . Practice, in proportion as *attention* and *exertion* are regarded as necessary to due *performance*, is termed *art*. *Knowledge*, in proportion as *attention* and *exertion* are regarded as necessary to *attainment*, is termed *science*. In the very nature of the case, they will be found so combined as to be inseparable. . . . Correspondent to every *art*, there is at least one branch of science; correspondent to every branch of *science*, there is at least one branch of art. There is no determinate line of distinction between *art*, on the one hand, and *science* on the other; no determinate line of distinction between *art* and *science*, on the one hand, and *unartificial practice* and *unscientific knowledge*, on the other.'

[3] Jeremy Bentham's *Economic Writings*, ed. W. Stark, 1952, Vol. I, pp. 223–4.

'the art of political economy' may draw on other *sciences* besides 'the science of political economy', such as the 'sciences' of ethics, politics, or legislation, it does not require or employ any *extra*—or *un*scientific value-judgments. The distinction between 'art' and 'science' as Bentham draws it has no element of the positive-normative distinction, because for him the distinction did not exist, 'normative' questions being questions of utility, which, in turn, were questions of fact and calculation.

(2) J. S. MILL, SENIOR AND MCCULLOCH

J. S. Mill, in his early essay *On the Definition of Political Economy*, uses the distinction between the 'art' and 'science' of political economy, and to a considerable extent seems to follow Bentham, as when, for example, he points out that an 'art' may draw on more than one science:

'Although the necessary foundation of all art is science . . . it is not equally true that every art corresponds to one particular science. Each art presupposes, not one science, but science in general; or, at least, many distinct sciences.'[1]

Elsewhere in the essay, however, Mill seems to depart from Bentham's ideas in suggesting that an art presupposes something essentially different in kind or mood from science. He criticizes Adam Smith's title *An Inquiry into the Nature and Causes of the Wealth of Nations* as

'liable to the conclusive objection, that it confounds the essentially distinct, though closely connected, ideas of *science* and *art*. These two ideas differ from one another as the understanding differs from the will, or as the indicative mood in grammar differs from the imperative. The one deals in facts, the other in precepts. Science is a collection of *truths*; art, a body of *rules*, or directions for conduct. The language of science is, This is, or This is not; This does, or does not happen. The language of art is, Do this; Avoid that. Science takes cognisance of a *phenomenon*, and endeavours to discover its *law*; art proposes to itself an *end*, and looks out for *means* to effect it.'[2]

Just how far, if at all, Mill had moved away from Bentham's concepts in this early essay it is difficult to say, but in the concluding sections of his *System of Logic* (1841) his concept of an art clearly

---

[1] *Essays on Some Unsettled Questions of Political Economy*, 1844, p. 152n.

[2] *Op. cit.*, pp. 123–4. It is interesting to contrast this criticism of Smith with Mill's Preface to his *Principles* of about twelve years later, where he takes *The Wealth of Nations* as his model. See below, Part II, Chapter 3, Section 6.

contains an admixture of an entirely different un-Benthamite quality
not derivable from science, an ethical or imperative component seen
as something completely distinct from the conclusions of any science:

'The art proposes to itself an end to be attained, defines the end,
and hands it over to the science. . . . The only one of the premises,
therefore, which Art supplies is the original major premise, which
asserts that the attainment of the given end is desirable. . . . But
though the reasonings which connect the end or purpose of every
art with its means belong to the domain of Science, the definition of
the end itself belongs exclusively to Art, and forms its peculiar
province. Every art has one first principle, or general major premise,
not borrowed from science. . . . These are not propositions of science.
Propositions of science assert a matter of fact: an existence, a co-
existence, a succession, or a resemblance. The propositions now
spoken of do not assert that anything is, but enjoin or recommend
that something should be. They are a class by themselves. A proposition of which the predicate is expressed by the words *ought* or
should be, is generically different from one which is expressed by *is*
or *will be*. . . .
  'A scientific observer or reasoner, merely as such, is not an adviser
for practice. His part is only to show that certain consequences
follow from certain causes, and that to obtain certain ends, certain
means are the most effectual. Whether the ends themselves are such
as ought to be pursued, and if so, in what cases and to how great a
length, it is no part of his business as a cultivator of science to
decide, and science alone will never qualify him for the decision. In
purely physical science, there is not much temptation to assume this
ulterior office; but those who treat of human nature and society
invariably claim it; they always undertake to say, not merely what
is, but what ought to be. To entitle them to do this, a complete
doctrine of Teleology is indispensable. A scientific theory, however
perfect, of the subject matter, considered merely as part of the order
of nature, can in no degree serve as a substitute.'[1]

These passages certainly seem to suggest that an 'art' does not
merely draw on more than one science but on something essentially
extra-scientific, 'generically different' from any science. Whether or
how far this idea is compatible with the utilitarian doctrine of ethics
as part of an empirical 'science of human nature', expounded by
Mill elsewhere, we shall not attempt to examine. Certainly Mill
concludes his *System of Logic* by claiming that he is in possession
of the 'complete doctrine of Teleology' which must underpin all

[1] *A System of Logic*, People's Edition, 1884, pp. 617, 619, 620 (Book 6, Chapter
XII, Sections 2 and 6).

practical policy recommendations, that is the general principle 'of conduciveness to the happiness of mankind, or rather, of all sentient beings'. But here he is quite reserved and even tentative in his claim and 'merely declares his conviction', without attempting any justification. On the other hand, in his *Principles of Political Economy*, in contrast with the criticism in his early essay cited above, Mill very deliberately adopted the broad treatment of Adam Smith, combining 'science' and 'art', in which 'Political Economy is inseparably intertwined with many other branches of Social Philosophy', as he puts it in the Preface. J. N. Keynes called attention to the contrasts between Mill's theory of method, as set out in his earlier essay *On the Definition of Political Economy*, and his practice as demonstrated in the *Principles*,[1] where he passes readily from 'science' to 'art' without noting that he is crossing some kind of significant frontier line, or introducing ethical or teleological assumptions. We would add that there are further contrasts, at least implicit, between the *Essay* and the *Principles* on the one hand and the closing sections of the *System of Logic* on the other. But in view of his emphasis in the latter on 'the generic difference' between 'science' and 'art', it is hardly justifiable to argue that Mill had no conception at all of the need for non- or extra-scientific ethical assumptions in the 'art' of political economy.[2]

In his *Outline* of 1836, probably his best-known work, Senior's treatment of the relation between the theoretical conclusions of political economy and its policy applications differed significantly from his first discussion of the subject ten years previously in his lecture of 1826, and again slightly from that in his subsequent lectures of 1847–52. In 1826 he regarded the science of political economy as consisting of two branches, the theoretic and the practical, and 'many conclusions, and those of the highest importance, in the practical branch, rest so immediately on the conclusions of the theoretic branch as to possess equal certainty and universality'.[3] But in the course of ten years he had become, as people sometimes do, much more cautious. In 1836, he confines 'the science of political economy', strictly to what he had called earlier the 'theoretic' branch, separating off the 'practical' branch and excluding it from the science, thus implicitly denying his earlier conclusion that practical conclusions followed immediately from 'theoretic'. Senior emphasizes the break he is making, not simply with his own earlier views, but with preceding writers such as McCulloch, Say, Steuart

[1] *The Scope and Method of Political Economy*, 1890, p. 19.
[2] See G. Myrdal, *The Political Element in the Development of Economic Theory* English translation 1953, p. 8; also J. A. Schumpeter, *History of Economic Analysis*, 1954, pp. 540–1.
[3] *Introductory Lecture on Political Economy*, 1826, pp. 8–9.

and others, who had included 'the practical branch' alongside 'the theoretic', and had indeed regarded the direct object of the science of political economy as the making of policy prescriptions. Whereas McCulloch had laid down the object of the 'science' as being 'to point out the means by which the industry of man may be rendered most productive of . . . *wealth*; to ascertain the circumstances most favourable to its accumulation; the proportions in which it is divided . . . ; and the mode in which it may be most advantageously consumed', Senior protests that 'such inquiries far exceed the bounds of any single Treatise, and indeed the powers of any single mind'. He continues:

'The questions, To what extent and under what circumstances the possession of Wealth is, on the whole, beneficial or injurious to its possessor, or to the society of which he is a member? What distribution of Wealth is most desirable in each different state of society? and What are the means by which any given Country can facilitate such a distribution?—all these are questions of great interest and difficulty, but no more form part of the Science of Political Economy, in the sense in which we use that term, than Navigation forms part of the Science of Astronomy. The principles supplied by Political Economy are indeed necessary elements in their solution, but they are not the only, or even the most important, elements. The writer who pursues such investigations is in fact engaged on the great Science of legislation; a Science which requires a knowledge of the general principles supplied by Political Economy, but differs from it essentially in its subject, its premises and its conclusions. The subject of legislation is not Wealth, but human Welfare. Its premises are drawn from an infinite variety of phenomena, supported by evidence of every degree of strength, and authorizing conclusions deserving every degree of assent, from perfect confidence to bare suspicion. And its expounder is enabled, and even required, not merely to state general facts, but to urge the adoption or rejection of actual measures or trains of action.

'On the other hand, the subject treated by the Political Economist, using that term in the limited sense in which we apply it, is not Happiness, but Wealth; . . . His conclusions, whatever be their generality and their truth, do not authorize him in adding a single syllable of advice. That privilege belongs to the writer or statesman who has considered all the causes which may promote or impede the general welfare of those whom he addresses. . . . The business of a Political Economist is neither to recommend nor to dissuade, but to state general principles, which it is fatal to neglect, but neither advisable, nor perhaps practicable, to use as the sole, or even the principal guides in the actual conduct of affairs. . . . The confounding of Political Economy with the Sciences and Arts to which it is subservient, has been one of the principal obstacles to its improvement.'[1]

Senior's distinction between 'Wealth' and 'human Welfare', or 'Happiness', is of some interest, as it seems to indicate his implicit rejection of 'economic welfare' as a useful concept or criterion, or at any rate as a concept or criterion conclusions as to which would justify the economist in 'adding a single syllable of advice'. It does not seem that Senior would have accepted the modern assumption, deriving from Pigou, of general harmony between 'economic welfare' and 'other branches of welfare'. But the main point we want to emphasize is that in proposing to exclude policy prescription from the province of the political economist, Senior, following Bentham, is not implying that they involve some non-scientific value-judgment different in nature from the 'scientific' conclusions of the political economist, but simply that policy recommendations have to draw on other branches of '*science*' (for example, 'the great Science of Legislation'). The distinction Senior was drawing was not, therefore, the same, or so fundamental, as the one the modern methodologist draws when he seeks to distinguish between positive analysis and value-judgments. Perhaps Senior got nearer to this modern distinction when in the last of his various pronouncements on this problem he stated: 'Whenever he gives a *precept*, whenever he advises his reader to do anything, or to abstain from doing anything, he wanders from science into art, generally into the art of morality, or the art of government. . . . We cease to be scientific as soon as we advise or dissuade, or even approve or censure.'[2] It is to be noted that Senior, typically, does not seem to envisage any difficulties in keeping quite separate or distinct, 'being scientific' from being 'dissuasive' (or persuasive).

J. R. McCulloch completely and explicitly dissented from Senior's doctrine that the economist is not authorized to give 'a single syllable of advice'. On the contrary, McCulloch brushes aside Senior's distinction between 'Wealth' on the one hand and 'Happiness' and 'human Welfare' on the other, and he argues

[1] *An Outline of the Science of Political Economy*, 1836, pp. 2–3. Senior was almost certainly much influenced by his Oxford colleague Whateley, on this point as on others (as Professor J. Viner has pointed out to me). Whateley argued strongly that political economy should be treated and regarded as ethically neutral and that the economist's 'proper enquiry was as to the means by which wealth may be preserved or increased: to enquire how far wealth is desirable, is to go out of his proper province: to represent it as the only thing desirable, is an error not *in* Political Economy, but apart from it'. (*Lectures in Political Economy*, 1831, 2nd Edition 1832, p. 21.)

[2] *Report of the British Association for the Advancement of Science*, 1860, pp. 183–4.

'that the economist is bound, whenever he sees cause, to dissuade, censure, and commend, quite as much as the politician, or anyone else. In treating, for example, of the influence of restrictions, is he not to censure those which, by fettering the freedom of industry, hinder the production of wealth? and is he not to commend the measures by which, and the Ministers by whom, such restrictions are abolished? The economist who confines himself to the mere enunciation of general principles, or abstract truths, may as well address himself to the pump in Aldgate as to the British public.'[1]

It would be very difficult to generalize as to how far economists tended, or have since tended, to follow Senior in his allegiance to the pump at Aldgate, on the one hand, or McCulloch, on the other. A tendency might possibly be discerned for the austere claims of Senior to be invoked as an impressive methodological programme, combined with much willingness, in practice, to assume the burdens of influencing public policy, as urged by McCulloch. Anyhow, neither Senior nor McCulloch envisaged or examined the question as to whether, or how far, positive, neutral theorizing *can* be kept distinct from, and pure of, normative, 'persuasive' elements. Senior held that it was possible and desirable, and McCulloch that it was undesirable, without suggesting that it was impossible.

(3) CAIRNES, SIDGWICK AND J. N. KEYNES

The later classical or post-classical writers, Cairnes, Sidgwick and J. N. Keynes, contributed much to clarifying and establishing the distinction between positive theory and normative policy recommendations as developed by J. S. Mill and Senior, and they argued strongly both for the possibility and desirability of a clear-cut separation. But they hardly went as far even as J. S. Mill in insisting on the 'generically different' extra-scientific character of the ethical or political assumptions necessary for policy recommendations, and sometimes seem to be clinging to the Utilitarian conception of the 'science' of ethics.

Cairnes was especially concerned to complain that Political Economy had come to be generally regarded 'as a sort of scientific rendering' of the maxim of *laissez-faire* and argued, on the contrary, that

'it has nothing to do with *laissez-faire* any more than with communism; . . . It stands apart from all particular systems, and is moreover absolutely neutral as between all. . . . It pronounces no judgment on the worthiness or desirableness of the ends aimed at

[1] *Principles of Political Economy*, new edition, 1843, p. IX.

in such systems. It tells us what their effects will be as regards a specific class of facts. . . . There are few practical problems which do not present other aspects than the purely economical—political, moral, educational, artistic aspects—and these may involve consequences so weighty as to turn the scale against purely economic solutions. On the relative importance of such conflicting considerations Political Economy offers no opinion, pronounces no judgment, thus, as I said, standing neutral between competing social schemes; neutral, as the science of mechanics stands neutral between competing plans of railway construction, in which expense, for instance, as well as mechanical efficiency, is to be considered.'[1]

Cairnes thus also seems—like Senior—to be rejecting the economic welfarist 'harmony' assumption that there is a presumption that, if the economic effects of a policy are beneficial, the other non-economic effects can be assumed not to outweigh them in respect of 'the other aspects of welfare'. Cairnes at one point insists on separating off a science from its practical applications with extreme sharpness:

'Whatever takes the form of a plan aiming at definite practical ends —it may be a measure for the diminution of pauperism, for the reform of land-tenure, for the extension of co-operative industry, for the improvement of the coinage . . . if its object be to accomplish definite practical ends, then I say it has none of the characteristics of a science. . . . Unfortunately, many who perfectly understand what science means when the word is employed with reference to physical nature, allow themselves to slide into a totally different sense of it, or rather into acquiescence in an absence of all distinct meaning in its use, when they employ it with reference to social existence. In the minds of a large number of people everything is Social Science which proposes to deal with social facts, either in the way of remedying a grievance, or in promoting order and progress in society. . . . Political Economy is a science in the same sense in which Astronomy, Dynamics, Chemistry, Physiology are sciences. . . . I think it, therefore, a matter not merely of theoretic, but of the utmost practical importance that the strictly scientific character of this study should be insisted on.'[2]

Cairnes takes the analysis further in his critique of Bastiat, emphasizing that 'The question, What is? and the question, What ought to be? are distinct questions'.[3] He complains that Bastiat fuses these two questions by using 'terms capable of lending them-

---

[1] J. E. Cairnes, *Essays in Political Economy*, 1873, p. 241 and pp. 255–6.
[2] Cairnes, *op. cit.*, pp. 252–3 and p. 261.
[3] Cairnes, *op. cit.*, p. 322.

C

selves at need to either point of view—capable either of simply expressing a matter of fact, or of connoting with the fact expressed a moral judgment'. Cairnes is calling attention to Bastiat's use of what, following C. L. Stevenson, have come to be called 'persuasive' terms or definitions—though Cairnes calls them 'passionate':

'Availing himself of the double meaning of such "passionate" terms as "principle", "value", "worth", "service" and the like, he has produced a theory which affects to cover both solutions—at once to explain and to justify the facts to which it applies. The economic vocabulary unfortunately lends itself only too readily to this sort of theorizing, and few writers have entirely escaped illusion from this cause.'[1]

Cairnes demands not simply the distinction, but complete separation:

'Even though the questions of Fact and Right, or Science and Morality, were conceived and argued as distinct, there would still be strong, and I venture to think, decisive reasons against combining them in the same scheme of speculation. . . . The student would be constantly solicited to overlook or ignore, or, on the other hand, to strain or overrate, data, according as they might seem to involve conclusions in one branch of the speculation in conflict with, or corroborative of, conclusions deemed to be of more importance in the other. Investigation thus pursued would no longer be disinterested; science would lose its singleness of purpose.'[2]

It is certainly a difficult methodological ideal, which Cairnes so trenchantly asserts; but he does not seem to envisage doubts as to its practicability.

Sidgwick begins his chapter on the scope of the subject by asking whether Political Economy is a Science or an Art, that is, whether it is concerned with 'what is' or 'what ought to be', thus conceiving 'Art' to be essentially normative, unlike, on the whole, Bentham. He answers that 'the former view is that which has been adopted, I believe, by all writers on economic theory in England for the last thirty years', though he points out that in Bastiat's conception of the subject 'science and art are completely fused'.[3] Like Cairnes, Sidgwick not only attacks Bastiat, but protests at the popular misunderstanding which more or less identified Political Economy with the doctrine of *laissez-faire*, and he even goes so far as to say that 'it remains true that English Political Economy, in whatever tone it

[1] Cairnes, *op. cit.*, pp. 322–3.
[2] Cairnes, *op. cit.*, p. 323.
[3] H. Sidgwick, *The Principles of Political Economy*, 1883, p. 12 and p. 21.

has been expounded, has generally included an advocacy of *laissez-faire*'. He argues that

'We shall gain in clearness, by distinguishing the problems of economic science from the political or ethical problems that are commonly combined with them, and stating the former in a purely positive way; asking not "What *ought* government, or workmen, or masters, or philanthropists, to do?" but "What will be the effects on their own wealth and that of others, if they do so and so?" For it should always be borne in mind that the answer to this latter question can rarely furnish more than a part of the data required for answering the former; and in some cases it will not supply the most important part.'

It is in problems of distribution (rather than production) that normative postulates have a specially large and obvious role, since 'there is no generally accepted axiom of ethics or politics which can be taken as a principle for judging of the rightness or goodness of different modes of division. In fact, we cannot consider Distribution as a practical problem without entering into the most fundamental controversies as to the ultimate basis and end of the political union'.[1] Again there seems to be a contrast here with Pigou's 'welfarist' assumption that distribution can significantly be pronounced upon simply in terms of *economic welfare*, and that 'economic welfare' can be assumed generally to move in harmony with 'other branches of welfare'.

However, though advocating the clearest possible separation of Science and Art, Sidgwick does not propose to 'confine the theory of political economy to economic *science* in the strictest sense'. Indeed the broad scope of Sidgwick's *Principles* is very similar to Mill's, except that Sidgwick—unlike Mill—explicitly labels his final book *The Art of Political Economy*. To the objection that in the realm of politics the exact measurements of economic science become impossible, Sidgwick answers that closer examination of the definitions of wealth and value 'seemed to lead to the conclusion that the real exactness of economic as compared with ordinary political estimates is generally over-rated'.[2] (This scepticism of Sidgwick is, incidentally, in some contrast with Marshall's, Pigou's and subsequent optimistic claims for 'the measuring-rod of money'.)

Sidgwick regarded 'Political Economy considered as an Art' as including

'besides the Theory of provision for governmental expenditure, (1) the Art of making the proportion of produce to population a maximum, taking generally as a measure the ordinary standard of exchange

[1] *The Principles of Political Economy*, 1883, pp. 22, 24 and 26.
[2] Sidgwick, *op. cit.*, p. 403.

value, so far as it can be applied; and (2) the Art of rightly distributing produce among members of the community, whether on any principle of Equity or Justice, or on the economic principle of making the whole produce as useful as possible.'[1]

Thus, what Sidgwick in his Book III called 'The Art of Political Economy' came nearer to what Pigou, a generation later, was to call 'The Economics of Welfare' (though Sidgwick rejected Pigou's main 'welfarist' assumption).

Sidgwick's attempt to revive the concept of an 'art of political economy' found no followers. It was explicitly criticized by J. N. Keynes and was rejected, or disregarded, by Marshall and Pigou. According to J. N. Keynes, the concept of the art of political economy either went too far or not far enough. If the art of political economy was confined simply to the practical applications of the science, its precepts would be conditional and lack finality. If, on the other hand, 'the art attempts a complete solution of practical problems, it must of necessity be to a large extent non-economic in its character and its scope becomes vague and ill-defined . . . and cannot with any advantage be separated from general political and social philosophy'. Keynes recommended a threefold classification of problems under the headings of (a) the 'positive' scientific study of economic laws; (b) applied political economy drawing on a much wider range of empirical and institutional material, and concerned with practical precepts for attaining given ends; and (c) the ethical norms and criteria required for policy recommendations.[2]

Keynes is especially insistent that 'we ought at least to recognize as fundamental a positive *science of political economy* which is concerned purely with what is. . . . The proposition that it is possible to study economic uniformities without passing ethical judgments or formulating economic precepts seems in fact so little to need proof, when the point at issue is clearly grasped, that it is difficult to say anything in support of it that shall go beyond mere truism'.[3] Keynes went on: 'It is not . . . the function of science to pass ethical judgments; and political economy, regarded as a positive science, may,

[1] *Op. cit.*, p. 403.

[2] *The Scope and Method of Political Economy*, 1890, pp. 31–6 and 57.

[3] *Op. cit.*, p. 36 and p. 40. Joan Robinson writes (*Economic Philosophy*, 1962, p. 74): 'It is true that in Cambridge we had never been taught that . . . the positive and the normative can be sharply divided.' On the contrary, J. N. Keynes, Sidgwick and Marshall plainly taught that the positive and normative could and should be sharply or clearly divided. But they held that economists should not necessarily confine themselves exclusively to the positive, so long as they distinguished clearly their positive from their normative statements. A strong interest in the fruit-bearing potential of a subject—whether medicine, economics, or even physics—does not, of course, imply the view that normative and positive cannot and should not be clearly distinguished.

therefore, be said to be independent of ethics.' However, Keynes adds, 'it is clear . . . that practical discussions of an economic character cannot be isolated from ethics, except in so far as the aim is merely to point out the practical bearing of economic facts, without any attempt to lay down absolute rules of conduct. . . . Purely economic data rarely by themselves suffice for the complete solution of practical problems'.[1]

Failure to make the positive-normative distinction, or 'the attempt to fuse together enquiries as to what is, and enquiries as to what ought to be, is likely to stand in the way of our giving clear and unbiased answers to any set of questions'.[2] Furthermore the public is confused and general agreement on 'positive' questions is obstructed. Some ambiguity may seem to remain in Keynes's account as between his statement that it is not the function of science to pass ethical judgments, and his Utilitarian-sounding references elsewhere to 'the *science*' of ethics.

(4) THE NEO-CLASSICALS AND THE RISE OF WELFARE ECONOMICS

Alfred Marshall generally agreed with Keynes, in particular in avoiding the term 'art', and with Sidgwick in holding that economists should not confine themselves to strictly scientific or narrowly economic questions, within the limits of which they could contribute very little to practical policy decisions—which Marshall fervently wished to do. But he strongly emphasized that a clear distinction should be kept between questions which lay within the compass of economic science, and those concerning the desirability of different social aims which, as he made clear, lay outside, (and it seems that he would probably have rejected, or at least had little use for, the concept of economic welfare, because it was apt to blur this distinction). In his inaugural lecture at Cambridge (1885), he stated:

'Sometimes indeed the economist may give a practical decision as it were with the authority of his science, but such a decision is almost always merely negative or critical. It is to the effect that a proposed plan will not produce its desired result. . . . It is true that an economist, like any other citizen, may give his own judgment as to the best solution of various practical problems, just as an engineer may give his opinion as to the right method of financing the Panama canal. But in such cases the counsel bears only the authority of the individual who gives it: he does not speak with the voice of his science. And the economist has to be specially careful to make this clear; because there is much misunderstanding as to the scope of his

[1] J. N. Keynes, *op. cit.*, Chapter II, p. 60 and p. 49.
[2] *Op. cit.*, p. 48.

science, and undue claims to authority on practical matters have often been put forward on its behalf.'[1]

He later concluded that normative and positive should (and therefore could) be clearly distinguished, but that the economist should not confine himself to the latter:

'Economic studies are not to be limited to matters, which are amenable to strictly scientific treatment. But those conclusions, whether in detail or in general, which are based on individual judgments as to the relative desirability of different social aims, or as to matters of fact which lie beyond the scope of any individual's special studies, *should be clearly distinguished* from those which claim to have been reached by scientific method'.[2]

The methodological principles laid down by Cairnes, Sidgwick and J. N. Keynes, to the effect that economics or political economy could and should be a 'positive', neutral science, clearly distinguished from policy recommendations requiring ethical or political judgments, though it was by no means universally accepted, seems to have been widely approved and agreed in principle by English and American economists, at any rate as a practicable and desirable rule of the game. How far the rule was actually adhered to in practice, on the field of play, how it was interpreted or misinterpreted, evaded or disregarded, are, of course, other questions. It could be argued that though this authoritatively proposed rule regarding the separation of value-judgments about the objectives of policies, from 'positive' theorizing, obtained a considerable measure of observance, it brought with it the disadvantage (as, for example, with Prohibition laws) that value-judgments were not always removed or distinguished, but were driven underground or remained disguised, which could be much more dangerous and confusing than their uninhibited expression.

With economics, in the neo-classical period, coming increasingly to be pursued as an academic discipline, one theme which met with some attention—which was to be masterfully treated by Max Weber —was that of the professional ethics of the university teacher of economics, and how far he should feel permitted to preach, indulge in propaganda, or take sides, in his university teaching and in public

[1] *Memorials of Alfred Marshall*, ed. A. C. Pigou, 1925, p. 165.

[2] *Industry and Trade*, 4th Ed., 1923, p. 676 (italics added). Moreover, Marshall expressed the view, perhaps over-optimistically, that this kind of methodological programme was being successfully carried out by 'the great body of economists who, working on parallel lines in many different countries, are bringing to their studies an unbiased desire to ascertain the truth'. *Principles of Economics*, 8th Ed., 1920, p. 13.

controversies.[1] J. N. Keynes referred to 'the importance of main-taining the strictly scientific standpoint in the *academic study* of political economy' and quoted C. F. Dunbar, the first professor of economics at Harvard, as follows:

'On the mixed questions of legislative policy and expediency it is not the province of the university to pronounce. They indeed involve questions of science, as they involve much else; but their solution is not an act of the scientific judgment. . . . The university may, and if successful in its true functions will, supply scientific data for the use of all who are concerned in the settlement of legislative and adminis-trative questions; but when to these data are added the many others which form a part of the basis for all practical decisions, the further declaration of opinion from the university chair becomes an *obiter dictum*, not necessary in the strict performance of duty and raising some difficult questions of expediency.[2]

Dunbar's views were approvingly expounded by Edgeworth in his inaugural lecture at Oxford:

'When we have done our best to correct our practical judgments, there will still be, as Mill says, "almost always room for a modest doubt as to our practical conclusions". This modesty and this doubt are particularly appropriate in the case of the academic teacher, who, expected to know something about all the branches of his subject, cannot be expected to have examined many of them closely and at first hand. . . . Therefore he should "teach, not preach", in the words of Professor Walker. Or, as it has been said by another eminent American economist, Professor Dunbar, . . . the instructor is not concerned with "the propagation of his own views". . . . Professor Dunbar specifies several good reasons why "the teacher's opinion upon some burning question of the day" should not be communi-cated to his pupils. There occurs to me as pertinent another case in which the teacher will not give an opinion—he may not have got one'.[3]

These views of J. N. Keynes, Dunbar and Edgeworth seem to have

[1] See Weber's paper 'Wissenschaft als Beruf' in *Gesammelte Aufsätze zur Wissenschaftslehre*, 1922.

[2] C. F. Dunbar, *Quarterly Journal of Economics*, July 1891, p. 411, quoted by J. N. Keynes, *The Scope and Method of Political Economy*, 4th Ed., 1917, p. 49n.

[3] *Collected Papers*, 1925, Vol. I, p. 10. For a more recent and very eloquent 'plea for detachment' in the social sciences, see Sir William Beveridge's farewell address as Director of the London School of Economics, reprinted in *Politica*, September 1937, pp. 459 ff.: 'The work of the social scientist and the work of the politician are different: they cannot be combined without harm to one or the other. . . . It is the duty of the scientist not to speak until he is sure' (p. 474).

gone very much out of fashion with their Oxbridge and Harvard successors, in spite of the much higher degree of specialization of modern economists compared with those of Edgeworth's day.

The rise of the marginal utility theory of value, and its successor, the analysis of consumer's preference and choice, with their emphasis on the subjectiveness of values and valuations, encouraged in a superficial way the view that social values, the ends of policy, and value-judgments generally, were relative and subjective, as contrasted with the 'objective', 'positive' propositions of economic science. In the new analysis of demand, 'utility', in some versions at any rate, was explicitly emptied of any ethical significance and simply meant 'desiredness'. The economist simply took consumers' tastes and desires—for beer or bibles—as given, and it was regarded as irrelevant or even 'illegitimate' for him to pronounce on their rightness or wrongness. Complete neutrality between consumers' valuations and preferences was the attitude the economist could and should adopt; and the same held good—it was implied—with regard to social desiderata and the objectives of economic policies.[1]

On the other hand, in other directions the marginal utility analysis, and the theories of economic policy with regard to production and distribution which were built upon it, at some points confused and blurred the boundaries between positive and normative, and the interpretation of the methodological rules proposed by Cairnes, Sidgwick and J. N. Keynes, just when these rules were obtaining wider acceptance or lip-service. In fact, the fundamental ambiguities of utilitarianism took on a new lease of life in the discussion of the principles of economic policy just when they were being abandoned elsewhere. In the neo-classical period, social value, or 'welfare', or 'economic welfare', became the area where the interpretation of the proposed rule of scientific neutrality caused the most controversy. It was not so much that the rule itself was called in question—though it was never universally accepted. As Pigou himself insisted, economics will not, indeed, cannot 'itself be an art or directly enunciate precepts of government. It is a positive science of what is and tends to be, not a normative science of what ought to be'.[2] 'Welfare' economics developed as an attempt to make policy recommendations while dispensing with value-judgments, or, at any rate, while reducing them to a minimum of one or two presuppositions generally accept-

---

[1] Cf. P. H. Wicksteed, *Alphabet of Economic Science*, 1888, p. 8, and H. J. Davenport, *The Economics of Enterprise*, 1913, p. 126: 'Peruna, Hop Bitters, obscene literature, indecent paintings, picture hats and corsets are wealth, irrespective of any ethical or conventional test to which they may or may not conform. Being marketable, price-bearing, they are wealth. . . . What is the economist, that he should go behind the market fact and set up a social philosophy of ultimate appraisals?'

[2] *Economics of Welfare*, 3rd Ed., 1929, p. 5.

able by all reasonable men. The change from 'political economy' to economics implied, or seemed to imply, that the subject was becoming more academic and specialized and more non-political, and the concept of 'economic welfare' emerged as a purely 'economic', non-political criterion for policies. There could hardly have been the same role for 'economic welfare', as a kind of non-political criterion, in classical 'political economy'. A key point in this Cambridge 'Utility-arianism' was, of course, the measurement of utility.[1]

(5) WALRAS, PARETO AND MAX WEBER

The starting-point, or certainly one main starting-point, of the controversy over 'welfare' economics, was what Marshall called 'the doctrine of maximum satisfaction', or the proposition that in some sense or other perfect competition represented some kind of social maximum or optimum. Marshall attributed this doctrine of maximum satisfaction in particular to Bastiat, in whose treatment of political economy, as we saw, 'science and art are completely fused',—that is, the positive analysis of the processes of a competitive economy was completely fused with the normative advocacy of free competition and even *laissez-faire*. Many or most of the more orthodox French economists of the middle and later part of the nineteenth century seem to have practised a similar fusion. When, therefore, Léon Walras mapped out the subject-matter of political economy—bitterly critical though he was of the dominant French liberal school in other respects—he hardly recognized a general distinction such as that developed by Cairnes, Sidgwick and J. N. Keynes, between 'science' and 'art' or between neutral positive analysis and normative prescription. Walras distinguished three component parts of the science of political economy: pure economics, or the abstract analysis of the competitive model, applied economics, which laid down principles of policy for the maximization of production or material welfare, and social economics, which prescribed principles for the property framework of the economy and for the just distribution of wealth.

---

[1] Cf. J. R. Hicks, *A Revision of Demand Theory*, 1956, p. 6: 'If one starts from a theory of demand like that of Marshall and his contemporaries, it is exceedingly natural to look for a welfare application. If the general aim of the economic system is the satisfaction of consumers' wants, and if the satisfaction of individual wants is to be conceived of as a maximizing of Utility, cannot the aim of the system be itself conceived of as a maximizing of Utility—Universal Utility, as Edgeworth called it? If this could be done and some measure of universal utility could be found, the economist's function could be widened out, from the understanding of cause and effect to the judgment of the effects—whether, from the point of view of want-satisfaction, they are to be judged as successful or unsuccessful, good or bad. Economists have always felt that such judgment or assessment was in some way part of their business.' (Senior and Cairnes?)

These three divisions of the subject all belonged to 'economic science' as Walras conceived it, no separation being made between positive analysis and normative prescription.

It was Walras's fusion, or continuation of the orthodox French fusion, of positive and normative, or Walras's 'metaphysics', as he called them, that Pareto indignantly rejected. He demanded a severely positivist methodology, and the exclusion of normative judgments from 'economic science', and he condemned economists in the most emphatic, even savage, terms for resorting to them. Like a good many other methodologists, Pareto did not seem always strictly to adhere to his own austere rule. But he did work out the application of the rule, decades in advance of other economists, to the highly controversial idea of a social maximum of utility and he provided the concept of 'a Pareto optimum'. As regards the contribution of the Austrian School to this question, its founder Carl Menger, at the end of his *Investigations on Method*, briefly indicated his dissent from the 'ethical' tendencies of the German historical school, for which he held there was no place either in theoretical or 'practical' economics.[1] The most distinctive contribution from later Austrian writers has been Mises's fusion of the science of political economy and the doctrines of extreme free-market liberalism on the lines of Bastiat.[2]

Max Weber's essays on *Objectivity in Social Science and Social Policy* (1904) and *The Meaning of Ethical Neutrality in Sociology and Economics* (1917) analyse these concepts more profoundly than any previous (and perhaps subsequent) work. Weber was primarily concerned with criticizing the methods of colleagues in the *Verein für Sozialpolitik*, and of German historical economists, notably Schmoller, in which social and economic studies were fused with the framing of policies for social reform, with little or no regard to any

[1] Cf. *Untersuchungen über die Methode der Sozialwissenschaften*, 1883, Anhang IX, pp. 288 ff.

[2] 'Therefore, when one reaches the conclusion, strictly by adherence to the canons of scientific procedure, that private ownership of the means of production is the only practicable form of social organization, this is neither an apology for capitalism nor an improper attempt to lend the authority of science to the support of liberalism. To the man who adopts the scientific method in reflecting upon the problems of human action, liberalism must appear as the only policy that can lead to lasting well-being for himself, his friends, and his loved ones, and, indeed, for all others as well. Only one who does not want to achieve such ends as life, health and prosperity for himself, his friends, and those he loves, only one who prefers sickness, misery, and suffering may reject the reasoning of liberalism on the ground that it is not neutral with regard to value judgments' (*Epistemological Problems of Economics*, L. von Mises, 1960, p. 39). Just previously, Mises had remarked (p. 37): 'What is impermissible, however, is the obliteration of the boundary between scientific explanation and political value judgment.' See also the earlier works of Mises, *Kritik des Interventionismus*, 1929, pp. 23–4, and *Liberalismus*, 1927, pp. 3, 78 and 170.

distinction or demarcation between positive and normative and the nature of the economist's 'authority' in the one field as compared with the other. The mainly historical economists of the *Verein* were, in their turn, to a large extent reacting critically against the claims to scientific neutrality and objectivity of English classical and neo-classical economists. Similar ideas were held by some of the early members of the American Economic Association, for example Ely. The issues were vigorously debated at a meeting of the *Verein* in 1909, in particular with regard to the concepts of productivity and welfare or well-being ('Wohlstand'), when Weber, with not much support except from Sombart, declared that the mixing of normative with scientific questions was 'the work of the devil' ('eine Sache des Teufels').[1]

In so far as the significance and possibility of 'objectivity' and ethical neutrality in historical studies may be even more problematic and difficult to assess than in general theoretical sciences, Weber was addressing himself to a larger and more intricate problem, and in so far as his conclusions have validity for the former, it might seem that they would follow *a fortiori* for the latter. As his translators have put it, Weber's essays are a demonstration of his

'pressing need to know the grounds for his own actions and his strong belief that man's dignity consists in his capacity for rational self-determination . . . as well as his contempt for those whose confidence in the rightness of their moral judgment is so weak that they feel the urge to support it by some authority such as the trend of history or its conformity with scientific doctrine in a sphere in which the powers of science are definitely limited'.[2]

We shall be quoting extensively from Weber in the following chapter.

[1] See *Schriften des Vereins für Sozialpolitik*, Band 132, 1910. For Schmoller's reply to Weber, see *Handwörterbuch der Staatswissenschaften*, 1911, Band VIII, s. 490 ff. Another distinguished supporter of the 'Wertfreiheit' doctrine was L. Brentano who in an article originally written in 1896 stated: 'It is very deplorable that the introduction of normative pronouncements in economics, and therewith the hopeless abandonment of the possibility of agreement, has rather increased than decreased in the last two decades.' *Archiv für Sozialwissenschaft und Sozialpolitik*, 1911, p. 701. A trenchant criticism of German 'ethical' ideas, as well as of the contemporary English 'welfarist' utilitarianism, was made by J. S. Nicholson in his Presidential Address to Section F of the British Association, 1893: 'To some extent the view prevails, especially in Germany, that it is the business of the economist to discover the general conditions of social well-being, and to show how they may be realized. If such an attempt were seriously made it could only end in the projection of the personality of the writer into an ideal, and one ideal would succeed another like a set of dissolving views.' *Report of the British Association for the Advancement of Science*, 1893, p. 846.

[2] See Max Weber on *The Methodology of the Social Sciences*, translated and edited by Edward A. Shils and Henry A. Finch, 1949, p. V.

(6) RECENT SCEPTICISM

With Pareto and Max Weber we are in reach of modern times. A gradual secular trend seems discernible—from Senior and J. S. Mill, through Cairnes, Sidgwick, J. N. Keynes, Pareto and Max Weber, towards establishing a clearer separation of positive and normative, and towards a wider, though never universal, recognition of the possibility and desirability of this separation as a methodological programme, however imperfectly the programme was actually carried out in practice. But even the programme was never fully accepted in Britain, and much less so in France and Germany. In a fuller account of this trend many other writers would be mentioned, for example, Fisher, Cassel and Schumpeter. We shall simply refer here to two important works which, in rather different ways, carried on this trend in the inter-war period, and which have been described by Hicks as 'classics of the positivist anti-normative tendency . . . which came into particular prominence at that particular time'[1]—Myrdal's *The Political Element in Economic Theory* and Robbins's *The Nature and Significance of Economic Science*. Myrdal's work did not then have such a wide influence since it did not appear in English till 1953, but Robbins's essay, though it came in for some criticism, undoubtedly had a very wide influence indeed. A principal difference between the two books was that though both agreed that economists could and should keep positive and normative elements distinct, Robbins held also that the maintenance of this distinction had in fact been 'the practice of economists of the "orthdox tradition" ever since the emergence of scientific economics' with Cantillon and Ricardo,[2] whereas much of Myrdal's book was devoted to showing that this normative-positive distinction had not been observed or maintained by economists, and in particular not by 'orthodox' economists. Robbins, for his part, repeatedly emphasized what he called the 'purely neutral analysis', and the 'perfectly neutral inference' of the economist, and that 'between the generalizations of positive and normative there is a logical gulf fixed which no ingenuity can disguise and no juxtaposition in space or time bridge over'. He relied on a clear-cut distinction between 'means' and 'ends' holding that 'Economics is entirely neutral between ends' and 'is not concerned with ends as such'.[3]

In the 1950s, however, there seems to have been a wave of criticism and scepticism regarding such confidently 'positivist' views. Though it has probably not often been argued that the economist should not *try* to keep normative and positive distinct, if he could, it has recently

---

[1] *Economic Journal*, December 1954, p. 793.
[2] *The Nature and Significance of Economic Science*, 2nd Ed., 1935, p. 151n.
[3] *Op. cit.*, p. 24.

frequently been implied that it is hardly worth while his trying, or that it is naïve self-deception to believe or claim that one could be successful in such an attempt. Here is a somewhat mixed anthology of recent quotations representative of this wave of thought, which we can begin by citing Myrdal's own account of his change of view over the last quarter of a century since the first publication of his book *The Political Element in Economic Theory*. In the introduction to the English edition of 1953 he states:

'Throughout this book there lurks the idea that when all metaphysical elements are radically cut away, a healthy body of positive economic theory will remain, which is altogether independent of valuations. . . . This implicit belief in the existence of a body of scientific knowledge acquired independently of all valuations is, as I now see it, naïve empiricism.'[1]

This shift in ideas represented by Myrdal seems to be part of a wider movement of thought, as a reference made a few years ago by David Riesman to 'American psychologists and sociologists' who 'still believe in a value-free social science and a deceptively neutral operationalism', and who do not realize 'the inescapable creative role of values in the scientific process itself'.[2]

Returning to economists, Smithies, in explicit opposition to the views of Robbins and Myrdal cited above, argues against 'hopes of making economics "scientific" ' by stripping it of its prescriptions and confining it to matters of analysis', holding that 'hardly any economic theory can be considered ideologically neutral', and that 'a sharp distinction between analysis and policy implications seems particularly difficult to maintain'.[3]

Paul Streeten, editing and enlarging upon Myrdal's views, held that 'we accept perhaps too easily the belief that the distinction between *is* and *ought* is always obvious, clear-cut and easy to draw'. He goes on: 'The strict separation of *ought* from *is* which dominates modern liberal economic theory (and in different versions modern philosophy) is not, as it claims to be, morally neutral', and he argues that a strict separation of ends from means is impossible.[4]

---

[1] *The Political Element in Economic Theory*, translated by P. Streeten, 1953, p. VII.

[2] *Individualism Reconsidered*, 1954, p. 21.

[3] *Economics and Public Policy*, Brookings Lectures 1954, 1955, pp. 2–3.

[4] P. Streeten in his Introduction to *Value in Social Theory* by G. Myrdal, p. XIII and p. XLIII. An anonymous review of this book in the *Times Literary Supplement* (August 15, 1958, p. 454) states 'the grand theme' of it to be 'that value premises are necessary in research and that no study and no book can be *wertfrei*, free from valuations'. The reviewer continues: 'When such a basic thesis becomes more generally accepted, shelf-loads of verbiage resting upon the

According to an economic historian:

'Even the purest of theories is based on certain logical (philosophical) assumptions about the nature and purpose of economic activity, and these assumptions predispose the theorist towards certain types of political action. Thus despite the economists' repeated and increasing claims of impartiality in the two hundred years or so since their discipline acquired the status of a recognized expertise, economic theory has been consistently permeated by the tradition of humanitarian liberalism'.[1]

Here is a particularly severe criticism apparently from a kind of neo-Marxist standpoint:

'Some [economists] would state that their task was to collect and collate facts and to reason from them, and that in doing this they were uninfluenced by value-judgments. But such people are the most potent apologists. . . . The claim to be uninfluenced by value-judgments is a sham one. It is not possible to play about with social facts, whether they be historical or contemporary, without allowing bias to count for something. One cannot even select facts without bias. . . . Objectivity in the social sciences is an illusion'.[2]

Those concerned with transmitting the increasing quantity of economic advice to governments have stressed the difficulty, or impossibility, of keeping distinct the role of the 'neutral' detached economic expert from that of the political decision-maker: 'That professional economists in government service should confine themselves to technique, leaving it to political leaders to set the objectives and take the decisions, is easier said than done. The border-line between the two roles is blurred: most social scientists are possessed of sufficiently strong political views to find it almost impossible to keep their impartial analyses genuinely impartial.' A former economic adviser to H.M.G. has stressed that 'it is an illusion to imagine that the dispassionate economist beloved of those who labour the distinction between ends and means, between normative and positivistic economics, can live in the practical world'.[3]

contrary assumption and now masquerading as the incarnation of wisdom in economics, political thought and sociology, will long since have been cast into outer darkness.'
[1] A. W. Coats, *Economic History Review*, August 1960, p. 40.
[2] V. L. Allen, *New Left Review*, January 1960, p. 60.
[3] R. L. Marris, *Economic Journal*, December 1954, p. 759, and Sir Robert Hall, *Economic Journal*, December 1960, p. 640.

Finally, to illustrate further the diversity of views, Colin Clark does not question the possibility so much as the desirability of economists abstaining from value-judgments, and complains of what he calls

'an intellectual disease which, like so many bad things in the modern world, appears to have reached the economists from the philosophers and particularly the Oxford philosophers. Economics, they say, is just a description of "how things happen" or of how to bring about certain objects which someone (not being an economist) desires to have brought about. But any statement by an economist about ends is forbidden because that constitutes a "value-judgment".'[1]

Now, of course, the points made in this variegated collection of pronouncements are of very different weight and validity. Some seem to be attacking ideas as to the scientific neutrality of economics which, in fact, nobody, or nobody of importance, recently has held, while others of the points quoted do not seem necessarily irreconcilable with the 'positivist' doctrines under criticism. Anyhow, let us emphasize that we are not trying to generalize about a change in economists' views in the last decade, or to claim that the long-term 'orthodox' trend from J. S. Mill and Senior, to Max Weber, Pareto and Robbins, has suddenly been completely reversed. In Germany support for Max Weber's views was probably considerably more widespread half a century later than at the time he proclaimed them. Economists' views on this question have never been uniform or agreed. Certainly many, and perhaps a majority of economists still agree, for example, with Friedman's views as expressed in his essay on 'Positive Economics' in which, after noting the 'confusion' that is rife on this question, he claimed that 'economics can be, and in part is, a positive science' and that 'positive economics is in principle independent of any ethical position or normative judgments' and 'is, or can be, an "objective" science in precisely the same sense as any of the physical sciences'.[2]

However, the wave of scepticism and criticism of what had, in Britain at any rate, to some extent hardened into an established orthodoxy for a hundred years or more, at least seems to suggest that further examination of the application of economic analysis to policy, especially in the light of recent fundamental policy disagreements, is not untimely or merely pedantic. For nearly all these pronouncements—except for Myrdal's series of essays—are thrown off as *obiter dicta*, before the writer passes on to another subject,

[1] *Encounter*, April 1958, p. 23.
[2] *Essays in Positive Economics*, 1953, p. 3 and p. 4.

without any attempt to get to grips with the opposite point of view.[1] Indeed, we come finally to the only case we have noticed where a defender of the 'orthodox' received view as to the scientific neutrality of economics has explicitly confronted and contradicted the new scepticism in a head-on clash. Even here we are simply given a summary quotation of one point of view, followed by a summary statement of the contradictory point of view, in the space of a page and a half, with little attempt to argue out the issues. But at least there is a recognition that the discussion of economic policies is starting not merely from different political value-assumptions, but from different views as to whether, or how far, value-assumptions and bias come in at all. Bauer quotes Myrdal as follows:

'There is no way of studying social reality other than from the viewpoint of human ideals. A "disinterested social science" has never existed and, for logical reasons, cannot exist. The value connotation of our main concepts represents our interest in a matter, gives direction to our thoughts and significance to our inferences.

'The recognition that our very concepts are value-loaded implies that they cannot be defined except in terms of political valuations. It is, indeed, on account of scientific stringency that these valuations

---

[1] For example, the usual trenchant logical incisiveness of Joan Robinson evaporates when she briefly takes up this issue, and, with a few rapid strokes, stirs it into incoherence. See *Economic Philosophy*, 1962, p. 14: '*It is no good trying to pretend that we can think or speak about human questions without ethical values coming in*. Perhaps Gunnar Myrdal is too sweeping when he says (speaking as an economist) that "our very concepts are value-loaded" and "cannot be defined except in terms of political valuations." It is true that economic terminology is coloured. . . . *All the same, taking a particular economic system as given, we can describe the technical features of its operation in an objective way. But it is not possible to describe a system without moral judgments creeping in.* For to look at a system from the outside implies that it is not the only possible system; in describing it we compare it (openly or tacitly) with other actual or imagined systems. Differences imply choices and choices imply judgment. . . . We cannot escape from our own habits of thought.' (Italics added.)

Apart from the question whether Gunnar Myrdal is too sweeping or whether he isn't, just how are we meant to reconcile, on the one hand, the *impossibility* of speaking 'about human questions without ethical values coming in', with, on the other hand, the *possibility* of describing 'the technical features' of the operation of an economic system 'in an objective way'? Moreover, where exactly is the crucial boundary line between describing 'the technical features' of a system, which can be done 'in an objective way', and describing 'a *system*', which is impossible 'without moral judgments'? Presumably what is being said is that it is possible to give an objective description objectively, but a normative description will be normative. Elsewhere Mrs Robinson writes: 'It is folly to reject a piece of analysis because we do not agree with the political judgment of the economist who puts it forward. Unfortunately, this approach to economics is very prevalent.' (*Collected Economic Papers*, Vol. II, 1960, p. 6). This seems to imply that one *can* separate clearly analysis from political judgments.

should be made explicit. They represent value-premises for the scientific analysis; contrary to widely held opinions, not only the practical conclusions from a scientific analysis, but this analysis itself depends necessarily on value-premises.'

Bauer counters this with a direct contradiction:

'The principal concepts of economics are surely not value-loaded; for example, concepts of opportunity cost, demand and supply as functions of price, the volume of output or of imports and exports, the consumption function and the multiplier, and the devices of aggregation, general and partial equilibrium analysis and period analysis. . . . The substantive propositions of positive economics embody the discernment of uniformities underlying the diversity of phenomena. Their validity is entirely independent of political positions. . . . When policies are proposed, value-premises and, more generally, bases for recommendation should be set out. But this is very different from the suggestion that the validity of economic propositions depend on value judgments. . . . The following appear to be some of the inevitable results and implications of the author's methodological position. It confuses the advancement of knowledge with the promotion of policy. It obscures the meaning of achievement of results: instead of meaning the establishment of successful and illuminating generalizations, it comes to mean the achievement of particular aims of policy. It prevents assessment of the competence of reasoning and of the validity of propositions, and thus also the establishment of minimum standards of technical competence, since criticism can always be ascribed to political differences. It destroys all possibility of reaching agreement even on elementary propositions, and it also prevents definition of the grounds of disagreement. It implies that the logical status of all propositions in economics is equal, because their validity depends on political acceptability or on their political results, and not on internal consistency or on correspondence with empirical evidence. . . . Such a position destroys economics as a systematic discipline.'[1]

We certainly agree with Bauer as to the possibly very serious consequences of abandoning all attempts to keep 'normative' and 'positive' concepts and statements distinct, as being naïve and delusory. Anything in the nature of scientific consensus and authority would then become impossible and the study of economics would come to consist of the cultivation of sophisticated rival propagandas. But warnings against such prospects, though they may or should

[1] P. Bauer, *Economic Journal*, March 1959, pp. 106-7, quoting G. Myrdal, *An International Economy: problems and prospects*, 1956, pp. 336-7.

D

stimulate the search for methods of warding them off, do not prove the complete possibility of such methods, or explain what they might be. The more or less 'orthodox' tradition coming down from Senior, J. S. Mill and Cairnes, to Robbins and Friedman, has been rather facile in simply proclaiming a clear-cut distinction between normative and positive, with the apparent implication that the mere proclamation of the distinction guarantees that it is easy to maintain it, and to exclude from 'economic science', or 'positive economics', both value-judgments and bias.

On the other hand, simply proclaiming—often, as we have seen, with an air of penetrating profundity—the ubiquity and inevitability of value-judgments and bias, without examining precisely at what points they enter, and how far they are inevitable, propagates a kind of helpless scepticism, or 'relativism',[1] as to any attempts at disciplined standards. It is easy here to pass from a healthy scepticism to the obscurantism of those who, primarily interested in propaganda and persuasion, will feel that they have freer scope if all attempts at disciplined distinctions can be dismissed as naïve and delusory. However, we note at this stage that recent scepticism regarding 'scientific neutrality' in economics, and the keeping separate of normative and positive, overtly at any rate, stresses rather its impossibility than its undesirability, and that it extends both to economic theorizing as well as to the discussion of policies.

---

[1] On 'relativism' see the addendum (pp. 369 ff.) to Vol. II of the fourth edition (1962) of K. R. Popper's *The Open Society and its Enemies*. Popper defines 'relativism' or 'scepticism' as follows: 'The theory that the choice between competing theories is arbitrary; since either, there is no such thing as objective truth; or, if there is, no such thing as a theory which is true or at any rate (though perhaps not true) nearer to the truth than another theory; or, if there are two or more theories, no ways or means of deciding whether one of them is better than another.'

CHAPTER 2

Types and Sources of Value-Judgments and Bias

'What is proposed here is that objectivity for
science lies at least in becoming precise about
what value-judgments are being made and
might have been made in a given enquiry.'

R. RUDNER
in *The Validation of Scientific Theories*
edited by P. G. Frank, 1961, p. 35.

'Discussion in general in this field is obscured
by a reluctance of many writers who insist that
valuations somehow seep into social analysis
to state clearly where precisely this seepage
occurs.'

P. STREETEN
Value in Social Theory
by G. Myrdal (edited and introduced by
P. Streeten), 1958, p. XXXVII.

(1) INTRODUCTION

The disagreements set out at the end of the previous chapter seem
wide and deep. They relate both to economic theorizing and to
discussions of policies. But it is impossible to tell just how wide and
deep these differences are, because, as we have noted, so many of
these sweeping pronouncements regarding economics and value-
judgments have been thrown out *en passant* before some main substantial theme is taken up.

We are now going to try to set out, and examine in some detail,
the types of value-judgment, or value-premiss, and of evaluative or
persuasive statement, proposal or prescription, which economists
make or have to make, or implicitly or explicitly assume. We shall
try to indicate as precisely as we can the stages at which they occur
or have to occur, and how far they conflict with or nullify claims to
scientific objectivity, political and ethical neutrality, or 'Wertfreiheit'.
We also examine where value-judgments play a part, often less
explicitly and more insidiously, in the form of biased subjectivity
and persuasiveness. From some sceptical critics one derives the
impression that all economic and social enquiry is so inevitably

impregnated, and almost unanalysably permeated, from start to finish, with value-judgments or persuasive biased statements of one kind or another, that any appearance of, or claim to, any measure of objectivity or neutrality, is bound to be spurious or naïve. But it is usually extremely difficult to find out from the generalizations of these sceptics exactly where and how the valuations creep in, their nature, and how far they are logically inevitable, or, on the other hand, due to conceivably avoidable errors or indiscipline, like false conclusions in logic or mathematics, the rules of which are not the less clear, or impossible to maintain, because they are frequently broken.

The disagreements mentioned in the last chapter as to how far value-premisses, and value-loaded or biased judgments and concepts, enter into economics, did not apparently turn on any significant differences, or on any inadequate clarity, regarding the nature of 'value-judgments' and ethical statements, or even on how these, or elements of these, when located, are to be distinguished from the theories and statements of 'positive' economics. We do not need, and it would take us much too far afield, to explore different theories of ethics, or the analysis of different kinds of value-judgment and ethical or evaluative statement or proposal, or the basis of their validity. For our purposes it suffices if we agree that these kinds of statement cannot be tested or refuted inter-subjectively in the same way as the 'positive' statements of science, and that a consensus regarding them cannot be reached of the same kind or in the same way. In marking off 'scientific' statements from 'non-scientific' statements and proposals (including ethical statements and value-judgments), we follow Popper's proposal of a 'demarcation criterion'. This is 'a fundamental proposal for an agreement or convention' to the effect that 'it must be possible for an empirical scientific system to be refuted by experience', that is, that scientific statements and theories must in principle be 'intersubjectively testable', and that their 'objectivity . . . lies in the fact that they can be intersubjectively tested'.[1] We do not need to insist on any particular precise or rigid view of the nature of ethical and evaluative statements and value-judgments. It suffices for our purposes that ethical and political value-judgments, value-premisses, 'proposals', prescriptions and persuasive judgments, can be broadly and adequately distinguished

[1] K. R. Popper, *The Logic of Scientific Discovery*, 1959, pp. 37, 41 and 44. For a further analysis by Popper of 'the dualism of facts and standards, or of propositions and proposals', the dissimilarities between them, and why in spite, also, of similarities 'they should be clearly and decisively distinguished', see *The Open Society and its Enemies*, 4th Ed., 1962, Vol. II, pp. 383–4. For the duality of 'propositions' and 'proposals', and for the nature of the latter, see L. J. Russell's paper, 'Propositions and Proposals', Library of the Tenth International Congress of Philosophy, Amsterdam, 1948, Vol. I, *Proceedings of the Congress*.

from the statements of an empirical science by such a 'demarcation criterion'. This is certainly not to say that ethical statements or value-judgments are 'nonsensical', or undiscussable, or beyond any rational examination. On the contrary, we shall argue that much more examination of them would often be helpful in discussions of economic policies. Often when some norm or objective for policy is urged—such as, for example, that price stability should be maintained—such a value-judgment will contain or imply a positive or descriptive element (such as that price stability will maintain a certain pattern of distribution). Further analysis can 'demarcate' or separate out for discussion the positive from the normative-evaluative elements in such a statement.

We shall be concerned mainly or entirely with two kinds of value-judgment, 'proposal', or value-premiss, and we emphasize the vital distinction between them with regard to the 'objectivity' of science. These are (1) the kind of value-judgments, 'proposals', or value-premisses involved (*a*) in choices of problems to be studied, and (*b*) in choice or adoption of the criteria or rules of procedure by which the problems are to be studied; and (2) ethical or political value-judgments and persuasive statements, overtly stated or latently implied, regarding the choices, objectives or 'ends' of policies in the widest sense. The first are logically inevitable in *any* science or study, and the second are logically necessary if policy recommendations are being put forward. We shall be concerned also (3) with biased subjectivity in positive empirical statements, and its possible points of entry and modes of operation in different parts of the scientific process, where political or ethical value-judgments can be said to have no logical or 'legitimate' place, but are nevertheless influencing and shaping hypotheses, theories, explanations and predictions.

(2) THE MAIN TYPES OF INEVITABLE 'PRE-SCIENTIFIC' VALUE-JUDGMENT

We start with the types of fundamental value-judgment or value-premiss which *have* to be made before any 'scientific' or disciplined intellectual process can begin, and which might, therefore, be called 'pre-scientific'. These value-judgments are logically inevitable, in a sense 'a priori', since they cannot possibly be avoided in any 'scientific' study of economic, social or any other problems, however detached, unbiased or cautious the scientist might be. There seem to be two main types:

(A) The acceptance of the presuppositions, rules of procedure and criteria of 'scientific' method and enquiry, involve a kind of value-judgment or 'proposal' in favour of engaging voluntarily in intellectual activity based on certain agreed conventions, or rules of

the game, or of 'scientific' discipline or procedure. To set out these
rules fully and precisely would require a whole treatise on scientific
method. There is much broad agreement as to the general form these
rules should take, though there are at the margin, and perhaps always
will be, differences over particular rules and their interpretation, and
controversial questions as to the best precise formulations of them.
For example, we shall discuss below (Section 9) vaguenesses and
differences regarding the rules of inductive inference and the precise
limits of the function of the 'scientist' regarding decisions in conditions of uncertainty. We shall take as broadly accepted rules of
scientific procedure the laws or conventions of logic and mathematics, the empirical testability of statements or theories and the
readiness to expose them to critical, objective testing, and the obligation to try to avoid ambiguity, in particular normative-positive
ambiguity, and to promote clarity in the use and interpretation of
language. Such fundamental presuppositions, in whatever precise
way they are formulated, are common to all 'sciences', and a kind
of value-judgment or 'proposal' is made when such rules or criteria
are proposed or accepted, or when the study of a subject is voluntarily pursued in accordance with such rules. The rules amount to a
programme, or procedure, as to how a scientific consensus is to be
attained (a consensus, of course, which is always provisional and
subject to revision) and as to how theories and statements for which
scientific status is claimed are to be arrived at, or selected.

It has been pointed out that the criteria of the scientific rules of
the game have not always controlled the general acceptance or
consensus regarding theories or the selection between conflicting
theories and generalizations:

'Obviously, fitness to support a desirable conduct of citizens or,
briefly, to support moral behaviour, has served through the ages as
a reason for acceptance of a theory. When the "scientific criterions"
did not uniquely determine a theory, its fitness to support moral or
political indoctrination became an important factor for its acceptance. It is important to learn that the interpretation of a scientific
theory as a support of moral rules is not a rare case but has played
a role in all periods of history.'[1]

As a historical generalization this is undeniable and it is obviously
illustrated throughout much of the history of economic thought. But
this is only to say that the scientific criteria or rules have been widely
disregarded, and still are sometimes disregarded, in spite of general

[1] P. G. Frank, 'The Variety of Reasons for the Acceptance of Scientific
Theories', in *The Validation of Scientific Theories*, edited by P. G. Frank (paperback edition, 1961, p. 19).

agreement as to what, broadly, the rules are, requiring, as they do, that 'every influence of moral, religious, or political considerations upon the acceptance of a theory'—or on its rejection—'is regarded as "illegitimate" by the so-called "community of scientists"—a view which 'certainly has had a highly salutary effect upon the evolution of science as a human activity'.[1]

We are concerned with economics as an enquiry or 'discipline' carried on in accordance with such rules or conventions, which most economists seem to claim their subject to be, even if the rules are not always obeyed or at some points even precisely agreed upon. A game of football remains a game of football even when the referee is frequently blowing his whistle for fouls, or even when there is no referee at all, or even when all the players do not completely know, or completely agree, as to every detail of the rules. At what precise point 'a game of football' ceases to deserve that description, and becomes 'a free-for-all', is a nice point of definition and judgment, of relevance, perhaps, to some debates between economists over economic policies.

Of course, nobody has to accept these procedures and rules, and the value-judgments underlying them, if he does not wish to do so.[2] He can, and some people do, more or less frankly, practise economics as a branch of political persuasion and propaganda, investigating problems and presenting explanations in the manner of party politicians before an election presenting their versions of recent economic history and critiques of future policies. Then, of course, propagandist victories and widespread *political* agreement may emerge, but not *scientific* consensus, or the kind of objective *scientific* status based upon it.

However, the main point we are concerned with here is simply that because value-judgments proposing or upholding scientific criteria, or a code of scientific ethics, are logically inevitable in any 'scientific' activity, the fact that this particular kind of value-judgment is, and has to be, made, does not nullify all claims to objectivity, value-neutrality, or *Wertfreiheit*, in the statements or theories arrived at by scientific enquiry.

(B) *Secondly*, and again this applies to *any* scientific enquiry, natural or social, the choice of problems for study depends on a kind of 'interest' or value-judgment. As one of the sceptical critics quoted above writes: 'The mere selection of economic problems for investigation involves value-judgments',[3] or, as Max Weber put it: 'The problems of the social sciences are selected by the value-

[1] P. G. Frank, *op. cit.*, p. 13.

[2] H. Albert, *Handbuch der empirischen Sozialforschung*, I Band, 1961, p. 48.

[3] A. Smithies, *Economics and Public Policy*, Brookings Lectures 1954, 1955, p. 2.

relevance (*Wertbeziehung*) of the phenomena treated. . . . The very recognition of the existence of a scientific problem coincides, personally, with the possession of specifically oriented motives and values.'[1] Here again the kind of value-judgment involved could be described as 'pre-scientific', and, in any case, scientific objectivity or neutrality can be, and should only be, claimed regarding the *answers* to the problems selected.[2] The 'interest', relevance, or *Wertbeziehung*, which shapes the choice of problems for scientific study, or which ranks one problem as more important than another, may range from a relatively detached intellectual interest to the most immediate and selfish prospect of material gain, and it may well serve also as an indispensable driving force to scientific achievement. Certainly it is a major political and sociological problem how, in different societies, different kinds of questions come to be selected for study, regarding different methods of air defence, space travel, or consumers' tastes, for example; how research resources are raised and allocated, or how the estimates of the uncertain costs of different kinds of research are weighed against the uncertain prospective returns from them. Obviously the most fundamental clashes of interests and values may be involved, and the issues fought out as crude struggles for power. Moreover, social or political pressure, or the researcher's own prejudices or beliefs, may prevent certain questions, or whole areas of enquiry, from being investigated scientifically at all. The scientist also may voluntarily or involuntarily be the servant of political or commercial masters who may dictate to him the questions he is to investigate, and may exploit, pervert or suppress the answers he arrives at. But 'a betrayal of the criteria of science is only committed where the investigator not merely answers a dictated question, but supplies a dictated answer, that is, allows the particular practical aims of his client to influence his conclusions'.[3]

[1] Max Weber on *The Methodology of the Social Sciences*, translated and edited by E. A. Shils and H. A. Finch, 1949, p. 21 and p. 61.

[2] 'The rules of scientific method do not tell us what it is important to work on.' M. F. Millikan, in *The Human Meaning of the Social Sciences*, edited by D. Lerner, Meridian Books, 1959, p. 179.

[3] T. Geiger, *Ideologie und Wahrheit*, 1953, p. 119. Cf. also I. Berlin, *Philosophy, Politics and Society* (Second Series), edited by P. Laslett and W. G. Runciman, 1962, p. 6: 'The mere fact that value-judgments are relevant to an intellectual pursuit is clearly not sufficient to disqualify it from being a recognized science. The concept of normal health certainly embodies a valuation, and although there is sufficient universal consensus about what constitutes good health, a normal state, disease and so on, this concept, nevertheless, does not enter as an intrinsic element into the sciences of anatomy, physiology, pathology, etc. Pursuit of health may be the strongest sociological and psychological (and moral) factor in creating and promoting these sciences; it may determine which problems and aspects of the subject have been most ardently attended to; but it is not referred

Furthermore, though there must be some preliminary selection of questions and problems to start from, their choice is not necessarily a once-and-for-all process but may be continually subject to revision, the questions being reformulated in the course of research. Sometimes only when an 'answer' has been propounded may it be seen precisely what question it is an answer to—perhaps quite a different one from that first posed. The historian faces special and weightier problems of selection (as we shall discuss very briefly below in Section 6 of this chapter), and he may seem to choose the detailed individual questions his history answers more or less as he goes along.

Nevertheless, the fundamental point remains valid that the *answers* to the questions eventually dealt with do not *necessarily* involve subjective valuations, and value-judgments and -premises, just because *the selection of the questions* does. Undoubtedly, 'the scientist decides what to study; he decides what model is adequate within which to pose his problem; he decides how, when, and where to make observations; he decides when to accept or reject a conclusion. As a decision-maker he is as much concerned with actions as is the executive.'[1] But, as a 'scientist' he has to take account of the rules and criteria of scientific procedure when making these decisions and choices, and, in any case, these are quite separate from the decisions and choices regarding, for example, which 'ends' and objectives of economic policies ought to be chosen or pursued.[2]

We thus have two basic types of value-judgment, choice and decision, which might be formulated, elaborated or sub-divided in different ways. They are involved in any scientific enquiry (natural, or social, or human), and are logically inevitable, or, in a sense, 'pre-scientific' or *a priori*, in that they cannot be avoided, in *any* science, even with the greatest, or most superhuman, measure of unbiased detachment or impartiality, or disciplined caution.

The economist is also involved with valuations, though not here in making a choice or decision, in that the social or human sciences (unlike, of course, the natural sciences) study people who are holding, expressing, projecting, fighting for, or living by, values of one

to in the science itself, any more than the uses of history or logic need be mentioned in historical or logical works.'

[1] C. W. Churchman, *Prediction and Optimal Decision*, 1961, p. 14.

[2] 'That scientific truth is a value worth pursuing is not a scientific truth but a value-judgment. And that X pursues knowledge for its own sake is the fruit of a fundamental valuation on his part according to which he puts scientific knowledge before many other objectives. It thus appears that a valuation by the will is somehow involved in every conceivable statement, and that all statements may be suspected of being value-loaded or ideological. The former conclusion is correct . . . the latter is not correct. . . .' T. Geiger, *Ideologie und Wahrheit*, 1953, p. 113.

kind or another. But claims for the 'objectivity' or neutrality of statements or theories *about* human activities are not invalidated by the fact that the activities themselves are expressive of, or impregnated with, values.

Moreover, the observers or enquirers are themselves 'bundles of prejudices' or 'masses of predilections' and impinge on, and are a part of, what they are observing or studying, though there is no necessity or inevitability in their coming to the subject as loaded with ideological and political prejudices as economists sometimes do, or that their loads should obstruct their entry even into what Pigou described as 'that first antechamber of knowledge' knowing that they do not know.[1] Also, as in the natural sciences, there is an inter-action of observer and observed, which may be much more pervasive in the social sciences, but which does not involve value-judgments or presuppositions different in kind or principle from those of the natural sciences.[2] Of course, new empirical knowledge may have profound effects on values, attitudes and policies, whether in the 'natural' sphere, relating, say, to nutrition, disease or new forms of energy, or in the 'social' or 'human' sphere, where the example is frequently cited of Booth & Rowntree's new facts about poverty in England stirring the social conscience. But no empirical or factual knowledge necessarily entails an attitude, standard or policy, or a change therein, without the addition of a value-judgment, and because facts and standards are relevant to, and interact on, one another, it does not follow that they cannot be sharply distinguished.[3]

It is obvious then that the economist's subject-matter is essentially concerned with human beings and their values, and that he may himself come to the subject stiff with moral and political prejudices. The logical inevitability is also clear of the two types of 'preliminary' value-judgments involved in accepting a discipline, or rules of procedure, and in selecting questions and problems. It may, therefore, be misleading to claim that 'positive economics is in principle independent of *any* particular ethical position or normative judgments'.[4] But, on the other hand, having recognized these inevitable value-premisses, it seems a serious misconception to argue that the necessity of these types of value-judgment, or involvement in valuations and choices, disposes of *any* significant claims to scientific objectivity. Nearly fifty years ago, as pertinently as one might today, Max Weber complained bitterly of objections, on these grounds, to

[1] *Economics of Welfare*, 3rd Ed., 1929, p. VI.

[2] K. R. Popper, *The Poverty of Historicism*, 1961 edition, p. 12, et passim; and E. Grunberg and F. Modigliani, 'Predictability of Social Events', *Journal of Political Economy*, December 1954, pp. 465 ff. See also below, Section 8.

[3] Cf. K. R. Popper, *The Open Society and its Enemies*, 4th Ed., 1962, Vol. II, pp. 383–4.

[4] M. Friedman, *Essays in Positive Economics*, 1953, p. 4. (Italics added.)

his defence of scientific objectivity or *Wertfreiheit*: 'In spite of all that I have said, the following "objections" have been raised in all seriousness: Science strives to attain "valuable" results, meaning thereby logically and factually correct results which are scientifically significant; and that further, the selection of the subject-matter already involves an "evaluation". Another almost inconceivable misunderstanding which constantly recurs is that the propositions which I propose imply that empirical science cannot treat "subjective" evaluations as the subject-matter of its analysis.'[1]

We are certainly not trying to prejudge the question to be examined throughout the rest of this chapter as to whether value-judgments or subjective, biased, persuasive or evaluative statements, must or do enter into economics at other points than these. But if, when it is stated, for example, that ' "a disinterested social science" has never existed and, for logical reasons, cannot exist',[2] this conclusion is based *simply* on the inevitability of the types of value-judgment and involvement in valuations which we have just discussed, then there can be no fundamental disagreement. We would simply complain regarding this statement, that if it is an analytical-tautological one, as it seems it might be, it might have been expressed as such more explicitly, and, furthermore, that the inclusion of the adjective 'social' is unnecessary and perhaps misleading. It seems logically essential for both social and natural 'sciences' that problems or questions have to be selected, that certain criteria and rules of the game have to be accepted in a 'scientific' discipline, and that the problems selected cannot be approached in a kind of mental vacuum, but inevitably with some 'load' of interests, values and preconceptions, if not with the cumbersome loads of political and ideological prejudice which are in fact frequently brought to bear.

(3) IDEOLOGY, 'VISION' AND POLITICAL PRESUPPOSITIONS

We have seen that the economist, like any 'scientist', is inevitably involved in kinds of value-judgment in selecting or accepting certain epistemological criteria or rules of his discipline, and in selecting his problems or questions. We have also noted that he starts, or may start, with something more than a mere detached intellectual interest in his question, but rather with a load of political presuppositions and prejudices. It is naïve empiricism, and the most suitable target for this common pejorative phrase, to suppose that a researcher can approach his problem with his mind a *tabula rasa*, and that his hypotheses and theories will, or can, emerge spontaneously from 'the facts', or automatically imprint themselves on this *tabula rasa*,

---

[1] Max Weber on *The Methodology of the Social Sciences*, translated and edited by E. A. Shils and H. A. Finch, 1949, p. 10.

[2] G. Myrdal, *Value in Social Theory*, ed. P. Streeten, 1958, p. 1.

or be 'given' simply by looking around him. To be able to make even a first tentative formulation of a question, in addition to some 'interest' in it, *some* initial equipment, however primitive and indefinite, is required, and this will include, or at any rate *may* include, various kinds of preconceptions, predilections, presuppositions or prejudices, as well as definitions, concepts and language, technical and 'everyday', which may, though not necessarily must, be heavily value-loaded. If it is necessary and inevitable to select questions and problems it is necessary and inevitable that there be some initial equipment or raw materials with which to formulate them.

In the first place, for example, the economist may approach his questions equipped more or less fully and intensively with an 'ideology', which may be regarded as a, or the, leading species of a large genus of preconceptions and presuppositions. We need not attempt a precise definition of ideologies, or of elements thereof. From one point of view they may be regarded as large-scale comprehensive explanations of the economic, social or political universe, infused with often passionately held value-judgments about it, and about the action that should be taken with regard to it; and they are often expounded with the aid of highly persuasive definitions, concepts and terminology.[1] Nor need we explore further how ideologies are formed, or the view that they may be conditioned by economic or social class. One usual feature is their systematic character, which fixes a limited exclusive framework within which questions can be formulated and answers propounded. Their comprehensive, large-scale, long-run character, involving sometimes whole historical epochs, tends to make them often practically impossible to test, or to frame in practically testable terms. It has been observed, incidentally, that the kinds of large-scale systematic ideologies, which flourished in the nineteenth and early twentieth centuries, seem today to be losing much of their influence on serious thinking in the western world, though it may be premature to conclude that they are disappearing for good.

However, ideology appears not only in comprehensive systems, but in bits and pieces as 'ideological' statements or elements. What we would regard as one of the main characteristics of 'ideology', whether in the form of some comprehensive system, or of a particular individual statement or theory, is the interweaving of normative and positive, the form or appearance of a positive empirical statement or theory being combined with, and shaped and biased to support (on the assumption of some widely held moral value-judgment), a more or less latent, crypto-normative, ethical or political component. The explicit moralist or preacher is not an 'ideologue' in this sense, and the explicitly moral or ethical statement has not, on this definition,

[1] See *Ideologie und Wahrheit* by Theodor Geiger, 1953.

the ambiguity of an 'ideological' statement. For separating, in the interests of clarity, the positive empirical content from the latent value-judgment, enquiring how the proposition is to be tested, or could be refuted, seems a useful and indeed essential procedure.

Not clearly distinguishable, at the margin, from 'ideologies' are the social and political philosophies, ideals or 'principles', with which the economist may approach the formulation of his questions and hypotheses, and which may inspire his views as to the objectives of society and policies. These may be less comprehensive and historically large-scale than ideologies in the narrower sense, and initially they may be more explicitly normative, that is, not so closely and intensively interwoven with 'positive' analysis and 'scientific' pretensions, as are ideologies. These political ideals or principles may, however, take on more of the ambiguous characteristics of ideologies when 'rationalized' by economists. Quite a number of economists, either before, or very soon after, they began studying economics, seem to have adopted very definite political principles and values, in terms, for example, of 'freedom' on the one hand, or 'equality' on the other, and to have devoted much of their subsequent efforts as economists to working out a kind of economic justification or rationalization of them.[1] Their pronouncements on economic policies then tend to amount to dressing up their political predilections in esoteric jargon or technical patter. Perhaps—perhaps not—one could find more cases falling into this category than one could find of economists—like Pareto—who modified their political principles and programmes as a result of, or at any rate in the course of, their economic studies—though the bold generalization has been made that the study of economics has a broadly conservative effect.[2] Anyhow, the whole impetus to and initial interest in economic problems seems, in some cases, to have consisted in the buttressing and rationalizing of political views and principles. Of course, we are not for one moment suggesting that economists should not hold strong political principles or values. Our question rather is, what effects these *may* exercise on their would-be, or should-be, 'positive' hypotheses and theories about economic processes—not that these effects will necessarily or always be to render them false, though they *may* frequently seem to have distorting tendencies.

Schumpeter, who, among economists, has examined the role of

---

[1] 'If science is a straight line, economics is a spiral. In science new discoveries extend our knowledge: as new truth accumulates, old error is discarded. But in economics we go round and round: each new generation rediscovers old error at about the same rate as it absorbs truth. . . . Perhaps the reason lies not in economics, but in economists. In brash youth we take up our theoretical positions, and spend the rest of our lives selecting the facts to fit them.' (G. D. N. Worswick, *New Statesman and Nation*, August 30, 1963, p. 256.)

[2] G. J. Stigler, *Quarterly Journal of Economics*, November 1959, pp. 522 ff.

ideology most acutely, uses the concept pretty broadly as the source of 'preconceptions about the economic process'[1] and of the 'visions', as he calls them, of the economic system, which have been the starting-point for the broader theorizing of great economists, in particular Smith, Marx and Keynes, of whose 'visions', and of whose subsequent scientific processing of their 'visions', he gives very interesting accounts. As Schumpeter says:

'Analytic work begins with material provided by our vision of things, and this vision is ideological almost by definition. It embodies the picture of things as we see them, and wherever there is any possible motive for wishing to see them in a given rather than another light, the way in which we see things can hardly be distinguished from the way in which we wish to see them.'[2]

As with comprehensive ideologies, the larger-scale and more comprehensive kinds of 'visions', which Schumpeter ascribes as their starting-points to Smith, Marx and Keynes, hardly have the same importance today. With increasing specialization and division of labour, the comprehensive book of *Principles*, or of *General Theory*, and the 'visions' of the economic cosmos which inspired them, or from which they started, have been to a large extent replaced by particular partial 'visions' and hypotheses about parts of the economic system, which are less difficult to 'process' and test scientifically, and in which, therefore, it should be less easy for ideological preconceptions and prejudices to survive—though, on the other hand, just because these are less blatant and systematic they may be more difficult to track down and neutralize or eradicate. Still, ideology and 'vision' may be drawn on for the answers to scientific questions, or the answers may be shaped by the desire to build up or strengthen ideology and 'vision'.

Sir Roy Harrod has claimed that 'experience suggests that many of those Englishmen who grew up to be professional economists, are born either little inflationists or little deflationists. It is something in the blood that they cannot get rid of.'[3] (Harrod claims that he himself was born, or is, a little 'flationist'.) Without taking overseriously this theory of the biological determination, in one particular branch of economic analysis and policy, of English economists' ideological 'vision' of, or preconceptions about, economic processes, one may recognize how just is its emphasis on the profound and almost (but not quite) ineradicable extent to which economists' visions and preliminary hypotheses may be shaped pre-scientifically. Fifty to a hundred years ago many economists might have been

[1] *American Economic Review*, March 1949, p. 347.
[2] *History of Economic Analysis*, 1954, pp. 41–2.
[3] *Policy against Inflation*, 1958, p. VII.

described, with some rhetorical exaggeration, as having been 'born' little free-traders or little protectionists. But the most general and important typological classification of economists' pre- or extra-scientific ideological visions, would be in terms of their views on the role of the state and central controls on the one hand, and of individualist enterprise and the market mechanism (and, in particular, the resulting distribution of income and the justice thereof) on the other hand. Some, perhaps many, economists would claim that they try, with Jevons, 'to judge each case upon its merits, interpreting with painful care all experience which can be brought to bear upon the matter'.[1] But in fact, to a considerable extent, many economists who pronounce on policy tend to bunch somewhat, or polarize or crystallize, into 'planners' or 'price-mechanists' of greater or less extremity. We must emphasize as strongly as possible that we are not attacking the maintenance of strong and definite political principles as such, or upholding expediency against principle. We are simply emphasizing the presence of these political principles, or elements of ideology, and how they *may* shape the selection of facts and factual generalizations about economic processes, which it is practically almost impossible to test conclusively, or only in the most tentative and uncertain way, and as to which no kind of scientific consensus has been reached. The economist coming with a more or less extreme belief in individual initiative and the price mechanism, on the one hand, and the economist believing, in a more or less extreme way, in socialist planning on the other hand, tend to assert as empirically valid widely differing and contradictory pictures of the economic world and of economic behaviour and its motivations. Their 'visions' and preconceptions shape, in turn, more specific and detailed hypotheses as to, for example, the effects of progressive taxation on the supply of effort, or of changes in interest rates on investment, or as to the extent of economies of large scale, or the diagnosis of inflation in terms of 'demand-pull' or 'cost-push', and as to a whole range of empirical questions about economic behaviour and processes. We discuss further examples in subsequent sections, drawing on a brilliant lecture by Lutz.[2]

In fact, wherever there is ignorance the gap is liable to be pseudo-scientifically filled in by ideology or biased 'vision', not merely left blank, thus obstructing entry even into that ante-chamber of knowledge, realization that one does not know. Edgeworth described as 'a peculiarity of our study':

'that in the race of the sciences we are as it were handicapped by

---

[1] W. S. Jevons, *The State in Relation to Labour*, 1882, p. 166.
[2] F. A. Lutz, 'Politische Überzeugungen und nationalökonomische Theorie', *Ordo*, Bd. IX, 1957. See Sections 5 and 7 below.

having to start at a considerable distance behind the position of mere nescience. An effort is required to remove prejudices worse than ignorance; a great part of the career of our science has consisted in surmounting preliminary fallacies.'[1]

And these 'preliminary fallacies' have not merely been those of the general public, but those introduced into the subject by economists' own ideologies and 'visions', and often tenaciously upheld without or against testing.

We have been concerned here with ideologies, 'visions' and elements thereof, at the 'pre-scientific' stage. They are in at the start, so to speak, or there is free and frequent entry for them. But it remains to be examined whether why and how they can and do survive the discipline of the scientific process, and how far their survival is inevitable.

(4) PERSUASIVE LANGUAGE AND VALUE-LOADED CONCEPTS

We have seen that economists, like other scientists, are inevitably involved in kinds of value-judgments regarding the choice of their problems and their epistemological criteria. We have seen also that, perhaps more than most other scientists, they come to their problems as 'bundles of prejudices', and that though it is not logically inevitable that they do so as heavily 'value-loaded' as they sometimes are, they cannot come in a mental vacuum, but must bring at least some minimum of pre-scientific interest, concepts or 'vision'. As they proceed to formulate their questions and answers more precisely, they have to choose also their language, concepts and definitions, a choice that certainly ceases to be pre-scientific and which could be said to involve a kind of value-judgment. In what sense, or how far, do such inevitable choices impair the objectivity or neutrality of 'scientific', or would-be 'scientific', theories and statements?

In recent years there has been much discussion of 'persuasive' definitions and 'value-loaded' concepts in economics.[2] Some of this discussion seems to confuse together questions of logic (or methodology) and questions of psychology. For the distinction sometimes seems not to be kept sufficiently clear between, on the one hand, the scientific criteria of the empirical testability and truth or falsity of statements, or, alternatively, their logical consistency; and, on the other hand, 'psychological' questions as to their effects on people's

---

[1] *Papers Relating to Political Economy*, 1925, Vol. I, p. 5.

[2] Cf. G. Myrdal, *Value in Social Theory*, edited by P. Streeten, 1958, p. 1: 'Our very concepts are value-loaded . . . they cannot be defined except in terms of political valuations.' Cf. also I. M. D. Little, *A Critique of Welfare Economics*, 2nd Ed., 1957, who states (p. 274) that his book 'might, in part, be described as a study of the usage of influential and persuasive language in economics'.

behaviour or their influence, or persuasiveness. It also sometimes seems almost to be suggested that claims to objectivity, or value-neutrality, *must* be false, because the making of *any* statement involves *choices* of concepts, definitions and language, and that these choices involve value-judgments.[1] To see what there is in these suggestions it is necessary to distinguish between different kinds of choice and to see how significant each kind is. Otherwise the suggestion might prevail that we are inevitably operating in an all-pervasive atmosphere of 'persuasiveness' and 'value-loaded' language. Let us then distinguish four kinds of choices with regard to language or definitions:

(1) In the first place a writer on any subject has to choose the language in which he is going to write or publish his statements, say English, German or Afrikaans, and whether he is going to use mathematical or literary symbols. Certainly a kind of value-judgment is involved here, and in some cases one which might have political relevance, but it is so obviously a pre- or extra-scientific one that we take it to be irrelevant to the issues we are concerned with.

(2) Secondly, for purposes of analysis economists have to define more precisely imprecise, everyday terms like 'wages', 'saving', 'income', 'rent', 'value', and so on; that is, they have to choose definitions. The history of economics has been full of confused controversies, and of a kind of terminological dogmatism, as to the 'right', 'real', 'essential' or 'best' definitions of words like 'value', 'welfare' and 'savings'. But such controversies would now be widely recognized as involving the fallacy of 'essentialism' (as Popper has called it), and it would be agreed that, subject to what is found to be generally convenient usage, all definitions should ultimately be tolerated, so long as the choice is clearly stated and consistently followed, and unless due warning is given. This represents simply a consensus and value-judgment in favour of clarity of communication and the rules of logic, and, as such, is preliminary or pre-scientific, though the 'convenience' of a definition may in turn depend on the pre-scientific choice of the question or theory in which the economist is interesting himself.

(3) Not essentially different, though rather more complex, is the frequent case where various choices for the measurement of a concept or the 'weighting' of index numbers are involved. The obvious point to make is almost the same as that in the previous paragraph. To imply that one particular index of 'national income',

---

[1] Cf. P. Streeten, 'Introduction' to *Value in Social Theory*, by G. Myrdal, 1958, p. XXI: 'The point is that the concepts and propositions of even the most purely empirical investigation derive their meaning and significance from a purpose, an interest, and involve choice and, therefore, valuation.'

E

for example, is the sole, real, uniquely significant measure, represents a kind of 'essentialist' dogmatism which might perhaps be 'persuasive' for the uninitiated public. But surely today it would be recognized by economists—though, of course, not by the general public—that, as the rules or conventions for the scientific use of language entail, there can be no one single, exclusively significant 'national-income' measurement, but only a series of indices which may at any moment be moving in different ways. Of course, which figure one gives more attention to, will, or may, depend more or less on one's pre-scientific interest, or choice of problem or theory. But the accuracy of any particular national income figure, for example, or of estimated changes in it, or of the effects of changes, are empirical, testable questions, and what the estimated figure or change entails is a logical one.

When indices of, say, 'national-income' come to be used in discussions of economic policies, or as policy objectives, goals or measures of 'progress', the danger of non-logical 'persuasiveness' obviously becomes more acute. There is often a tendency for what one is able, or had decided, to give a measure or index of (say 'real national income-per-head'), gradually, and perhaps more or less unconsciously, to take on a highly questionable normative significance.[1] Here the connection between terminology, or definitions and 'interest' goes further. But *simply* from *'scientific'* statements involving such indices, whether they are definitional as to how they have been composed, or empirical as to how they behave, or logical as to what their movements logically entail, no valid normative conclusions or recommendations can logically be drawn.

(4) When it is argued that some sorts of concepts or definitions are incompatible with scientific neutrality, or that there is a whole range of national-income definitions and measurements between which a choice has to be made, and a relative interest expressed, more is meant, presumably, than simply that any choice of words or definitions can be said to involve a value-judgment of some kind.[2] It is implied that there may be a more or less intentionally propagandist, persuasive or evaluative element in the terms, concepts and

---

[1] Andrew Shonfield has commented on how 'we' (Western economists) have 'wished . . . our own techniques for measuring economic progress on to the underdeveloped countries. . . . We had observed that they had responded by forcing the pace of those particular things we had decided to measure. . . . As so often happens, the devotion to the ideal of precision at all costs leads the technicians to attach inordinate importance to the factors that they happen to be able to measure—whereas the truth about these factors is often not that they are important but that they are just familiar to the people who have been responsible for setting up the conventional methods of measurement.' *Encounter*, December 1961, pp. 60–63.

[2] P. Streeten, Introduction to *Value in Social Theory* by G. Myrdal, 1958, p. xxi.

definitions that are chosen, rendering the statements and theories in which they are used not merely, or purely, positive or descriptive, but, to some extent, also normative. This may be so. But the precise 'scientific' relevance of this point must be questioned, and the fundamental distinction insisted on between, on the one hand, questions of the empirically testable truth or falsity of statements, or their logical consistency or inconsistency, and of what they logically entail, and, on the other hand, their possible or actual effects, influence, or persuasiveness, or of the psychological reactions to them, or of the motives or suggestibility of those who discuss them. 'Scientific' criteria and rules of procedure are only concerned with the former and not with the latter questions, and only with the testable content or aspects of empirical statements and theories.

In any case, the concept of persuasive definitions, if it is not to be obfuscatory, must be sufficiently clearly defined and delimited, or the impression may be given that *all* definitions and concepts are, or may be, in some significant sense, impregnated with persuasive or evaluative overtones. As C. L. Stevenson, the inventor of the concept, makes clear, *any* definition expresses an interest, or a kind of value-judgment of the pre-scientific type involved in the choice of a problem for study, since it suggests that the concept, or what the concept refers to, is worth discussing.[1] All definitions must be 'persuasive' in this sense, but this is not enough to make them 'persuasive' in a significant moral or political sense.

Stevenson emphasized that merely because a definition (e.g. of national income) involves a choice and direction of interest, it is not thereby 'persuasive' in the sense he introduced:

'When a scientist introduces a technical term, in no matter how detached a manner, he indicates his interest in what he names—his estimation of the importance of talking about it, or of predicting its occurrence—and he often leads his readers to have a similar interest. It would be quite misleading to call all such definitions "persuasive".

'. . . The distinction depends on whether the term defined has a

[1] 'It will be obvious that no definition, however severely intellectual and detached it may be, can be wholly divorced from certain bearings, direct or indirect, upon human inclinations or purposes. Thus Russell, writing not of ethics but of logic and mathematics, has remarked: 'A definition usually implies (i.e. leads one to suspect) that the definiens is *worthy* of careful consideration. Hence the collection of definitions embodies our *choice* of subjects and our judgment as to what is more important." Now a choice of what is judged important or worthy of attention is a reflection of the speaker's attitudes, and may serve to redirect the attitudes of the hearer. If this is the usual effect of any technical definition (and Russell's observation seems beyond intelligent objection) then how are persuasive definitions to be distinguished from others?' C. L. Stevenson, *Ethics and Language*, 1945, p. 282.

strong emotive meaning, and upon whether the speaker employs the emotively laden word with dynamic purposes—with the predominating *intention* of changing people's interests. . . . When a definition is given mainly for the purposes of distinction or classification, when it is used to guide only those interests which (like *curiosity*) are involved in making the classification understood, and when it in no way suggests that this is *the one* legitimate sort of classification,then the definition will not be called "persuasive".'[1]

The sort of words, it has been pointed out, which mostly come in for definition,of this kind are 'those which have a relatively vague "conceptual" meaning but a very rich emotive meaning. . . . People seek to steal the good-will (or bad-will) which belongs to the word and use it for their own ends'.[2] Thus 'welfare', or 'economic welfare', has, or had, a fairly rich emotive meaning and a relatively vague conceptual meaning, but 'national income' has a relatively clear, (though far from fully precise), conceptual meaning, and not such a richly emotive meaning.

To be 'persuasive' in Stevenson's sense, therefore, a definition must influence more simply than the limited range of attitudes regarding what is judged important as a part of knowledge, and which, as we have seen, shape the scientist's preliminary choice of questions. They must influence what is judged important or desirable in other political or ethical respects. Above all, as Stevenson concludes, because the scientist is essentially involved in making definitions which inevitably involve judgments or evaluations of what is important or interesting knowledge, this does not mean, as he puts it, 'that science totters',[3] or is inevitably involved in evaluations as to what is politically or ethically desirable.

In any case, the influence, or persuasiveness of a sign, word, phrase or concept, depends on what happens to be the reactions of those who use or discuss it. To hold that any word is somehow *inherently* or *essentially* persuasive, normative or value-loaded, would be to profess a kind of terminological 'essentialism'. Economists, especially, can understand that a 'good' is not necessarily 'good'.

It is perhaps worth stressing further that it takes two to complete a process of persuasion, a persuader and a persuaded, and that to

[1] *Mind*, July 1938, p. 336.

[2] M. Warnock, *Ethics since 1900*, 1957, p. 101.

[3] *Op. cit.*, p. 290: 'There is unquestionably a possibility that interests in knowledge should be opposed, and lead to evaluative controversy, within science itself, about what is worth speaking of, or what classifications or distinctions are worth making. At times these issues are complicated enough to stand in the way of scientific agreement and must be debated by many of the methods that we have illustrated for ethics. But there is no occasion for philosophical fear, on this account, that science totters. The evaluative aspects of science involve only interests in knowledge.'

the extent that economics is pursued as, or economic problems discussed in terms of, a 'scientific' discipline, economists are not concerned with persuading one another or being persuaded as to what is politically or ethically good, right, just, beneficial or desirable, to any extent beyond simply the implication that the subject or question is of some interest and importance, and worth studying in accordance with 'scientific' criteria. A rule of using and understanding language non-persuasively broadly coincides with the rules of procedure regarding empirical testing and testability and mathematical deduction. Of course, all these rules are constantly broken. But if one makes the preliminary claim or value-judgment, that it is worth practising economics as a 'scientific discipline', then there is an implied obligation to make a reasonable attempt to keep these rules, which, though some absolute ideal purity may, by definition, be unattainable, are not impossibly difficult to keep to within practicable human limits. Of course, if economists want to, and do, act as persuaders, hidden or open, as is certainly sometimes the case, then they are, of course, directly interested in propagandist effects and persuasiveness. Scientific rules or 'discipline' in the use and understanding of language, or the rules of logic and of testing and testability, then go by the board, or come a bad second.

Myrdal claims that in economics and the social sciences inevitably 'our very concepts are value-loaded'.[1] If these value-loads simply consist in the implication that the problems of economics and the social sciences, or, indeed, of any sciences, are of interest, or worth studying, then this is certainly true and is perhaps almost or actually a tautology, or, at any rate, a triviality. We could not or would not introduce or define concepts if we had not some 'interest' in them, or in what they referred to. If Myrdal means, on the other hand, that economists often, though not always and inevitably, approach their problems, and proceed to conceptualize them, very heavily and intensively loaded with political and ethical predilections, then this certainly seems a valid generalization, though one which one could imagine having to be mitigated at least to some extent. But, important though these considerations are, Myrdal might well be taken to imply a good deal more, and this, we think, must be rejected. The 'value-load' in that unfortunate term 'welfare' may be so heavy that

[1] *Value in Social Theory* by G. Myrdal, edited by P. Streeten, 1958, p. 1. Elsewhere, in a comprehensive omnibus statement on the subject, Myrdal writes: 'Valuations enter into social analysis, not only when conclusions concerning policy are drawn, but already in the theoretical endeavour to establish what is objectively true—in the choice of a field of enquiry, the selection of assumptions, even the decision as to what is a fact and what is a value. Our concepts are, therefore, "value-loaded".' See his contribution ' "Value-loaded" Concepts' in *Money, Growth and Methodology*, Essays in Honor of Johan Åkerman, 1961, p. 274.

it is practically impossible to unload it completely. But such unloading as is necessary is quite practicable with most of the main concepts of economics, and if it has not been achieved as thoroughly as it could (and should) have been in all cases, it is quite possible, and an outstanding analytical task, to push the unloading further—if it is desired to cultivate a disciplined subject, free, or as practicably free as possible, of value-loads. As regards Myrdal's example that 'economic integration' is a value-loaded term, because it 'carries the implication that the attainment of economic integration—in some sense—is desirable', there is certainly no logical implication here, and even the persuasive suggestion is rather tenuous, easily neutralizable, and highly questionable—and, in any case, it is scientifically irrelevant.

The argument we are attempting to present has been summarized with admirable trenchancy as follows:

'That everyday language is value-loaded and that the problems of the social sciences are rooted in everyday life and of vital interest to society is undeniable. But this also holds good for the natural sciences which have likewise only gradually freed themselves from normative elements. Why should this not be achieved in the social sciences? The vocabulary of modern sociology has to a considerable extent been practically neutralized. In cases of doubt the convention suffices for purposes of scientific discussion that the terminology in question is to be taken as neutral and free of valuations. Infringements of this rule, just like infringements of the rules of logical deduction, can immediately be corrected, as in fact often today occurs. The rules of the game in a positive science are certainly in other ways not very easy to follow. Circular definitions, false proofs, faulty deductions and contradictions are common. One can only rely for their elimination and correction on the institutionalized mechanism of sanctions which operates in scientific discussion, which can also see to it that the language of science is generally kept neutral and free of valuations. . . . That the valuations of other branches of culture may diverge (from those of the scientist) and that such conflicts of values may create personal difficulties where one and the same person seeks to combine the social role of the scientist with those of, for example, the politician, the business man, the teacher or the pastor, is undeniable. In the field of politics a value-loaded language can be more useful than neutralized, analytical conceptual tools. Implicit valuations and pseudo-objective arguments may well prove more effective than logical deductions from explicit value-premises. The languages of political agitation and scientific argument diverge in opposite directions from that of everyday speech.'[1]

[1] H. Albert, *Schweizerische Zeitschrift für Volkswirtschaft und Statistik*, 1958, p. 339.

The history of economics has been full of persuasive, value-loaded language and definitions, and indeed Stevenson himself took the majority of his examples from our subject: 'productive' and 'unproductive' labour, the 'sterile' class, definitions of 'value' (particularly in terms of labour), 'natural' values and incomes, 'equilibrium', 'exploitation' and, above all, 'welfare'. As we saw in the last chapter, J. E. Cairnes, in 1870, was complaining 'of the double meaning of such "passionate" terms as "principle", "value", "worth", "service" and the like', and that 'the economic vocabulary unfortunately lends itself only too readily to this sort of theorizing and few writers have entirely escaped illusion from this cause'.[1] To a modern economist it may possibly seem a little strange to find another economist describing such terms as 'value' and 'service' as 'passionate'. Although today in many contexts such words may be used 'passionately' or 'persuasively', in the context of economists' theorizing about value and the pricing of productive 'services', all, or nearly all, 'passion' has long been spent, all persuasiveness neutralized, and such terms are readily understood in a quite neutral, non-persuasive and non-evaluative sense — which illustrates that words or concepts are not inherently or essentially normative, persuasive or value-loaded, not even such words as 'value', 'goods' or 'services'. There is such a thing as 'progress' in logical and scientific analysis and an important element in this consists of the neutralizing of the value-loads or persuasiveness of the everyday language economists start from. In fact, today, increasing sophistication and awareness make it difficult for an economist to get away with persuasive usages for very long, or very far, *vis-a-vis* other economists. Of course, persuasive usages will continue to be perpetrated just as the rules of logic and mathematics will continue to be broken, but the scientific processes of critical analysis are not ineffective in checking them. An economist may well succeed in 'persuading' himself, or his immediate school or disciples, with his persuasive language, and, of course, in an extra-scientific context such as a letter to a newspaper or a broadcast talk, he may 'persuade' members of the general public unversed in the discipline of scientific usage. Graphical methods particularly offer scope for public 'persuaders' on television. Prices or G.N.P. can, according to taste, be made apparently to have rocketed up, or remained almost stationary, by choosing the appropriate scale. But in scientific or disciplined contexts neither verbal nor graphical persuasiveness is likely today to have a significant influence for any length of time.[2]

[1] J. E. Cairnes, *Essays in Political Economy*, 1873, p. 322.
[2] A recent example of a comparatively subtle use of a persuasive definition seems to have occurred in respect of the concept of equilibrium in international trade, according to which the presence of import restrictions entailed, by defini-

The major recent example of a persuasive definition or concept is that of 'welfare' or 'economic welfare', and 'real national income' has also been cited.[1] But if we compare such a 'persuasive' statement as 'This policy will increase the welfare (or "real income") of the community' with such statements as 'This policy will increase the rate of growth' (or level of employment, or stability of prices), it is not obvious that there is inevitably and inherently something 'persuasive' about the former, and not about the latter, which certainly *can* be taken in a purely descriptive, positive sense.[2] It seems dogmatic to try to insist that the former statements (concerning 'welfare' and 'real income') *cannot*, or *must* not, be taken in the same positive mood as the latter, if this is made sufficiently clear, though certainly it might be urged that the terms had best be scrapped altogether.

Economists have often complained of the difficulties they are under in having to start with imprecise or ambiguous everyday language, and the normative-positive ambiguities in everyday language may be more dangerously confusing than purely positive ambiguities. It would be almost impossible to avoid *all* everyday words which started with some sort of persuasive overtones—'value', 'monopoly', 'equilibrium', and so on. But it was, of course, inviting normative-positive confusion to introduce such a highly-charged word as 'welfare' right into the centre of the discussion of economic policies, and to set it up as the main title and main concept of a whole branch of economics, as has been done over the last fifty years. On the whole, it would seem advantageous if the word 'welfare' was never uttered again by an economist, or, at any rate, never allowed out unless firmly shackled between inverted commas. It would surely be clearer simply to define a choice or efficiency criterion, or a movement in a particular national income index, without mentioning the word 'welfare'.

---

tion, 'disequilibrium', so that these had to be removed if 'equilibrium'—implicitly or explicitly suggested as the ideal—was to be reached. But this device was promptly exposed by other economists, who completely refused to be persuaded and neutralized its persuasiveness,—as they would have corrected it if it had been an error in logic or mathematics. Cf. F. Machlup, *Economic Journal*, March 1958, p. 23: 'The objections against persuasive definitions of equilibrium are not based on the fear that gullible people may actually be persuaded to stand up for the measures of policy "deduced" from arguments in which such an equilibrium concept is employed.'

[1] Cf. I. M. D. Little, *A Critique of Welfare Economics*, 2nd Ed., 1957, p. 275: 'Many economic statements, which appear at first sight to be merely descriptive, have value implications. Among the most important of such phrases are "increase of welfare" and "increase of real income".' J. de v. Graaff (*Theoretical Welfare Economics*, 1957, p. 2) states that 'we must place questions regarding "real income" in the normative division'. It is not clear what sort of 'must' this is.

[2] Cf. G. C. Archibald, 'Welfare Economics, Ethics and Essentialism', *Economica*, November 1959, p. 324.

There has been much progress in recent decades in the rapid neutralization of persuasiveness, and a reasonable standard of observance of the rule of non-persuasiveness is not impossible to attain if there is a general, critical consensus in favour of it, in spite of the economist's handicap of having to use, or start from, everyday language. Persuasive language and concepts do not represent some kind of inevitable all-pervasive 'value-loadedness' in economics. As Popper says:

'Ordinary language is not rational, but it is our task to rationalize it, or at least to keep up its standards of clarity. . . . We ourselves and our ordinary language are, on the whole, emotional rather than rational; but we can try to become a little more rational, and we can train ourselves to use our language as an instrument not of self-expression (as our romantic educationists would say) but of rational communication.'[1]

At least this seems to be 'our task', and an inevitable value-premiss, if we are claiming to cultivate our subject 'scientifically', or arrogating to ourselves any 'scientific' objectivity. Of course, in so far as economists take on the role of political persuaders and ideologues —and quite a number of them do—such tasks and value-premisses do not arise.

(5) BIAS IN HYPOTHESES AND THEIR TESTING

When the scientific processes of critical analysis and testing get started, the analytical part of them will begin with wringing out imprecisions and ambiguities (including 'persuasive' ambiguities) in everyday language, so as to arrive at workably precise definitions permitting of workably precise questions and hypotheses. Relations between the more precisely defined concepts are then analysed deductively, definitional equations and taxonomies can be drawn up, and purely deductive models can be constructed on postulated conditions. Only the rules of logic and mathematics, and testing as to the observance of these rules, are involved here, and a good deal of —though not, of course, all—'theorising' in economics has been of this purely analytical kind. Logical consistency is the only test in this case, and empirical testing is irrelevant since, at this stage, only definitions and analytical statements, without empirical content, are being dealt with. At the same time, and more or less linked with this analytical work, empirical hypotheses may be set out, either taken over from extra-scientific ideologies or 'visions', or based on 'hunch',

---

[1] K. R. Popper, *The Open Society and Its Enemies*, 4th Ed., 1962, Vol. III pp. 278 and 357.

introspection, impressionism, casual empiricism, or more systematic empirical investigation, and these call for the essential scientific process of the empirical testing of hypotheses and the collection and examination of evidence to test them. The 'objectivity' of scientific statements depends on this inter-subjective testing.

We are now faced with the well-known difficulty of the critical and rigorous testing of hypotheses, theories and statements in the economic and social field.[1] The practical possibility of testing theories critically and significantly often hardly exists, and the strong wish to see the facts in one particular way, as expressed in an initial ideologically biased hypothesis, may mean that there is not even a will to test, in the sense of a genuine critical attempt to falsify. It is all too easy, even when the scientific process of refining, testing and attempting to falsify hypotheses has begun, for economists to retain their belief in what they want to believe.

Let us, however, consider a highly optimistic account of how ideological prejudices and subjective biases and preconceptions, and the disagreements they lead to, are purged away by the discipline of the scientific process of selection by inter-subjective testing. Under the heading 'The Objectivity of Economic Science', Oskar Lange wrote in a well-known essay:

'The statements of economic science have objective validity. This means that two or more persons who agree to abide by the rules of scientific procedure are bound to reach the same conclusion. If they start with the same assumptions, they are bound, by the rules of logic, to derive the same theorems. If they apply the same rules of identification and verification, they are bound to reach agreement as to whether the theorems should be accepted as "true" or rejected as "unverified" or "false". The test of verification decides whether the assumptions are adequate or not. In the latter case they have to be replaced by new ones which lead to theorems able to stand the

[1] Cf. M. Friedman, *Essays in Positive Economics*, 1953, pp. 10–11: 'Unfortunately, we can seldom test particular predictions in the social sciences by experiments explicitly designed to eliminate what are judged to be the most important disturbing influence. Generally, we must rely on evidence cast up by the "experiments" that happen to occur. The inability to conduct so-called "controlled experiments" does not, in my view, reflect a basic difference between the social and physical sciences. . . . The denial to economics of the dramatic and direct evidence of the "crucial" experiment does hinder the adequate testing of hypotheses; but this is much less significant than the difficulty it places in the way of achieving a reasonably prompt and wide consensus on the conclusions justified by the available evidence. It renders the weeding-out of unsuccessful hypotheses slow and difficult. They are seldom downed for good and are always cropping up again. . . . One effect of the difficulty of testing substantive economic hypotheses has been to foster a retreat into purely formal or tautological analysis.'

test of verification. The final verdict with regard to any statement of economic science is thus based on an appeal to facts, i.e. to empirical observations.'[1]

Lange traced disagreements between economists, which he admitted were many and profound, to three sources, which are 'all due to failure to abide by the rules of scientific procedure and can be resolved by strict application of these rules'. The first of these sources of disagreement consists of differences as to social objectives, which depend on differences in value-judgments, the remedy being to state these explicitly so that agreement can be reached on what particular measures promote, or fail to promote, different objectives. Next there may be disagreements owing to a failure to abide by the rules of logic—which have an obvious remedy. It is the disagreement described by Lange as 'disagreement about facts' with which we are concerned here and for which his remedy seems especially optimistic:

'Such disagreement can always be removed by further observation and study of the empirical material. Frequently, however, the empirical data necessary to resolve the disagreement are unavailable. In such cases the issue remains unsettled. The conclusion that the issue cannot be settled with the data available has interpersonal validity. Agreement is reached to withhold judgment.'[2]

Lange is describing how, in his terms, ideally, or 'on paper', the rules of the game 'should', or might be hoped to, operate. We can only emphasize how wide is the range of questions in economics, and particularly of policy questions, where 'the empirical data necessary to resolve the disagreement are unavailable'. We can only point out how much of the empirical content of economic theorizing remains untested, or even practically untestable, at any rate sufficiently significantly to remove disagreement, and how little disposed 'to withhold judgment' economists show themselves to be, especially when they feel the urge to discuss policy recommendations. As we have already noted, often when scientific criteria 'did not uniquely determine a theory, its fitness to support moral or political indoctrination became an important factor for its acceptance'.[3] Whether it is the effects of changes in interest rates on investment, income-tax

---

[1] 'The Scope and Method of Economic Science', reprinted from the *Review of Economic Studies*, No. 13, 1945–46, in *Readings in the Philosophy of Science*, edited by H. Feigl and M. Brodbeck, 1953, p. 748. It seems that Lange may subsequently have come to harbour reservations as to some of his arguments in this paper.

[2] *Op. cit.*, p. 749.

[3] Cf. P. G. Frank, 'The Acceptance of Scientific Theories', in *The Validation of Scientific Theories* (ed. P. G. Frank), paperback edition, 1961, p. 19.

rates on the supply of effort, levels of employment on price levels, levels of profits on the policies of firms, or the extent of possible economies of scale—just to begin what could be an almost endless list—the issues indeed 'remain unsettled', though it certainly does not follow that 'agreement is reached to withhold judgment'. Lange's conception of a smooth, rapid and almost automatic process to agreement is as far from the reality of economic controversy as a model of a smooth, rapid and almost automatic tendency to full long-term equilibrium throughout the economic system is from economic reality. In fact, it may be doubtful how significant it is to assume even a 'tendency' towards it. Nevertheless, Lange undoubtedly states the formula for agreement and scientific consensus, and this *could* be followed out if there was a will to do so, though clearly a great deal of 'withholding judgment' would be required.

Schumpeter also describes how the scientific process of analysis and empirical testing tends to crush out the influence of ideology:

'The rules of procedure that we apply in our analytic work are almost as much exempt from ideological influence as vision is subject to it. Passionate allegiance and passionate hatred may indeed tamper with these rules. In themselves these rules, many of which, moreover, are imposed upon us by the scientific practice in fields that are little or not at all affected by ideology, are pretty effective in showing up misuse. And, what is equally important, they tend to crush out ideologically conditioned error from the visions from which we start. . . . And if this process is allowed to work itself out completely, it will indeed not protect us from the emergence of new ideologies, but it will clear in the end the existing ones from error. It is true that in economics, and still more in other social sciences, this sphere of the strictly provable is limited in that there are always fringe ends of things that are matters of personal experience and impression from which it is practically impossible to drive ideology, or for that matter conscious dishonesty, completely. The comfort we may take from our argument is therefore never complete. But it does cover most of the ground in the sense of narrowing the sphere of ideologically vitiated propositions considerably, that is, of narrowing it down and of making it always possible to locate the spots in which it may be active.'[1]

Perhaps realizing that his emphasis here was slightly over-optimistic Schumpeter went on to add the following qualifications:

'We have had to recognize, on the one hand, that although there exists a mechanism that tends to crush out ideologies automatically, this may be a time-consuming process that meets with many resist-

[1] *History of Economic Analysis*, 1954, p. 43 and p. 44.

ances and, on the other hand, that we are never safe from the current intrusion of new ideologies to take the place of the vanishing older ones.'

To say that the process of reaching agreement—including agreement to withhold judgment—is, in economics and the social sciences, a 'time-consuming' one 'that meets with many resistances', is certainly an understatement rather than an overstatement. It is not simply that the tests of a hypothesis, or of the evidence regarding it, may be so selective that it is only exposed to those which it will pass, that is, that they are no tests at all. There will often be an unwillingness simply to set out the evidence and accept its inconclusiveness. Rather an attempt will be made to weigh the evidence up, or interpret it in favour of the hypothesis, so that it is protected rather than tested. Alternatively, there may be a retreat into what Popper calls 'conventionalist stratagems' by elastically modifying the assumptions or definitions involved to protect the hypothesis against falsification, ultimately removing all falsifiable empirical content by reducing it to a tautology.[1]

An economist may come to an economic problem 'loaded' with ideological prejudices or political 'principles', the most important implications of which are the desirability of certain social objectives and of policies to promote them. It has been all too easy for such an economist to support his political and economic policy objectives by persisting in the assertion of those empirical propositions from which they can most easily be derived, that is, from which they follow on the basis of the most widely acceptable value-judgments. The process has been aptly described as follows:

'The question arises how to justify [policy] objectives by theoretical reasoning. Two ways are open to the theorist. One is faulty, i.e. elusive or contradictory reasoning; the other is the choice of suitable assumptions from which theoretical conclusions are logically deduced, supporting the political and economic objectives. The first way, though often followed, is theoretically less interesting. As to the second way, it is clear that if the choice of assumptions were free one could prove what one pleases. Actually, the choice is not free because assumptions which are obviously contrary to known facts cannot be used. But many facts in the field of economics are not known, about others only little is known, and many are controversial. Very often the quantitative significance of one or the other fact is debatable. If the theorist then attaches great significance to one fact and little to another his conclusions may well be in direct opposition to those at which he would have to arrive if he reversed his quantitative appraisal. It is here where the theorist has a wide field of

[1] v. K. R. Popper, *The Logic of Scientific Discovery*, 1959, pp. 82–4.

activity where social ideals often determine, without difficulty from the logical point of view, the "objective" conclusion.'[1]

Von Mering shows this process at work in contrasting theories of interest, the history of which right down to the present day is rich in instances of the influence of ideological and political preconceptions.[2] International trade, tax incidence and public debt are other subjects where von Mering cites interesting examples, and the 'stagnation' thesis is another case.[3] Those with contrasting political preconceptions—in favour, say, of economic individualism, on the one hand, or socialist planning, on the other hand—do not merely differ in their valuations of social and economic objectives, they tend to uphold as valid quite different sets of factual generalizations about economic behaviour and processes, and persist in upholding them whether they have withstood testing or not.

The process of describing a situation, or diagnosing a disease, in terms which suggest or imply that the kind of remedial measures required—given certain fairly widely accepted value-judgments—are ones which the doctor wished to have adopted *anyway*, can probably be illustrated from the debate in the early and middle 'fifties as to whether inflationary processes in the British economy came about through 'demand-pull' or 'cost-push'.[4] It was very

[1] O. von Mering, *Social Ideals and Economic Theory*, Kyklos, Vol. IV, 1950, p. 175.

[2] O. Hobson (in *Not Unanimous*, edited by A. Seldon, 1960, p. 87), criticizing the report of the Radcliffe Committee, writes: 'Its left-wing members started with a fundamental antagonism to the idea that regulation of a modern industrial community must hinge on control of its money supply. In the endeavour to meet this antagonism, an alternative theory, which one may call the "liquidity structure theory", has been elaborated and adopted by the whole Committee.' The process here described works, of course, both ways, from left to right, so to speak, as well as from right to left. But we are not concerned with how far a *'tu quoque'* may be justifiable regarding *'right*-wing' experts who 'started with a fundamental antagonism' to central regulation and discretionary controls, and were concerned to establish the theory of the effectiveness of acting on the quantity of money. Our point is simply the pervasiveness of political bias and latent value-premises in theorizing about monetary processes and policies, the desirability of making one's premises much clearer and more explicit, and of acknowledging the role of bias in the selection and weighting of evidence.

[3] 'Observation teaches us that liberal economists usually reject the assumption of a deficiency of private investment opportunities, while economists sympathetic to planning very willingly make use of it.' F. A. Lutz, 'Politische Überzeugungen und nationalökonomische Theorie', *Ordo*, Bd. IX, 1957, p. 14. See below, Section 7 of this chapter.

[4] 'The economist may be tempted to stress one set of arguments because he believes this supports a policy which is desirable in any case for other reasons.' E. Devons, *Essays in Economics*, 1961, p. 44. The role of latent ideological or political 'visions' or preconceptions in macro-economic theorizing has been described as follows: 'Attitudes to inflation are coloured by very general, more or less implicit, assumptions about how the economy works; and in particular

difficult, if not practically impossible, to devise tests of whether it was 'demand-pull' processes rather than 'cost-push', or *vice versa*, which were predominantly at work in the actual inflationary situation. In fact, these two concepts were often not precisely defined or delimited. On the empirical question as to which process was predominantly at work there was, for some years, no agreement and no tests sufficient to eliminate one or other of the alternative answers. On the contrary, one or the other formula was championed with exclusivist fervour, and, to a considerable extent, it seemed, in accordance with preconceived political predilections. Those generally favouring free markets and opposed to the extension of central controls tended to favour the 'demand-pull' description, as this implied that no essential expansion of central regulation or discretionary controls was necessary. The 'cost-push' description suggested or implied—given other widely supported policy objectives—that a significant extension of the range of central controls was necessary, and this tended to be supported by those who had expressed an inclination—or no disinclination—to such extension, for other reasons. Not that the mechanism, stressed by Schumpeter, 'that tends to crush out ideologies automatically', has not been operative in gradually taking some of the exclusivist political sting out of the controversy, but, as he said, it 'may be a time-consuming process'.[1]

Another very broad and somewhat vague empirical generalization, which seems liable to be shaped in opposite senses by conflicting political preferences, concerns the extent of economies of scale in modern industries. Socialistically inclined economists are apt to emphasize the prevalence and growing importance of economies of scale, and of a trend to widespread monopolistic conditions, as a reason for nationalization or for public ownership or control. For example, according to H. D. Dickinson:

about the degree to which it is sensitive to "market forces". It is difficult to bring such general preconceptions to the test of evidence, without first making them explicit.' (J. C. R. Dow, *Economic Journal*, September 1958, p. 613.) It still remains very difficult to test them when they *are* made explicit.

[1] In his 1959 address to the Royal Economic Society, the then Economic Adviser to H.M.G. stated: 'Economists have been, and to some extent still are, broadly divided' as between the 'demand-pull' and 'cost-push' descriptions or diagnoses. (*Economic Journal*, December 1959, pp. 647–8.) Two years later, however, the effects of Schumpeter's 'time-consuming process' were, to some extent, apparent in the form of a certain *détente* in expert opinion: 'The experts . . . were at one time divided into two schools: one laid stress on the pull of demand . . . ; the other stressed the upward push of negotiated rises in rates of pay, initiating rises in cost. More recently the experts have found more common ground. There is now a wide measure of agreement that both "demand-pull" and "cost-push" have been active.' (Fourth Report of the Council on Prices, Productivity and Incomes, July 1961, p. 15.)

'In the early and middle period of capitalism, diminishing costs did
not often occur . . . equilibrium was possible under competition.
. . . But more recent times have seen the rapid growth of decreasing-
cost industries. . . . What is needed, at any rate for the large-scale
sector of the economy, is a system of production by public bodies
. . . not obliged to make profits.'[1]

Jewkes, on the other hand, contradicts this generalization and
asks 'Where is the evidence in support of the view that "indivisibilities" are of growing importance?' He asserts that 'we are not
really confronted with the awkward choice between monopoly and
inefficiency', and that 'it is difficult to believe that indivisibilities do
really create a new situation in industry which now makes inappli-
cable the general case for a free economy'.[2] Of course, no proof can
be offered that economists' political attitudes are liable to determine
their beliefs about industrial technology, rather than that their
beliefs about industrial technology shape their political beliefs. But,
at least, the former seems not impossible.[3]

We must add here that the biased support of hypotheses and
assumptions when the evidence is inadequate or disputed, may not
always stem from *political* preconceptions. An economist, or school
of economists, may see and weigh the evidence, as he or they want
to see and weigh it, out of a determination to uphold his or its
particular theory, without political preconceptions playing a part.
Moreover, there is often a strong desire to come to *some* general
conclusion, to have something reasonably succinct and coherent to
say, rather than to have no definite conclusion to offer at all, and if
the conclusion is unusual or novel so much the better.[4] Even if no
political or ideological preconceptions and no policy issues are
involved, there may be a tendency to selective simplification, or
'modellization', either quite independently of any political bias, or,

[1] *Humanitas*, Autumn 1946, quoted by J. Jewkes, *Ordeal by Planning*, 1948,
p. 43.
[2] J. Jewkes, op. cit., pp. 42–3. An interesting reversal in the discussion of this
issue has emerged in the debate over the economic gains or losses from Britain
joining the Common Market. Socialistically inclined economists, who tended
to be politically opposed to Britain joining, were to be found categorically
denying the general significance of economies of scale: 'There is nothing in the
argument that we need a larger internal market for such an improvement' (in
investment and innovation). T. Balogh, *The Observer*, October 21, 1962. We are
not accusing anyone of outright contradiction, but are simply suggesting that
there may be a certain mutability of factual generalization—rather like Orwell's
'mutability of the past' in *1984*.
[3] See below the quotations from F. Lutz in Section 7 of this chapter.
[4] 'It is simply a fact that many of our best economists are irresponsible. They
would as lief be wrong in an interesting way as be right along with the mob.'
P. Samuelson, *Problems of the American Economy*, Stamp Memorial Lecture,
1961, 1962, p. 19.

more probably, effectively reinforcing it. This process has been cogently analysed by H. G. Johnson, with reference to the theory of international trade:

'In order to choose between the impossible number of alternatives with which even a relatively simple analytical problem confronts him, the theorist is strongly tempted to eliminate some of the cases by prejudging the results of measurements he does not and perhaps could not make, either by illegitimately assuming that a number of qualitative statements can be added up into a quantitative fact, or by postulating an ideal world in which only the cases he chooses will exist. This temptation is particularly dangerous when questions of economic policy are involved, because then the desire for simplicity may be reinforced by personal preferences in prompting the exclusion of possible cases.'[1]

We wish to emphasize, however, that in spite of its well-known difficulties, and the deep and powerful psychological resistances at work, the mechanism of intersubjective testing often does its work of wringing out ideological prejudices and presuppositions, and of modifying 'visionary' hypotheses, at least sufficiently effectively to render complete and wholesale scepticism unjustifiable. It *could* be made to work more rapidly and efficiently. This does not mean that an attempt should be made to prohibit guess-work, particularly with regard to practical policy problems which cannot wait. It does mean that guesses, and particularly conflicting guesses, should, at least, be acknowledged as such, that is, as statements or theories that are untested or inadequately tested. When we discuss below (Section 8) predictions required for the elucidation of the choice of policies, we shall have to consider the controversial question of how far economists are 'entitled' to base these on various kinds or degrees of judgment or hunch.

We have seen that the economist has to select his questions or problems, and the scientific criteria or rules of the game by which he conducts his studies. He also selects, in a sense, his language, concepts and definitions. None of these kinds of selection or valuation, which are common to all sciences, need, or indeed should, be held to destroy scientific objectivity, or the possibility thereof, in any significant sense. We have also seen that whatever ideological or political prejudices or presuppositions he starts from, the scientist cannot, according to his rules of procedure, 'select' his theories, hypotheses, or answers to his questions, but must let the selection be settled in accordance with the rules of logic and mathematics, and of critical intersubjective empirical testing, which he himself has set

[1] *Economic Journal*, December 1951, p. 827.

F

up, preferably showing at least some disposition to admit that the evidence is inconclusive. That is the position we have reached so far. But we shall have to examine the view that the scientist does, and must, in the nature of his task, select causes and hypotheses. Let us first, however, briefly consider the problem of selection and bias in writing history.

(6) BIAS AND OBJECTIVITY IN HISTORY AND HISTORICAL SELECTION

We referred previously (in Section 2 above) to the problem of selection in history, and we must now enquire rather further as to whether, how far, and in what way, value-judgments may be involved in historical selection. We might avoid this problem, on which, of course, there is a large and controversial literature, by claiming that we are concerned simply with the premisses and methods of economics, and with economic analysis and its application to policies, and not with economic history. But this would be something of an evasion. For economists are constantly concerned with questions of economic history, with the explanation of particular events and episodes, and especially with recent and contemporary history. They are constantly trying to establish conclusions, or illustrations, concerning longer or shorter periods of history, and they do this especially when discussing policies. Moreover, the frontier between economics and economic history, never in practice very clearly and explicitly marked or observed, has become much more frequented and blurred as more and more explicit attention has been given to the problems of economic growth and development. In fact, the study of economic growth, in general comprehensive terms, unless the questions are very cautiously formulated, offers an open invitation to 'historicist' ambitions, to the propounding of historical 'laws' and stages, and to the value-loaded teleology which often accompanies these efforts. But while we do not feel obliged to investigate at all thoroughly controversial issues of the methodology of history, such as the problem of historical objectivity, or the role of value-judgments in historical writing, we cannot neglect this frontier altogether.

A theoretical science is concerned both with general and particular statements, but especially with establishing general statements or laws, particular statements providing only test statements, or—and this is important—the specifications of the conditions (or 'assumptions') for applying a general law to a particular case for purposes of making a prediction. The historian, on the other hand, though inevitably using general statements and laws, is not concerned to establish these, but only particular, singular statements. Like the theoretical scientist he is involved in a kind of *a priori* value-judgment in accepting criteria for evidence and in selecting questions for study. But it may seem that the historian not merely has to select his questions but to some extent selects the answers he proposes, or selects what is relevant to an answer. It is argued, for example, that the historian cannot possibly give a *complete* account of an historical episode and all its antecedents, or reproduce it in its entirety, and that value-judgments are inevitably involved in his selection of what to include as relevant.

To some extent, at least, this argument can be countered by observing that if an historian does not start from a very precise question, as historians often do not, then what is relevant to his answer will be imprecise and will continually be requiring selection, involving a kind of value-judgment, as he goes along. If he does not make, *a priori*, the question selected (and the value-judgments involved) clear and precise, then these value-judgments will emerge in the answer he gives, and in the selection as to what is relevant which it reveals. If he starts out to write 'The History of Europe (or of Economic Thought) 1860–1960', he will have to select at some stage, or as he goes along, what, for him, 'the history of Europe (or of economic thought) 1860–1960' consists of. If he starts from a vague question such as 'What were the causes of the industrial revolution?' he will have to select the 'relevant' causes, or what is relevant to the 'causes'. On the other hand, if he starts from relatively precise questions such as 'Where, When and How did Hitler die?' or 'What was the increase in population, or steel output, in Britain between 1900 and 1950?' then what is 'relevant' will be comparatively clear-cut.

However, the peculiarly historical problem of selection arises from the absence of a standard of relevance of the kind which exists in theoretical sciences. Popper has pointed out that whereas theoretical sciences have laws and generalizations 'as centres of interest to which observations are related, or as points of view from which observations are made', there are no universal historical laws which can possibly fulfil this function:

'It must be taken over by something else. For undoubtedly there can be no history without a point of view; like the natural sciences, history must be *selective* unless it is to be choked by a flood of poor and unrelated material. . . . The only way out of this difficulty is, I believe, consciously to introduce a *preconceived selective point of view* into one's history; that is, to write that history which *interests us*. This does not mean that we may twist the facts until they fit into a framework of preconceived ideas or that we may neglect the facts that do not fit. On the contrary, all available evidence which has a

bearing on our point of view should be considered carefully and
objectively. . . . But it means that we need not worry about all those
facts and aspects which have no bearing upon our point of view
and which therefore do not interest us.'[1]

As Popper stresses, maintaining historical objectivity involves
being conscious and critical of one's own selective point of view and
its limitations. It is quite possible to maintain this to a reasonable,
if not to some absolutely pure and ideal extent. To claim objectivity
for an historical account, or that one account is more objective or
less biased than another, is not just meaningless naïveté. One achieves
a measure of 'objectivity' by stressing the 'subjective' elements in
one's answers. We need hardly add that to uphold this possibility
and practicability of reasonable objectivity is not to deny how much
of economic history, and of the history of economic thought, has
been written with a strong underlying desire to attack or defend
particular economic policies and systems, or to suggest the need for
particular sorts of policy.

The theoretical economist needs and uses economic history to
provide examples of a particular theoretical model, or to suggest
(given certain normative assumptions which may or may not be
explicitly stated) the desirability of particular policies. Obviously the
scope for bias in selecting and defining historical examples may be
very wide, and the accuracy of statistical estimates used as examples
may be highly questionable — as, for example, in discussions of
'the' rate of growth of the British economy where the dates of the
period taken for measuring 'the' rate of growth make a significant
difference.[2]

The difficulties of presenting an objective historical account
become immense when an attempt has to be made to present
historical facts not only for purposes of a discussion of policy, but
sufficiently succinctly and graphically to be understood by the
general public. For example, in its first report (1958), the Council
on Prices, Productivity and Incomes stated:

'It has been our aim to present the relevant facts about the movements in recent years in prices, productivity and incomes in language
intelligible not only to economists but to all who may be interested
in these questions and to comment on those facts.'[3]

[1] *The Poverty of Historicism*, paperback edition, 1961, p. 150.
[2] See the controversy over '*the*' British rate of economic growth between C. G.
Clark and F. W. Paish where, mainly as a consequence of taking different periods
of years, they arrived at estimates 70 per cent apart (1.3 per cent and 2.2 per cent).
See *The Listener*, July 6, 13, 20 and 27, 1961.
[3] Council on Prices, Productivity and Incomes, First Report, 1958, p. 1.

At different points it took its review back to 1850, 1938, 1946 and 1949. Historical selection, or value-judgments of a kind, were inevitable as to what, very roughly, was 'relevant' to the comprehensive and imprecise policy objectives set out in the terms of reference: 'the desirability of full employment and increasing standards of life based on expanding production and reasonable stability of prices'. What is 'relevant' is a vague question to which the answer must depend on one's interests. But that is quite a distinct question from that of the truth or falsity of whatever factual material is produced.

Historical explanation, furthermore, involves discovering and asserting the sufficient conditions for historical events. Often, or usually, these conditions are impossible to ascertain fully, and historians give, and can only give, what they hold to be the main, or most important, or fundamental causes. Here there is wide scope for subjectivity and bias—as one finds in debates over 'the causes' of particular wars and economic depressions—and sometimes not even a reasonable measure of objective consensus emerges. Statements assigning causal weights to different factors in historical processes, though not inevitably and in principle devoid of objective substance, are, in practice, often highly vague and subjective. As Nagel concludes:[1]

'Doubtless the basic trouble in this area of inquiry is that we do not possess at present a generally accepted, explicitly formulated, and fully comprehensive scheme for weighing the evidence for any arbitrarily given hypothesis so that the logical worth of alternate conclusions relative to the evidence available for each can be compared. Judgments must be formed even on matters of supreme practical importance on the basis of only vaguely understood considerations; and, in the absence of a standard logical canon for estimating the degree in which the evidence supports a conclusion, when judgments are in conflict each often appears to be the outcome of an essentially arbitrary procedure. This circumstance affects the standing of the historian's conclusions in the same manner as the findings of other students. Fortunately, though the range of possible disagreement concerning the force of evidence for a given statement is theoretically limitless, there is substantial agreement among men experienced in relevant matters on the relative probabilities to be assigned to many hypotheses. Such agreement indicates that, despite the absence of an explicitly formulated logic, many unformulated habits of thought embody factually warrantable principles of inference. Accordingly, although there are often legitimate grounds for

[1] See 'The Logic of Historical Analysis', by E. Nagel, reprinted in *Readings in the Philosophy of Science* edited by H. Feigl and M. Brodbeck, 1953, p. 700.

doubt concerning the validity of specific causal imputations in history, there appears to be no compelling reason for converting such doubt into wholesale scepticism.'

Among the 'other students', whose findings are put in doubt by these considerations, are students of economics, and Nagel's perhaps optimistic arguments lead on to our next problem as to the role or scope for subjectivity and value-judgments in analysing causal processes, and with regard to inductive inferences, prediction and the treatment of uncertainty.

(7) BIAS AND THE SELECTION OF CAUSES AND 'DETERMINANTS'

We have seen how the writing of history involves selection, and have noticed the problem of the 'weighting' of historical causes. It is arguable that the complex interdependence of economic, social and political phenomena, and the impossibility of isolating processes to test out the relative weights of 'causes' and 'effects' by laboratory experiments, means that the economist has, inevitably, more or less subjectively to select and 'weigh' causes. He can do this by simplificatory postulates in an abstract model, say, of the business cycle. But in *applying* any model to explaining or predicting in an actual historical case, the economist has to select or 'weigh' what he considers to be the actually important forces at work. Inevitable ignorance of the precise causal 'weights' to be assigned to different factors has to be, or at any rate often is, filled out by subjective impressionism, guesses and hunch, not in principle untestable, but practically not at the moment testable, or tested to the extent that some measure of consensus emerges. In the taking of practical decisions, which will not wait, this will often be unavoidable. But, of course, largely untested subjective guesses and hunch may be shaped by political and ideological bias and presuppositions. The problem has been well described by Lutz:

'Every change of an economic condition spreads its effects fan-wise throughout the whole system. Such a change in data sets off causal chains running in all directions. It is not possible for the theorist to follow out *all* of them completely and there is nothing for it but to leave aside some of them and take up the others under the never really valid assumption of *ceteris paribus*. He therefore has to make a judgment as to which causal chains he holds to be more important. But it is always at least conceivable that his judgment is quite unconsciously influenced by his political convictions. It must always be remembered that the theorist seldom detaches himself from the normative implications of his subject. So when he has followed out, purely analytically, some of the causal chains, he will always be thinking instinctively of how the effects he has analysed, if they seem to him unfavourable, can be counteracted or removed by policy measures. According to his attitude in principle to state intervention, he may, possibly, from the start, search for those causal chains which justify interventionist measures, or the reverse. One economist, for example, will emphasize unfavourable frictions which will obstruct the reaching of a new equilibrium when a change in data occurs. Another economist will make light of such frictional resistances and will push his analysis rapidly through to the new equilibrium condition in which everything is all right again.'[1]

An example of different or contrasting types of causal processes which have strong political implications is the somewhat misleadingly named division into 'short-period' and 'long-period' processes. The 'weighting' given to these two different types of process in general abstract economic theorizing, or in the explanation of particular historical processes, may be, and seems often to be, guided by political and ideological presuppositions. As Lutz says:

'The theorist is always free to interest himself solely in the short-period effects of a change or in the long-period effects. Keynes, for example, explicitly favoured the short-period treatment, as the assumptions underlying his system regarding given productive equipment clearly show. This choice between the short period and the long period leaves room for political presuppositions. The classics who always kept in view the beneficial long-period effects were non-interventionists, while today, economists who limit themselves to short-period effects—and these always consist of the unfavourable frictions before a new equilibrium is reached—appear rather to be interventionists. It remains an open question whether the classicals concentrated on the beneficial long-period effects because they rejected state intervention on the grounds of their political attitude regarding the role of the state, or whether they limited the economic role of the state as a result of their long-period treatment. The former seems to me by no means impossible.

'The same question arises regarding modern theorists who confine themselves to short-period effects . . . Whether an inclination to state intervention gives rise to short-period treatment, or the other way round, also remains an open question. Both are possible. I believe that the path is very often *from* the attitude regarding state intervention *to* the choice of short-period treatment, and not the reverse. My experience of theoretical discussions with colleagues has shown me that, nearly always, liberal economists are much more ready to apply

[1] F. A. Lutz, 'Politische Überzeugungen und nationalökonomische Theorie', *Ordo*, Bd. IX, 1957, p. 15.

long-period treatment than their opponents who incline to state intervention and put short-period disturbances in the forefront. . . .

'I cannot provide any concrete proofs because, of course, no economist will say straight out that he uses a short-period treatment because he favours state intervention, or a long-period treatment because he is opposed to it. These influences work at the sub-conscious level. But the possibility of this influence certainly exists and I personally have no doubt at all that it is actually at work in many cases.'[1]

Lutz goes on to cite an example of the selection of short-period and long-term causal processes in international trade theory.

The relation between the simplificatory selection of causes, and political bias, is also apt to be specially close in those mono-causal theories which used to be more influential than they are today (e.g. the labour theory of value and some versions of the marginal utility theory stressing 'consumers' sovereignty').[2] Sometimes, also, some elements will be stressed as 'causal' and others not, because the latter are held to be data which are unalterable, or which *should* not be altered. For example, if a country is in balance of payments difficulties those whose political attitude leads them to rule out devaluation will stress other elements, for example, perhaps wages, as the 'cause' of the difficulties, rather than an over-valued currency —or *vice versa*.[3] An analysis of causal responsibility or imputation is confused or combined with an analysis of moral or political responsibility, 'guilt', scapegoat-hunting, or with a kind of 'essentialist' dogmatizing as to what the 'real' cause is.

If the economist selects or assigns weights to different causes in a highly complex process, in partial ignorance of what these weights or the 'causes' at work actually are, on the basis of largely untested hunch or impressionism, agreement and consensus will be unlikely. The ideal—perhaps almost Utopian—recipe is Lange's formula of 'agreement to withhold judgment', or else guesses and hunches must be put forward as such, so that at least some measure of agreement to differ, pending further evidence, may be attainable.[4]

[1] F. A. Lutz, *op. cit.*, p. 16. Cf. also J. Viner's essay, 'The Short View and the Long in Economic Policy', in *The Long View and the Short*, 1958, pp. 103 ff. Viner holds that 'this habit of taking the long view is not only characteristic of the orthodox economic theorist, but in the discussion of matters of economic policy it is often the principal characteristic by which he can be distinguished from other professional economists or even from the intelligent layman' (p. 107).

[2] Cf. H. Albert, 'Die Problematik der Ökonomischen Perspektive', *Zeitschrift für die gesamte Staatswissenschaft*, 1961, p. 438 ff.

[3] Cf. H. Giersch, *Allgemeine Wirtschaftspolitik*, Grundlagen, 1960, p. 43.

[4] Cf. E. Devons, *Essays in Economics*, 1961, p. 46: 'There might be more understanding by the public of the issues involved if economists exercised self-restraint and confined themselves to attempting to explain the nature and complexity of the problems, rather than providing conflicting and widely divergent solutions.'

(8) BIAS IN ECONOMIC PREDICTIONS

Our examination of how political prejudices and valuations get into and can survive in the shaping of economic theories and hypotheses, applies also as regards economic predictions. For a prediction, of a strictly scientific type, is, as we shall discuss below, simply one aspect, or implication, of a scientific theory. Scientific explanation is simply 'prediction written backwards'.[1] We are adding this discussion of prediction to what we have said about causation, because of the contradictory attitudes economists take about prediction, and for the further illustrations afforded of the operation of subjectivity and bias.

As with causal explanations, the difficulties of precise and critical testing make it easy for contradictory predictions to be maintained and even retrospectively to be defended. We cannot explain completely and we cannot predict completely, and our incompletenesses, or ignorance, are apt to be filled in according to bias and ideology. It may be that in some cases the predictions of economists have been so shaped by bias that they predict what they want to happen, as when a Marxist economist predicts a socialist revolution. But, more often, these events are predicted which are not so much wanted by the predictors for their own sakes, but because they will, on widely agreed normative assumptions, require, as remedial measures, policies which the predictors want anyway (e.g. that there will be inflation, and/or stagnation, unless there is much more central planning—or, alternatively, much less).[2]

Some economists stress prediction as the ultimate purpose of economic science, and perhaps a majority would broadly agree.[3]

[1] A. Marshall, *Industry and Trade*, 1919, p. 7, quoted by R. C. Tress, 'The Contribution of Economic Theory to Economic Prognostication', *Economica*, August 1959, p. 194.

[2] As Lord Robbins has observed (*Politics and Economics*, 1963, p. 111): 'The fact is, I suspect, that when it is a question of diagnosing what we believe to be present evils, we economists are particularly liable to the temptation to drive home our point by warnings which go considerably further than the circumstances of the case would in fact justify. The appendix to Sir John Sinclair's *History of the Public Revenue* (Third Edition, 1803) contains a most salutary list of unfulfilled predictions of imminent catastrophe by English economists; and it would be very easy indeed to bring it up to date.' The point is that all these dire warnings are not uttered out of a sheer delight in inspissated gloom for its own sake, but, very often, in order to persuade governments to adopt policies the predictors of catastrophe want *anyway*.

[3] Cf. M. Friedman, 'The Methodology of Positive Economics', in *Essays in Positive Economics*, 1953, p. 7: 'The ultimate goal of a positive science is the development of a "theory" or "hypothesis" that yields valid and meaningful (i.e. not truistic) predictions about phenomena not yet observed.' Also, G. J. Stigler, *Five Lectures on Economic Problems*, 1950, p. 23: 'The purpose of the study of economics is to permit us to make predictions about the behaviour of economic phenomena under specified conditions. *The sole test of the usefulness*

But others appear to reject economic prediction completely, or almost completely, though without holding, apparently, to a purely historical method and conception of the subject. For example, Jewkes holds 'that economists cannot without stepping outside their discipline predict in the sense of telling us what will happen in the future', and he rejects 'predictions as an activity proper to economic science'. By attempting predictions (or, at any rate, some kinds of predictions), Jewkes holds that economists may allow 'their authority completely to lapse by seeking to bluster a way into the ranks of the politicians through making bogus claims for the power of their science'.[1]

Jewkes supports his case by pointing out how often economists' predictions have been wrong ('the long list of appalling errors') and suggests that this may be due to the fact 'that economists, like other scientists, are biased', so that 'different economists looking at the same evidence frequently reach very different conclusions about the future'[2] (and about the present and the past, it might be added).

However, later on in his analysis, it appears that Jewkes's objections do not apply to *all* predictions of any and every kind (if they did, one might wonder what use there could be for economic knowledge). In fact, Jewkes argues that economists should have made *more* of *some sorts* of prediction, and complains that they 'have so frequently been reluctant to recommend the processes of the free market, the forces of supply and demand, as the most effective system for correcting economic maladjustments'. He indicates the kinds of prediction—surely very difficult—which he would like to see economists attempting—for example, with regard to the 'danger point' for progressive taxation.[3]

of an economic theory is the concordance between its predictions and the observable course of events.' (Italics added.)

[1] J. Jewkes, in *Economics and Public Policy*, Brookings Lectures, 1954, 1955, pp. 82 and 99. F. H. Knight also has very fundamental objections to prediction in economics: 'I must say, dogmatically if you like, that prediction or control, or both, do not and cannot apply in a literal sense to social science. . . . Science in this sense—knowledge used for prediction and control—simply does not apply in a society with freedom and equality.' *Intelligence and Democratic Action*, 1960, p. 69.

[2] J. Jewkes, *op. cit.*, pp. 85–6.

[3] *Op. cit.*, pp. 92 and 98. For a further statement of Jewkes's views see *Lloyds Bank Review*, April 1953, where he complains of 'this neurotic hankering after prediction', and holding that 'the purpose of a science is understanding and not the power to predict'. He states: 'It cannot be too strongly emphasized that there is nothing in economic science which enables us to foretell events. Those who claim otherwise are dragging their subject down to the level of astrology . . . for better or worse, in economic science we must, as Lecky put it, "endure the sufferings of suspended judgment" (pp. 24, 27 and 29). However, subsequently Jewkes has published an important prediction, or at any rate 'belief', that the entry of Britain into the Common Market 'will, over the next decade, be likely to put us in a better position than we will occupy if we stay out with all that that is likely to involve' (*The Times*, October 8, 1962).

We wish strongly to emphasize the view at this point that the rational application of economic knowledge by way of making or discussing policy recommendations *must*, to some extent, or in some ways, involve prediction. We believe that the opposite view that economists can make, or advise as to, policy recommendations, without making or implying *some kinds of* prediction is dangerously confusing, since prediction is essentially involved in any kind of 'rational' choice. For example, it has been authoritatively denied that the economist's 'advisory power is confined within the narrow limits of his predictory power'.[1] The term 'advisory power' is a little imprecise. Of course, political persuasion and propaganda can be undertaken without any, or any clear, predictions being made. Gnomic maxims can be uttered to the effect that the welfare of the community should be maximized, or such vacuities as that a policy should be adopted if it makes at least one person better-off and nobody worse-off. Approved ideology can be purveyed, or political principles can be enunciated to the effect that no policy should be adopted if it diminishes freedom of choice on the one hand, or, alternatively, equality of distribution, on the other, or that '*laissez-faire* should be the general rule'.[2] But such utterances, however admirable—or the reverse—one holds them to be, should surely not be regarded as 'advice' based on economic knowledge, but as political maxims. Harrod went on to take the example of an import duty on wheat and claimed that the economist:

'may be able to say outright and with substantial authority that on the whole the individuals of the community will be in a worse position, *even although his power of predicting the actual course of prices and incomes is negligible.* Any definition of the economist's advisory scope which does not recognize this is unrealistic, and fails to do justice to the usefulness of the economist, even with his present limited powers.'[3]

[1] R. F. Harrod, 'Scope and Method of Economics', *Economic Journal*, September 1938, p. 390.

[2] Cf. J. S. Mill, *Principles of Political Economy*, Ashley's edition, 1909, Book V, Chapter XI, Section 7.

[3] R. F. Harrod, *op. cit.*, p. 391, italics added. Theoretical economists sometimes take the repeal of the Corn Laws in 1846 as the classic instance of a major policy decision being clinched or demonstrated by economic theorizing. Certainly Ricardo's general theorizing, a quarter of a century before, may have had some influence, though he advocated gradualness in repeal. But when it came to the point in the 1840s, of the four leading classical economists of the day, Torrens opposed repeal, J. S. Mill was dubious and almost silent, Senior was favourable but circumlocutory, and McCulloch was in favour of reduction but not complete repeal. Real and important policy issues can never be decided by a demonstration that one particular policy can, potentially, make some people better-off and nobody worse-off. (See W. D. Grampp, *The Manchester School of Economics*, 1960, Chapter 2.)

Harrod based this claim for the advisory power of the economist on his possession of 'his criterion of individual preference'. But, quite apart from the fact that it inevitably involves a not necessarily universally-shared value-judgment, a criterion is useless if there is nothing relevant to apply it to, and there can only be something relevant to which to apply a criterion if the effects of different policies are to some extent predicted.

As Harrod stressed, the power of prediction in economics at the present juncture is severely limited. It would be encouraging if the confidence and authority with which the economist could 'advise' the public was not restricted in this way. But we must repeat our view that there may be a misleading delusion here. Of course, the economist's predictions may be wide 'interval' predictions rather than 'point' predictions. Of course, they will be conditional, and yet still remain significant predictions with falsifiable predictive content, however difficult to test in practice. It seems, however, a questionable posture to deliver extremely conditional or hypothetical predictions and leave it entirely to the statesman, or decision-maker, to predict as to the applicability of *all* the conditions and hypotheses, *including all those concerned with economic processes.* Certainly 'the statesman' might be expected to predict regarding the more political contingencies (the result of the next election or international crisis).[1] But it is surely doubtful whether one should claim the status and authority of an expert adviser, while refusing to commit oneself to any non-trivial, falsifiable predictions whatsoever.

However, as there seem to be some pretty fundamental disagreements regarding prediction as a task for the economist, let us attempt some further clarification of what may be meant by 'prediction'.

Let us exclude altogether from 'predictions' analytical or empirically unfalsifiable statements such as 'If demand for exports is elastic a reduction in their prices will, other things being equal, result in an increase in receipts'. Such a statement, like any analytical statement, *might* be useful in elaborating the logical implications of a prediction, *if one were ventured,* to the effect, say, that the demand for exports was elastic. But it is not *itself* a prediction and has no predictive

---

[1] P. A. Samuelson, *Problems of the American Economy,* Stamp Memorial Lecture, 1961, 1962, p. 17: 'We laugh at students who, instead of answering the examination question as set, try to brazen it out by answering some quite different question. Some scholars are like that: when you ask them what would be the effects of a cut in personal income tax rates, they say you should be making a study of the effects on the balance of payments of an appreciation of the currency. Or they reply: "On the assumption of an *n*-person economy, with indifference curves that are homothetic and production functions that are homogeneous, and assuming workers save nothing and non-workers save all, tax rates enter merely as . . . blank, blank, blank . . . " — leaving you to decide how relevant is the answer and how it must be modified to give a tolerable approximation.'

content, since it is empirically unfalsifiable and remains true whatever happens.[1] It is often correctly—though sometimes rather uncritically—repeated that economic predictions, like all scientific predictions, are conditional. But the conditions have to be reasonably precisely stated, and leave some non-trivial, refutable content in the proposition, if it is to represent a significant prediction for policy-making.

Let us next make a two-fold division of 'predictions'—retaining the term for the two types together—into (a) 'scientific prognoses' based on tested scientific laws as to which a measure of scientific consensus has been reached; and (b) 'forecasts' which *may* make *some* use of scientific laws and theories, but which go beyond these in prophesying or forecasting what will happen, outside the range of tested scientific laws and theories.

This is certainly not a clear-cut distinction, or one as to which there would be immediate clarity and agreement as to just where the line between the two should be drawn. Exactly which statements deserve the description of 'scientific laws' or theories, and which do not, would not be immediately and clearly agreed in the social and economic sciences. We have also left vague the extent, and the manner in which, what we have called a 'scientific prognosis'—as contrasted with a 'forecast'—is 'based' on a scientific law or theory. But, though there is an ambiguous area on the frontiers between the two concepts, they are sufficiently distinct at their centres.

The nature of 'prognoses' based on scientific laws or theories has been set out very precisely by Popper, and he brings out very clearly the close relation between causal explanations, testing and prediction:

'I suggest that to give a causal explanation of a certain *specific event* means deducing a statement describing this event from two kinds of premisses: from some *universal laws*, and from some singular or specific statements which we shall call the *specific initial conditions*. For example, we can say that we have given a causal explanation of the breaking of a certain thread if we find that this thread could carry a weight of only one pound, and that a weight of two pounds was put on it. If we analyse this causal explanation, then we find that two different constituents are involved. (1) Some hypotheses of the character of universal laws of nature; in this case, perhaps: "For every thread of a given structure S (determined by its material, thickness, etc.) there is a characteristic weight W such that the thread will break if any weight exceeding W is suspended on it"; and "For every thread of the structure S_1, the characteristic weight W equals one pound". (2) Some specific (singular) statements—the initial

---

[1] Jewkes (*op. cit.*, p. 89) very cogently distinguishes 'economic logic' from prediction, i.e. such statements as 'If the supply of money increases by 100 per cent, everything else remaining equal, prices will rise'.

conditions—pertaining to the particular event in question; in this case, we may have two statements: "This is a thread of structure S_1," and "The weight put on this thread was a weight of two pounds". Thus we have two different constituents, two different kinds of statements which together yield a complete causal explanation: (1) *Universal statements of the character of natural laws*; and (2) *specific statements* pertaining to the special case in question, called the "*initial conditions*". Now from the universal laws (1) we can deduce, with the help of the initial conditions (2), the following specific statement (3): "This thread will break". This conclusion (3) we may also call a specific *prognosis*. The initial conditions (or, more precisely, the situation described by them) are usually spoken of as the *cause* of the event in question, and the prognosis (or, rather, the event described by the prognosis) as the *effect*; for example, we say that the putting of a weight of two pounds on a thread capable of carrying only one pound was the cause, and the breaking the effect.

'Such a causal explanation, will, of course, be scientifically acceptable *only if the universal laws are well tested and corroborated*, and if we have also some independent evidence in favour of the cause, i.e. of the initial conditions. . . . The use of a theory for *predicting* some specific event is just another aspect of its use for *explaining* such an event. And since we test a theory by comparing the events predicted with those actually observed, our analysis also shows how theories can be tested.'[1]

The difficulty in economics and the social sciences is, of course, that (1) there is not a substantial body of precise 'well-tested and corroborated' universal laws in the fields in which predictions are wanted, ventured or required to support rationally the policies adopted; and (2) the 'independent evidence' in favour of all 'the initial conditions' which are often so much more numerous, complex and difficult to isolate than in the natural world, is often practically impossible to ascertain with sufficient precision and reliability. That is, it is practically impossible to ascertain that the social and economic 'threads' are precisely of 'the given structure', and will remain so, undisturbed for the period of the prediction. For if predictions useful for practical policies are to be obtained, these initial conditions must themselves be reasonably precise, not too numerous, and themselves predictable.[2]

[1] K. R. Popper, *The Poverty of Historicism*, paperback edition, 1961, pp. 122–4. We have added the italics for the words '*only if the universal laws are well tested and corroborated*'.

[2] 'A typical law in the physical sciences is stated precisely, usually in mathematical terms, and is quite free of ambiguity. It has been tested repeatedly and has withstood the tests. The usual law in the social sciences, on the other hand, is ordinarily couched in Big Words and a great deal of ambiguity.' J. G. Kemeny,

One of the most relied-on general laws, and the cornerstone of price theory, is broadly to the effect that, subject to conditions regarding tastes, expectations, incomes and other prices, a rise in the price of a good, other than a 'snob' or 'Giffen' good, will be followed by a fall in the quantity demanded. But the predictive usefulness of such a law or generalization is much impaired by the fact that the initial conditions with which it needs to be combined to yield a scientific prognosis in a specific case are numerous, complex and not easily ascertainable or predictable.

In fact, prediction in economics and the social sciences has often to be attempted not on 'well-tested and corroborated laws', but on tentative imprecise generalizations regarding trends and tendencies. In any case, no prediction, of course, can have absolute certainty. But most or many predictions based on the physical sciences can be corroborated by checking and re-checking the initial conditions and the law. But in economics and the social sciences only personal or subjective probability can usually be indicated.[1]

There is, in fact, a whole range of 'predictions' from, at one extreme, scientific 'prognosis', on the basis of physical or chemical laws, involved in engineering, or bridge or aeroplane building, through different types of medical prognoses, meteorological prognoses and detailed weather 'forecasting', population forecasting, the forecasts involved in insurance, economic forecasting of next year's G.N.P., stock-market forecasts and 'investment analysis', and the expert tips of horse-racing and football forecasters. There is something like a spectrum here in which a change of quality obviously takes place. This change turns on the degree of precise reliance on scientific laws, and is here described as moving from 'scientific prognoses' to 'forecasting'—though the transition is so gradual as to render rather arbitrary any clear-cut dividing line. Perhaps the spectrum can be continued through the 'hunch' and 'feel', or tradi-

---

A Philosopher Looks at Science, 1959, p. 244. This comparison does not seem seriously unfair, nor to be entirely refuted by Popper's perhaps rather optimistic list of examples of tentative 'sociological laws and hypotheses': 'You cannot introduce agricultural tariffs and at the same time reduce the cost of living.'— 'You cannot, in an industrial society, organize consumers' pressure groups as effectively as you can organize certain producers' pressure groups.'—'You cannot have a centrally planned society with a price system that fulfils the main functions of competitive prices.'—'You cannot have full employment without inflation.' Popper gives further examples from the realm of power politics. See *The Poverty of Historicism*, paperback edition, 1961, p. 62.

[1] Jewkes (*op. cit.*, p. 88) lays down 'the golden rule' that 'the economic expert should be most scrupulous' in 'indicating the degree of probability that attaches to each' of his assumptions, when he attempts a prediction. But, however scrupulous the economist may be, he will usually only be able to give 'guess-timates' of the most subjective kind, regarding degrees of probability, from which those of other economists might widely diverge.

tional weather-wisdom, of sailors and farmers, on through non-rational superstitions, to astrology and fortune-telling. We have already noted the contrasting views economists take regarding economic prediction generally, and there would probably be much disagreement as to just where in this broad spectrum different kinds of economic predictions were to be placed. For example, by some, the use of economic statistics for the forecasting required for some types of policy is regarded as little better than a magic ritual or astrology.[1]

In the most important recent treatment of 'Economic Forecasts and Policy', Theil endeavours to lay down the requirements which predictions should meet if they are to merit 'the weighty adjective "scientific" '. But he does not seem able to make these requirements very precise or restrictive. His requirements simply are that predictions must be 'verifiable', which implies that they must be unambiguous as regards the concepts and timing they contain. But, however verifiable (or falsifiable) and unambiguous a prediction may be, it may merely be 'the result of the forecaster's imagination'. As Theil puts it:

'It is therefore not sufficient that the predictions themselves can be verified afterwards; it is, in addition to this, necessary that the line of thought which underlies the prediction can be verified. . . . It is not easy and even not fruitful to generalize about this point, but this at least can be said: the forecasting procedure must be based on theoretical considerations—however simple—and on empirical observations obtained beforehand—however scanty and crude.'[2]

In other words, it is impossible to mark off very strictly or clearly predictions which merit 'the weighty adjective "scientific" ' from those that do not. Samuelson appeals to what he calls 'loose' scientific

[1] Cf. E. Devons, *Essays in Economics*, 1961, p. 135: 'Decisions must be taken, and even if it is exaggerated confidence in the statistics which helps the Government to decide rather than dither, should we complain? Considered in this light there seem to be striking similarities between the role of economic statistics in out society and some of the functions which magic and divination play in primitive society.' See also J. Brunner, 'The Dash for Planning', *The Listener*, May 10, 1962, p. 796. After examining the forecasts of the Ridley Committee, 1951, Brunner concludes: 'Fuel forecasting is no more of a science than astrology. And if this is true in an industry where there is the maximum exchange of information, where there are hardly any exports, and where the nature of the product ensures a comparative stability of demand, how much more true is it of forecasting in more volatile industries.' Perhaps these sceptical quotations should be balanced with a quotation from Marshall (*Industry and Trade*, 4th Ed., 1923, p. 506): 'Greater risks are taken where no attempt is made to forecast the future, while considering methods of action or inaction that will largely affect the future, than by straining inadequate eyes in reading such faint indications of the future as can be discerned by them.'

[2] *Economic Forecasts and Policy*, 2nd Ed., 1961, pp. 11–14.

method.[1] But it is just the inevitable scarcely definable 'looseness' which lets in subjectivity and bias. Moreover, a consensus of experts as to a prediction cannot necessarily be said to lend it a firm objectivity since, if aware of one another's predictions, they may be clustering together simply for mutual reassurance.[2] But certainly an economic prediction might seem to begin to take on some measure of objectivity and independence of political bias, if various economists agreed on it who were known to hold conflicting political viewpoints on the issue concerned. For example, if *both* those economists, who one had reason to believe were opposed to Britain entering the European Common Market on political grounds, *and* those who were politically in favour, agreed on an economic prediction as to one or other of the likely economic effects, say, that the resulting economies of scale were likely (or unlikely) to be of importance, then such an economic prediction would acquire at least a minimum basis of expert objective consensus (though, of course, it might be false). But this is often just what one does *not* get. Those politically opposed discover that economics of scale will be negligible, and those politically favourable tend to predict their importance.

Nevertheless, it might be argued that whichever methods of prediction or forecasting are adopted, *some* canons of expertise, and at least some measure of consensus regarding what is a respectable procedure for building a forecast, and what is not, do exist. It therefore seems impossible to accept the view that all forecasting, and even all prediction, should be banned as too dubious and disreputable for the 'scientific' economist. It is obviously much more deplorable to adopt such an austere attitude towards the predictions required for the kind of policies one dislikes, while urging more boldness as regards the predictions required—given widely accepted value-premisses—for the types of policies which one approves.

It seems clear that if the economist confined himself strictly to 'scientific prognoses', on the basis of 'well-tested and corroborated' scientific laws, he would be able to offer very little genuinely useful advice—though not absolutely none. But as regards most important realistic policy-issues, the scope of his advice would be extremely limited or negligible, unless he resorted to judgments and hunches on

---

[1] *Problems of the American Economy*, Stamp Memorial Lecture, 1961, 1962, p. 21.
[2] Cf. P. Samuelson, *op. cit.*, p. 28: 'Forecasters are if anything too homogeneous, too much in touch with one another, too sheep-like in their shifts of optimism. We have an apt saying: "Economic forecasters are like many eskimos crowded into the same bed. You can be sure of one thing, they will all turn over together." The reasons are not hard to find; what one fool can do, so can another; opinions mingle; finally it is safer to be wrong with the crowd than take the chance that you may not be right, all by yourself.' It must be emphasized that the eskimos' 'consensus' is not the same thing as genuine scientific consensus —however 'expert' eskimos they may be.

which different experts will often not agree, and which are inevitably
liable, especially in the field of economic policy, to ideological
prejudice or bias. To expect or suggest that in the vast majority of
realistic policy issues an economist can or should 'demonstrate' the
economic gains of one policy as compared with another—like the
proof of a geometrical theorem, beyond all reasonable disagreement
—is to indulge in intellectual delusion.[1] To state that there are significant economic gains from adopting one policy rather than another,
one has to make predictions as to what the effects of the different
policies will be. Logical, mathematical or geometrical 'demonstration' *may* illuminatingly analyse or elaborate a prediction when made.
But in the majority of realistic cases it is the quality of the judgment
in predicting or forecasting which is essential.[2]

The question arises then as to how far the economist's judgment
or hunch is 'better', or more often 'right', than the non-economist's,
with regard to economic predictions or forecasts; and how far he is
entitled to claim or assume some measure of 'expert' authority for
predictions in which subjective judgments are or may be present in
differing degrees. In the case of one of the most important issues of
British economic policy to be faced for many decades, admittedly a
case involving extremely open, complex and long-term predictions,
regarding the economic effects of Britain joining the Common

---

[1] 'It cannot be stated too emphatically that no economist of any standing in
this country has alleged, much less demonstrated, that significant economic gains
would accrue to this country on entering the Common Market.' E. J. Mishan,
The Times, October 2, 1962. We are not concerned with what economists ('of any
standing' or otherwise) *alleged* on this issue, but with the epistemological misconception of suggesting, even as a remote practical possibility, that any conclusions about economic gains or losses could be '*demonstrated*'—either from
Britain entering or from her staying out of the Common Market.

[2] Cf. the classic pronouncement by Sir James Fitzjames Stephen: 'The one
talent which is worth all other talents put together in human affairs is the
talent of judging right upon imperfect materials, the talent if you please of
guessing right. It is a talent which no rules will ever teach and which even experience does not always give. It often co-exists with a good deal of slowness and
dullness and with a very slight power of expression. All that can be said about it
is, that to see things as they are, without exaggeration or passion, is essential to
it; but how can we see things as they are? Simply by opening our eyes and looking with whatever power we may have. All really important matters are decided,
not by a process of argument worked out from adequate premises to a necessary
conclusion, but by making a wise choice between several possible views.' (*Liberty,
Equality, Fraternity*, 2nd Ed., 1874, p. 352, quoted by A. S. Ashton, *Lloyds Bank
Review*, October 1962, p. 30.) Stephen's recipe of 'simply . . . opening our eyes'
may seem a little *simpliste*. But he is surely right that the 'batting averages' are
not likely to be very high of the ideologue (with his 'passion') or the geometrician
concentrating on processes of argument 'from adequate premises to a necessary
conclusion'. Unfortunately, so much economic education concentrates exclusively on these logical or geometrical processes as 'the one thing necessary', to
the neglect of developing at least an awareness of the need for judgment—which
itself may not be so completely unteachable as Stephen suggests.

Market, one distinguished economist took the view that 'the only position for an economist with a respect for the facts is: . . . there is so much we don't know that it is a case of "your guess is as good as mine" '.[1] Rightly or wrongly not many other economists in Britain seemed to take such an austere view, suggesting usually that 'your' guess (whoever 'you' were) was not nearly as good as theirs (unless it agreed with it).

It is to this kind of large-scale, long-term, highly complex and 'open' prediction as to, say, the economic effects of Britain joining the Common Market that the following sceptical conclusion would apply (whether or not to the subjectivity, uncertainty and possible bias of the 'positive' predictions of the multifarious economic effects is added some large, if latent, value-judgment, striking a balance and weighing up the net outcome, as favourable or unfavourable). M. F. Millikan writes:[2]

'Our best formal models are still partial; they explicitly exclude consideration of some of the factors at work in any actual situation. The relative weight of the factors explicitly analysed can seldom be measured, and their combined influence seldom computed. Prediction of a sort is, of course, a necessary component of policy-making. Any decision to act must be based upon a judgment that the net consequences of the preferred course of action will be more favourable than those of some alternative. But in social situations such a judgment can seldom be effectively made by "scientific" procedures. If the policy-maker simply desires advice as to what he should do, he had better rely on the intuition of a man of wide experience and demonstrated understanding rather than on the intellectual skills and techniques of the social scientist. . . . A net predictive judgment in most human situations can be made more safely by the successful journalist, novelist, diplomat or businessman than by any social science research team.'

But there are many different kinds of economic, or politico-economic, predictions or forecasts, and, with regard to some, the sceptical conclusion that 'anybody's' guess will be as good as the economist's is less justified than with regard to others—though

[1] R. G. Lipsey, quoted in the *Observer*, October 14, 1962, p. 5. Lipsey was classified as regarding the economic arguments for and against Britain joining the Common Market as 'evenly balanced'. But there is, of course, a vital distinction between a confident belief on convincing evidence that the balance of advantages is about even, or is likely only to veer very slightly either way, and a belief that in view of the extensive ignorance of many of the factors affecting the various kinds of advantage and disadvantage involved, a fifty-fifty toss-up is as rational a method of decision as any other.

[2] *The Human Meaning of the Social Sciences*, edited by D. Lerner, Meridian Books, 1959, pp. 165–6.

economists can probably be found predicting with equal cheerfulness in both kinds of cases. In contrast with his colleague Millikan—the contrast being, perhaps, more apparent than real because they are probably dealing with different types of prediction—Samuelson has claimed that though economists *'cannot forecast well . . . they forecast the economy better than any other group thus far discovered.* Empirical statisticians, clairvoyants, down-to-earth businessmen, hunch-players—all these turn out to have a worse "batting-average" than government, academic and business economists'—though not, it seems, very much worse.[1] No one is better qualified to assert such a generalization than Samuelson, though it is not clear on how much systematic evidence he bases it, and it obviously holds only for some economists and not for all. Moreover, it should be noted that Samuelson's claim might be taken simply, or mainly, as covering, say, the forecasting of next year's G.N.P. for the United States, and not many other sorts of prediction (e.g. with regard to the economic effects of Britain joining the Common Market) which economists attempt.

Anyhow, a considerable complication regarding predictions in the social and economic field arises from the interaction of observer and observed, or the influence of the prediction on the predicted event—the 'Oedipus effect' as Popper calls it. It is as though meteorologists had to forecast the weather in conditions where private and/or governmental rain-making (as well as counter rain-making) agencies could, and did, frequently and effectively operate. But it has been shown that however much 'Oedipus' effects may complicate prediction they do not make it impossible, or render it, in the social field, completely different in principle from prediction in the natural sciences.[2] The problem, rather, which we are centrally concerned with here would be presented by a situation where some meteorologists were passionately interested financially and otherwise in outdoor activities, while others were passionately committed to indoor activities, and where these ideological prejudices and presuppositions affected their weather forecasts.

We conclude that because scientific 'prognosis' on the basis of 'well-tested and corroborated scientific laws' has, at any rate for the time being, a limited range, insufficient to support the wide policy

[1] P. A. Samuelson, *Problems of the American Economy*, Stamp Memorial Lecture 1961, 1962, p. 23. I. M. D. Little holds that it 'cannot be taken for granted' that 'economists are better at forecasting, and better at judging the economic consequences of alternative policies, than are administrators or bankers', but that their training does give them certain advantages. (*Lloyds Bank Review*, April 1957, p. 35, 'The Economist in Whitehall'.)

[2] v. K. R. Popper, *The Poverty of Historicism*, paperback edition, 1961, pp. 12–17; and E. Grunberg and F. Modigliani, 'Predictability of Social Events', *Journal of Political Economy*, December 1954, p. 465.

ambitions of peoples and governments, much or most social and economic prediction *has* to consist of forecasting on the basis of hunch, judgment, guesswork and insufficiently tested generalizations, which may well be shaped by subjective optimism and pessimism stemming from political and ideological presuppositions. It does, however, seem reasonable to expect that one be given as clear indications as may be practicable as to how far the different elements —empirical generalizations, tendencies, hunches and 'guess-timates' —on which different predictions are based, consist of well-tested and corroborated laws and their initial conditions, on which a consensus exists, and how far they are untested and subjective, and therefore specially liable to bias. As we have already noted, we have the authority of Marshall for the view that 'economic studies are not to be limited to matters which are amenable to strictly scientific treatment'. He went on:

'Those conclusions, whether in detail or in general, which are based on individual judgments as to the relative desirability of different social aims, or as to matters of fact which lie beyond the scope of any individual's special studies, should be clearly distinguished from those which claim to have been reached by scientific method.'[1]

We would simply add that the conclusions 'based on individual judgments', which should be clearly distinguished from those claimed 'to have been reached by scientific method', should also include forecasts and predictions other than what we have called 'prognoses' firmly based on acknowledged scientific laws and generalizations; and should also include, as we shall discuss further below, attitudes to risk—of preference, aversion or neutrality— which are inevitably subjective.

The uncertainty and subjectivity of predictions and forecasts in economics leave a wide scope for the possible workings of bias and 'prejudice'. To some extent, and in no pejorative sense, a kind of prejudice may be inevitable in venturing a prediction as a basis for a policy recommendation. Just as, in Keynes's phrase, 'animal spirits', or 'a spontaneous urge to action rather than inaction', rather than reasonable calculation alone, is the basis of 'most, probably, of our decisions to do something positive, the full consequences of which will be drawn out over many days to come',[2] so a kind of intellectual high spirits prompting one to say something rather than nothing are the basis for some, if not many, kinds of predictions and forecasts. As Hazlitt said in his *Paragraphs on Prejudice*:

'Without the aid of prejudice and custom, I should not be able to

[1] *Industry and Trade*, 1919, p. 676.

[2] J. M. Keynes, *The General Theory of Employment Interest and Money*, 1936, p. 161.

find my way across the room; nor know how to conduct myself in any circumstances, nor know what to feel in any relation to life. Reason may play the critic, and correct certain errors afterwards, but if we were to wait for its formal and absolute decisions in the shifting and multifarious combinations of human affairs, the world would stand still. Even men of science, after they have gone over the proofs a number of times, abridge the process, and *jump at a conclusion*.'[1]

There is nothing wrong in stating one's 'prejudices' provided one makes it quite clear that that is what they are, not trying to pass them off as scientific conclusions with claims to what Popper has called 'the authority of objective truth'.[2]

(9) THE 'SELECTION' OF HYPOTHESES?

We now come to a more fundamental thesis as to the inevitability of value-judgments and subjectivity in science, whether natural or social. This thesis asserts that the scientist *has* to make value-judgments in having to assess evidence or accept or reject hypotheses. The leading statements of this thesis seem to have a strong pragmatist or even techno- (or sciento-) cratic flavour, and we had better say at once that we do not accept its central point or main assumptions. Nevertheless, it does focus attention on important problems and difficulties in keeping normative and positive distinct, which have not been faced by the more facile exponents of 'positive economics' and of a clear-cut distinction between positive theories and policy recommendations.

Here is a specially forthright statement of this thesis:

'Since no scientific hypothesis is ever completely verified, in accepting a hypothesis on the basis of evidence, the scientist must make the decision that the evidence is *sufficiently* strong or that the probability is *sufficiently* high to warrant the acceptance of the hypothesis. Obviously our decision with regard to the evidence and how strong is "strong enough" is going to be a function of the *importance*, in the typically ethical sense, of making a mistake in accepting or rejecting the hypothesis. Thus, to take a crude but easily manageable example, if the hypothesis under consideration stated that a toxic ingredient of a drug was not present in lethal quantity, then we would require a relatively high degree of confirmation or confidence before accepting the hypothesis—for the consequences of making a mistake here are exceedingly grave by our moral standards. In contrast, if our hypothesis stated that, on the basis of some sample, a certain lot of machine-stamped belt buckles was not defective, the degree of con-

[1] Quoted by Krsto Cviić, *The Listener*, December 13, 1962, p. 1008.
[2] *Conjectures and Refutations*, 1963, p. 375.

fidence we would require would be relatively lower. *How sure we must be* before we accept a hypothesis depends on how serious a mistake *would be*.'[1]

We cannot accept Rudner's rather dramatic conclusion based on this argument that 'we are confronted with a first-order crisis in science and methodology'. But, certainly, important questions are being raised as to what precisely the rules and scope of scientific procedure are, particularly with regard to statistical hypotheses, and conclusions or decisions based on them, and as to what is, or should be, the demarcation line between the duties and functions of 'the scientific expert', and those of the choice-making customer or political authority, in conditions of uncertainty. In fact, the possibility of 'the involvement of inductive logic in evaluative considerations',[2] as it has been described, raises the question as to whether in practice, and if so how, or at what point, 'the decision-making animal' can, or should, be split up into a 'choice-animal' and an 'information animal' in conditions of uncertainty (that is, in most realistic conditions).[3]

The kind of decisions discussed by exponents of the thesis we are examining is, at any rate, realistic, in that it involves uncertainty. But the examples are drawn, on the one hand, from choices and decisions regarding the problems and costs of scientific research, or, on the other hand, are concerned with problems of pharmaceutical or industrial quality control. It could well be argued that the former may be classified as 'preliminary' or 'pre-scientific' (in the sense discussed in Section 2 above of this chapter), and that, as regards the latter, value-judgments are certainly and admittedly involved in, so to speak, 'post-scientific' applications in the form of policy recommendations about quality control.

There is no question as to the scientists' need to make choices and

[1] Cf. 'Value Judgments in the Acceptance of Theories', by R. Rudner, in *The Validation of Scientific Theories*, edited by P. Frank, paperback edition, 1961, p. 33. See also R. B. Braithwaite's lecture 'Moral Principles and Inductive Policies', 1950, and his *Scientific Explanation*, 1960, Chapter VII, 'The Choice between Statistical Hypotheses'. Also C. W. Churchman, *Prediction and Optimal Decision*, 1961, *passim*, and the discussion by R. C. Jeffrey and C. W. Churchman, in *Philosophy of Science*, July 1956, pp. 237 ff., and by I. Levi, *Journal of Philosophy*, May 1960, p. 345.

[2] R. B. Braithwaite, *Scientific Explanation*, paperback edition, 1960, p. 253.

[3] Cf. H. Theil, *Economic Forecasts and Policy*, 2nd Ed., 1961, p. 414: 'One of the problems in the decision-making process is the great diversity of tasks which the policy-maker has to face. He must not only make a choice (and bear the responsibility for it), but he must also be a forecaster. Naturally, the question arises whether it is possible to delegate at least the latter task to another man or to a staff, so that the "decision-making animal" is then split up into a "choice animal" and an "information animal".' Churchman (*op. cit.*) argues very strongly that this 'splitting up' is impossible—of course, not simply in economics.

decisions with regard to the projects they undertake and their possible costs. Rudner suggests that:

'. . . it would be interesting and instructive, for example, to know how high a degree of probability the Manhattan project scientists demanded for the hypothesis that no uncontrollable pervasive chain reaction would occur before they proceeded with the first atomic bomb detonation or even first activated the Chicago pile above a critical level. It would be equally interesting and instructive to know how they decided that the chosen probability value (if one was chosen) was high enough rather than one that was higher; on the other hand, it is conceivable that the problem, in this form, was not brought to consciousness at all.'[1]

It is not denying the immense importance of these decisions, or the significance of the values involved, to describe them, and the choices emphasized here, as 'preliminary' or 'pre-scientific'. No valuations or value-judgments enter into statements as to whether or how atomic explosions are possible, because of the crucial valuations and decisions involved in launching a Manhattan project and incurring the huge costs and possible risks. So when Churchman counters the thesis that 'science ends in summarizing its evidence, and it has no part in the evaluation of policies' with the argument that 'science obviously makes decisions of its own in both theoretical and applied science' and 'must decide to take certain steps in its procedures, and these steps must presumably be evaluated by science',[2] we can certainly agree with regard to the choice of research projects and of scientific criteria and rules of the game. But, so far, no conclusion follows at all that the scientist has to pass value-judgments regarding social and political policies, unless one simply asserts, in a question-begging way, that this is within his duties.

The other examples, taken from the field of medical and industrial quality control, might be described as *'post-scientific'*. For example, how highly probable, or virtually certain (because, of course, literally absolute certainty is out of the question), must the hypothesis be that a new drug does not have harmful effects of some kind or other before it is made publicly available? Such a decision only arises when there is an application of scientific knowledge to policy, and when particular policy objectives are being laid down. Then, in any case, a value-judgment is, indisputably, logically necessary, though one which is widely held to belong clearly with the 'choice animal'

---

[1] R. Rudner, 'Value Judgments in the Acceptance of Theories', in *The Validation of Scientific Theories*, edited by P. Frank, paperback edition, 1961, p. 33.

[2] C. W. Churchman, in *The Validation of Scientific Theories*, edited by P. Frank, paperback edition, 1961, p. 29.

rather than the 'information animal'. Anyhow, as pointed out, the strength of the evidence required might be very different depending on the policy objectives involved—or whether, for example, the drug being tested was intended for humans or animals. A parallel case with regard to social investigation would be the elaborateness of a sample, or the accuracy of a statistical estimate, being determined by the importance of the policy decisions and objectives to be based on the information it yielded. Certainly, here the functions of 'the choice animal' and 'the information animal' seem to merge together. But not, we would suggest, inextricably so, at any rate analytically.

Nassau Senior, for example, took the view of the scientist's functions that he 'does not presuppose any purpose beyond the acquisition of knowledge', and he ascribed to the distinct realm of 'art' that which 'is intended to influence the will' since 'it presupposes some object to be attained'.[1] In methodological programmes, though not so much in practice, this is a view for which much support could be found in the writings of 'orthodox' economists. To some, this view might seem rather too passive or quietist, but according to it the task for the scientist is simply to set out the evidence for and against different hypotheses as far as it goes, and not 'accept' or even 'reject' them in any stronger sense than this. Scientific investigation does not have 'to terminate with the replacement of doubt by belief'. Probabilities may be assigned to hypotheses and predictions, but in the economic and social field these will mostly be highly 'subjective' or 'personal' without often anything. or much, of the 'objectivity' which a consensus of expert opinion might give, and therefore very liable to bias. Moreover, there are obvious practical difficulties in setting before the 'choice animal' or 'statesman' complicated probability distributions under numerous possible assumptions regarding the eventual decisions. As Theil puts it: 'The task of informing the "choice animal" about the stochastic consequences of his measures can easily become inconvenient and cumbersome. . . . Few policy-makers will appreciate their staffs providing them with information of such an elaborate and refined nature.'[2] However elaborate (or concise) may be the range of information which 'choice animals' or policy-makers 'appreciate', it is clearly their function to decide on action on the basis of *their* valuations of policy objectives and of the seriousness of mistakes.

In contrast with Senior's quietist view, a more activist scientocratic view may be urged on behalf of 'those who don't want science to stop just before it gives an answer'. Such a view may, of course, be held not only by scientific 'information animals' but by lay

[1] *Report of the British Association for the Advancement of Science*, 1860, pp. 183–4.
[2] Cf. H. Theil, *Economic Forecasts and Policy*, 2nd Ed., 1961, pp. 414–15.

'choice animals'. What the 'scientist' should or should not do, and how strictly he should confine himself, as Marshall put it, only to 'matters which are amenable to strictly scientific treatment', is, of course, a question of pre- or extra-scientific value-premisses. Certainly the application of these maxims, in particular practical cases, may inevitably turn on pretty fine shades of emphasis in the presentation of evidence for economic hypotheses and predictions that are being applied to policies.

There is, however, undoubtedly a kind of value-judgment arising out of risk and uncertainty, which is inevitably involved in policy decisions, and which seems to deserve more emphasis than it has received. The presentation of the evidence for prognoses or forecasts, and estimates of their probabilities, seem to lie in the field of 'the information animal', though often it will be impossible to eliminate subjectivity and thus the possibility of bias or prejudice. But, in any case, the attitude to risk and uncertainty, however these are presented or weighed up, involves a kind of value-judgment which definitely belongs to 'the choice animal' or political decision-maker, or is a part of his utility function. Even if the probability of a prediction could be formulated not merely in subjective personal terms, but in the precise, 'objective', quantitative terms of a gamble at roulette, which is surely quite unrealistic for most of the kinds of decisions involved in economic policy-making, and even if, also, the values of the outcomes or objectives, in terms of certainties, which (continuing to stretch the realism of the example) the political authority must be assumed to be clear about, there is an inevitable further value-judgment, or element of valuation, involved in the adoption of a particular attitude to risk, whether of risk-preference, risk-aversion or risk-neutrality. It is clearly for the 'choice-animal' to choose whether to adopt a more cautious 'minimax' type of attitude or a Bayesian or 'maximin' attitude. If two decision-makers take different attitudes of this kind in a similar situation, 'no one else, not even the scientists, can say which one is right when one adopts a Bayesian attitude and the other decides on the basis of pessimism'.[1]

It has been pointed out by Giersch that democratic governments may tend to an attitude of risk aversion, while oppositions may tend to urge attitudes of risk preference.[2] It is, in practice, often very difficult to distinguish the separate influences on a policy decision of the values or preferences of a decision-maker (as they would be between certainties) from his risk attitude: that is to distinguish between a high estimate of the possible costs of a possible unfavourable outcome of a policy—say an ambitious 'growth' policy—from a cautious, minimax risk-attitude to a choice between uncertainties; or,

[1] C. W. Churchman, *Prediction and Optimal Decision*, 1961, p. 166.
[2] *Allgemeine Wirtschaftspolitik*, Grundlagen, 1960, p. 336.

in the reverse case, to separate a high valuation of a possible out-standingly successful outcome from a bold attitude of risk preference. In fact, it is important to distinguish with regard to the concept of 'responsibility' in policy proposals, how far it signifies a particular pattern of valuations holding good for choices between certainties, and how far it relates rather to the attitude to risk. But, because of different risk-attitudes, two decision-makers could differ over and choose different policies, even if they were in agreement in their valuations of all choices between certainties, and also as regards all relevant 'positive' predictions and their probabilities.

However, the difficulty in distinguishing, in practice, between risk-attitudes and policy preferences does not matter for the problems of marking off analytically the functions of the 'choice-animal' from those of the 'information-animal'. For both the risk-attitudes, and the choices or valuations of objectives, are surely for the 'choice animal' to determine. Consequently, the scientist does not seem logically or inevitably to be involved in value-judgments simply because of the need for valuations or choices of risk-attitudes in conditions of uncertainty, any more than he needs to be involved in value-judgments because policy decisions, as between certainties, involve choices between, and valuations of, different outcomes or objectives. It is in the setting out of the evidence or 'probabilities' regarding the different possible outcomes of alternative policies that the vital frontier, with which we are concerned in this book, may become blurred, and a demarcation line between the functions of the 'information animal' and those of the 'choice-animal' may be difficult to ascertain precisely in practice.

The history of economic theorizing, of the more orthodox type at any rate, has been largely one of deductive theorizing and model-building, and of the analysis or logic of choice between certainties, whether for the individual consumer choosing consumption goods, or in the 'welfarist' logic of the choice of economic policies.[1] It has been mainly concerned with choice in 'transparent' conditions of 'perfect knowledge', with indifference curves and possibility lines, representing highly complex but *certain* knowledge and information, sweeping with smooth certainty across the page or blackboard. At least until comparatively recently the application and applicability to the actual world of conclusions arrived at by deductive logic were often left largely to impressionism, casual empiricism, or hunch.

---

[1] Cf. J. Buttrick's criticism (in *Theories of Economic Growth*, edited by B. Hoselitz, 1960, p. 160) of neo-classical theories: 'A model in the social sciences in which no stochastic elements are present, i.e. one in which relationships among variables are presumed to be exact and in which the variables themselves can be measured, is a model constructed for heuristic rather than "practical" (i.e. predictive) purposes.' Cf. also, T. W. Hutchison, *The Significance and Basic Postulates of Economic Theory*, 1938 and 1960, pp. 86–8.

As regards choices between certainties, the demarcation line between the functions of 'the choice animal' and 'the information animal' seems perfectly clear-cut. In fact, some of the more facile pronouncements and programmes regarding a clear-cut distinction between positive and normative seem, like so much of economic theory, to be assuming away uncertainty. But, in conditions of uncertainty, where decisions have to be taken on the basis of uncertain predictions, this demarcation line—though not, I would say, analytically impossible to draw—will often become in practice very difficult to ascertain, particularly if ideological and political value-loads may be shaping the predictions. The thesis we have examined in this section, whether or not one agrees with its assumptions about the scope of the scientist's functions, certainly draws attention to the problems of inductive and statistical inference, of the weighing of evidence and the uncertainty of predictions, which are the source of considerable practical difficulties in demarcating clearly in practice, in the social and economic field, the roles of the neutral, scientific expert and the political decision-making authority.

(10) 'MEANS' AND 'ENDS'

According to the conception of economics as a neutral, positive science, which might perhaps still just be called the 'orthodox' conception, not only can economic theories be kept free from value-judgments, subjective bias and 'persuasiveness', but, within a particular limiting framework, the discussion of economic policies can be also. This framework is often described in terms of the categories of 'means' and 'ends'. The 'scientific economist', it is held, should not, and indeed cannot 'as such', pronounce or advise on ends, but *given* the ends, by abstract assumption for the purposes of a particular model, or as laid down by a political authority, he can pronounce on the means which will promote them. The means-ends categories are thus regarded as providing a clear and precise formula for delimiting normative from positive and the frontier of positive economics. Means and ends are broadly treated as corresponding or parallel in discussing economic policies in the teleological mood, to 'causes' and 'effects' in the positive mood of economic theory.

In the first place, analysis in terms of means and ends is apt to suffer from the usual oversimplification of the 'certainty' assumption, treating the choice of 'ends' as a choice between known certainties, as discussed in the previous section. But it is a different line of criticism of the means-ends categories which we wish now to examine. The use of the means-ends categories has been criticized by several of those who are sceptical of the possibility of neutral positive economics. It is argued that it is not possible to mark off sharply 'means' from 'ends' so that the economist can clearly confine his pronouncements to the former. For example, Smithies writes: 'Attempts to draw sharp distinctions between means and ends can be misleading and dangerous. The means chosen to achieve particular ends today may alter the ends of tomorrow.'[1] Myrdal describes the common use of the means-ends categories as follows:

'The basic idea of this principle is this: By splitting economic processes into (1) a given initial situation, (2) alternative means, and (3) the hypothetical end, it should be possible to concentrate all value-judgments on the third link, viz. the purpose. This is particularly important for relativists. They can now discuss purely scientifically not only the initial situation, but also the means. They can conduct a teleological argument objectively. Values are attached to the means only indirectly, via the values attached to the end which the means can serve. In themselves, means are supposed to be neutral, value-free. . . .

'Now it is quite obvious that values are attached not only to "ends" but also to "means". Means are not ethically neutral. The value-judgment must compare and choose between alternative courses. Value-judgments thus refer always to whole sequences, not merely to the anticipated final outcome. . . . Moreover, as we have seen, by "end" we do not normally mean the *total* final situation (nor by "means" the total sequence), but only a relevant section of it. (Otherwise a discussion of alternative means would be impossible: only exceptionally do different means lead to precisely identical total results.) Therefore, even if it were possible to isolate means as neutral, we would still have to discuss the by-effects which may not be neutral. . . . The political value judgment refers not only to the end but to every component in all possible alternative sequences which are to be compared.'[2]

As Myrdal subsequently concluded:

'It is simply not true that only ends are the object of valuations and that means are valued only as instrumental to ends. In any human valuation means have, in addition to their instrumental value, independent values as well. The value-premiss which has to be introduced in order to allow policy conclusions to be reached from factual analysis has therefore to be a valuation of means as well as ends.'[3]

[1] *Economics and Public Policy*, Brooking Lectures 1954, 1955, p. 3.
[2] *Value in Social Theory*, by G. Myrdal, edited with an introduction by P. Streeten, 1958, pp. 210–11.
[3] *Op. cit.*, p. 49.

Let us make a comment first on a purely definitional point. In elaborating and supporting Myrdal's argument, Streeten describes as a 'trick' the defining of anything to which value is attached as an 'end', leaving 'means' to be, by definition, neutral, with no values attached to them.[1] Such a definition hardly seems to us to amount to a 'trick', but to represent perhaps the most suitable, or 'correct', definition of the terms as they are widely understood. What seems criticizable is not so much defining 'means' as neutral, but including under 'means' what can only be considered neutral by an arbitrary value-judgment. But this point is mainly terminological. We would prefer to express the substantial point which Myrdal and Streeten are making, which is valid and important, as being that the means-ends categories are often misleadingly used because what are described as 'means', and as having by normal implication no intrinsic values attached to them apart from the ends they promote, are not 'means' or pure 'means', because they have, or may well be thought to have, their own intrinsic values. The means-end categories are only applicable, that is, to what may be called purely technical problems where the 'means' are generally agreed to be neutral. Otherwise the 'ends' are being incompletely stated and are spilling over into what are being misleadingly described as neutral 'means', so that hidden persuasion and concealed value-judgments, possibly of a highly controversial kind, are being inserted in implying that no value-premises are involved in the choice of 'means'. But in the social world policies and institutions cannot be treated as purely neutral 'means', except by the insertion of an often highly arbitrary value-judgment which may sometimes, when the means-end categories are used in the most crudely mechanical way, lead on to the tyrannical error of treating people and their ways of life as 'means' or 'human material'.[2]

This confusion is apt to originate from the definition of economic science as a relationship between ends and scarce means. Being neutral, the argument proceeds, economics does not choose between or pronounce value-judgments on different ends, and it is implied that no value-judgments are involved in recommending 'means' to

[1] *Op. cit.*, Introduction, p. XXI. For example, there does not seem to be any 'trick' involved in the following treatment of means as 'purely technical': 'Where ends are agreed, the only questions left are those of means, and these are not political but technical, that is to say, capable of being settled by experts or machines like arguments between engineers or doctors.' I. Berlin, *Two Concepts of Liberty*, 1958, p. 3.

[2] Cf. A. Huxley, *Ends and Means*, 1938, who observes: 'The end cannot justify the means, for the simple and obvious reason that the means employed determine the nature of the ends produced. . . . The means whereby we try to achieve something are at least as important as the end we wish to attain. Indeed they are more important. For the means employed inevitably determine the nature of the result achieved' (p. 9 and p. 52).

given 'ends'. The point may then be illustrated by an example from the life of Robinson Crusoe where he has to choose between the 'ends' of warmth and protection in allocating his scarce means—a quantity of timber—between fires and fences;[1] or, alternatively, a housewife is described allocating her pennies between different household wants. Here the 'means' are represented by units of money or commodities. They can justifiably be assumed to be neutral and interchangeable means, having no intrinsic values of their own, except in so far as they promote the ends which are unambiguously and completely given by Crusoe's preferences for warmth and protection. The problems may be described as 'technical', and this use of the means-end categories *can* be, as far as it goes, unobjectionable. But these are not problems of social or political economy, and it is highly dangerous to extend this use of the means-end categories to questions of policies and institutions such as the choice between monetary and fiscal policies and the nationalization or de-nationalization of the steel industry. The 'means' here are not neutral (or rather are not pure 'means') and can only be assumed to be neutral by an arbitrary value-judgment, since the choice between them affects the whole distribution of powers, and ways of life, of the community.[2] The 'end', therefore, cannot be taken as unambiguously given—in terms simply of the stabilizing of prices or the efficient production of quantities of steel—except by a value-judgment regarding the neutrality of the 'means' which would not be widely agreed, even if it was explicitly inserted, but which in any case is often left implicit. The confusion is particularly serious in the discussion of problems of the economic development of poor countries whose institutions and ways of life are sometimes treated as purely neutral 'means' subordinate to the 'end' of 'economic growth', which is defined in terms of an index of real income-per-head. Max Weber was, in fact, dealing with an example from this field when he pointed out that 'strictly and exclusively empirical analysis can provide a solution only where it is a question of a means adequate to the realization of an absolutely unambiguously given end'.[3] It is just this absolutely

---

[1] Cf. L. Robbins, *Essay on the Nature and Significance of Economic Science*, 2nd Ed., 1935, p. 34.

[2] 'In every proposal of economic policy there lies an often undisclosed preference for a society integrated in one way rather than another.' M. Oakeshott, *Rationalism in Politics*, 1962, p. 37.

[3] Max Weber on *The Methodology of the Social Sciences*, translated and edited by E. A. Shils and H. A. Finch, 1949, p. 26; cf. also p. 37 and p. 45: 'The evaluations are unambiguous *only* when the economic end and the social context are definitely given and all that remains is to choose between several economic means, when these differ only with respect to their certainty, rapidity and quantitative productiveness, and are completely identical in every other value-relevant aspect. It is only when these conditions have been met that we evaluate a given means as "technically most correct", and it is only then that the evalua-

unambiguous statement of the ends, or objectives of policies, which in real-world policy discussions—as contrasted with abstract 'technical' models—is so difficult to achieve without arbitrariness and incompleteness.

The misuse of the means-ends classification and the confusions it perpetuates have played an important part in the perennial debates between those inclining to policies based on free markets and those favouring policies based on central controls and public ownership. Many examples could be cited from recent political debates, in particular from the Labour Party's reconsideration of its nationalization policies. We may take an example of a confusing and value-loaded use of the concept of 'means' from A. P. Lerner's *Economics of Control*. Lerner contrasts his concept of the 'controlled' economy with that of the 'mixed' economy:

'The term "mixed economy" is sometimes used to designate something like our controlled economy which has elements of collectivism as well as elements of private enterprise for profit. This is a very bad name because it suggests the absence of any single controlling principle but a confusion of different and perhaps contradictory principles. The fundamental point of the controlled economy is that it denies both collectivism and private enterprise as *principles* for the organization of society, but recognizes both of them as perfectly legitimate *means*. Its fundamental principle of organization is that in any particular instance, the means that serves society best should be the one that prevails.'

Anyone is—like Lerner—quite entitled to proclaim that he personally is indifferent as to whether there is a greater measure of public or social control or a greater measure of free individual enterprise in an economy; but he is not entitled to expect or imply that all 'rational' citizens will agree with his indifference. Nor is he entitled to argue that it is wrong or 'bad' to suggest that there is indeed a conflict of values and ends (or 'principles' as he calls them).[1] The

tion is unambiguous. In every other case, i.e. in every case which is not purely a matter of technique, the evaluation ceases to be unambiguous and evaluations enter which are not determinable exclusively by economic analysis. . . . It should be emphatically recalled that the possibility of the exact definition of the end sought for is a prerequisite to the formulation of this problem.'

[1] A. P. Lerner, *Economics of Control*, 1944, p. 4. See also the penetrating criticism by M. Friedman, *Essays in Positive Economics*, 1953, pp. 301 ff. Lerner is at one point (p. 85) prepared to take some marginal account of political values in admitting that 'anything that may contribute to the safeguarding of democracy is of great value'. He continues: 'The controlled economy may consider that even some sacrifice of efficiency in the allocation of resources is worthwhile as a contribution to the safeguard of democracy, though the kind of government that would take this into account could put up adequate safeguards even if it were 100 per cent collectivist.' What is misleading is treating different types of

whole task of economic analysis is surely to bring out conflicts of 'ends' or 'principles' and to elucidate the choice society has to make, and not to smother or obscure these by empty formulae about 'what serves society best'. There *are* conflicts between freedom and justice, progress and security, and so on, and all too often economists have tended to obscure the inevitable necessity of choice by obfuscatory formulae such as 'maximizing welfare' or 'utility'. Collectivism and private enterprise cannot be treated as purely neutral 'means', nor can fiscal policy and monetary policy be treated as purely neutral 'means' towards the 'end' of economic stability, without latent political value-judgments. Certainly, as Boulding has put it, 'publicness' has tended to become an end in itself among the socialists, 'privateness' among the libertarians, and such value-judgments may be explicitly questioned.[1] Certainly also, one may object to the Utopian dogmatism of some economists who present one system or the other as disposing of the problems of conflict and cost, and the need for choice, because *their* system realizes a maximum of *all* ends, freedom, distributive justice, stability, growth and everything else, while suggesting that what their system does not maximize or minimize is not worth bothering about. One does not clarify the issues by invoking a formula such as 'what serves society best', but by setting out explicit value-premises. As has been well said: 'In controversial matters there is always a tendency to conceal questions of ends and to pretend that every question is one of means only—as for instance in politics, where it is "claptrap" to announce portentously that we all desire the welfare of the community and to pretend that we differ only in our view of the best way of attaining it; what we really differ about is our ideas of the welfare of the community.'[2] In other words it is 'claptrap' to set up 'welfare' as the single 'agreed' end of policies and then discuss different kinds of policies, of very different significance in terms of political values, as purely neutral 'means'.

The means-ends categories are so often confusing and dangerous because in the social world there are few—or perhaps it might be said *no*—policies, institutions or arrangements which can be assumed to be purely neutral 'means' with no possible intrinsic value of their own.[3] The use of the distinction too often amounts to an

economy, say, 100 per cent, 50 per cent, and 5 per cent collectivist economies, simply as different machines, or pure techniques, for generating 'economic welfare', unless it is made quite clear that the analysis is strictly in terms of abstract models from which no policy conclusions are being, or can be, directly drawn.

[1] K. Boulding, *Principles of Economic Policy*, 1959, p. 138.

[2] N. Campbell, quoted by B. Wootton, in *Testament for Social Science*, 1960, p. 120.

[3] Cf. J. A. Passmore, 'Can the Social Sciences be Value-Free?' in *Readings in*

incomplete and garbled statement of policy objectives or value-premises, and hence the kind of inconclusive wrangling which results from crypto-normative and pseudo-neutral assumptions. We agree with Dahl and Lindblom when they hold that the means-ends framework is not necessarily always unusable. But, as they put it: 'Because most "ends" are themselves means in a lengthy chain of means-and-ends; because an end in one chain of means-ends may be a means in another chain of action; and because a means in one chain may be an end in another, sometimes the language of means-ends is slippery and cumbersome.'[1] They make use of a distinction between a 'prime' and an 'instrumental' goal, the former representing 'a direct source of satisfaction in itself', while the latter 'has value only because it facilitates the attainment of one or more prime goals'.[2]

Another useful distinction is Stevenson's between 'extrinsic' and 'intrinsic' values, the former values existing exclusively in the *consequences* of something, and the latter in the thing for its own sake. Apart from its consequences, Stevenson emphasizes that something, an institution, process or policy objective, can have both intrinsic and extrinsic value, the one reinforcing the other. For example, a decrease in unemployment *can* be regarded as, at the same time, both an end in itself and also as a means to a higher or better distributed national income. Of course, the same thing can be both 'means' and 'end' simultaneously, and can be an 'end' at one moment and a 'means' at another. Also, many, or most, so-called 'economic ends' are not, except for thoroughgoing materialists, at all *ultimate* 'ends' but rather 'instrumental goals'. In fact, that the pleonastic expression 'ultimate end' seems required points to the inadequacy in terminology.

Nevertheless, all this does not justify the view that means-ends statements are *inevitably* value-loaded and that the distinction cannot be drawn. It simply signifies that in the discussion of policies the

---

the *Philosophy of Science*, edited by H. Feigl and M. Brodbeck, 1953, p. 675: 'Scientists sometimes profess to be giving "merely technical advice" when in fact they are tacitly assuming a particular social policy. This gives encouragement to the view that "positive social sciences" are a sham. But, of course, genuine technical problems can also be found; they are contained within the sham sort; what the sham sort does is to include in the technical specifications factors which it does not mention.'

[1] Cf. R. A. Dahl and C. E. Lindblom, *Politics Economics and Welfare*, 1953, p. 26.

[2] C. W. Churchman deals with the point in terms of 'act-preference' (e.g. for buying in a favourite shop when the price of an 'identical' good is lower elsewhere): 'The dichotomy of the act and the goal (i.e. the means and the end) is primarily one of conceptual convenience, and there is no reason why a scientist might not want to make act-preference measures the inseparable components of goal values.' *Prediction and Optimal Decision*, 1961, p. 197.

'ends' are often very nebulously and incompletely formulated, and that 'ultimate ends' and 'instrumental goals' or objectives are often not adequately distinguished and elaborated—not that they cannot be.[1] It also seems to point to the desirability of an alternative terminology. Valuable though it has been to expose these inadequacies, and the tendentious crypto-normative arguments based on them, the conclusion does not seem warranted, on this ground at any rate, that the economist must inevitably resort to value-judgments in discussing policies, or that he cannot separate quite clearly positive propositions about the consequences of policies from the assertion or assumption of value-judgments about the desirability of policy objectives (which latter can and will often include what have been mis-classified as 'means').[2]

What tend to get mis-classified as 'means' are often differing political or social institutions (e.g. free markets or controls, or the nationalized or private organization of an industry). The mis-classification involves making, inexplicitly, arbitrary political and social value-judgments. Moreover, what often seems to happen is that these inexplicit political presuppositions are shaping extremely speculative economic generalizations. But then by arbitrarily treating, explicitly or inexplicitly, the political choices of institutions as simply questions of 'means', the impression is given that crucial politico-economic issues can be and are being decided by purely economic expertise. It is a very similar procedure to that of the 'welfarist' economist pronouncing on 'economic welfare', while arbitrarily assuming, perhaps inexplicitly, that the non-economic effects—on 'other aspects of welfare'—are neutral, negligible, or generally move in the same direction as the economic effects. We are certainly not complaining that political value-judgments as to different political and social institutions and processes often seem to determine political preferences or decisions, but that they are not explicitly acknowledged as doing so. If the 'purely economic' effects of measures—of, say, monetary or fiscal policy—are very difficult to predict and weigh up, or even if they are not, it may be entirely reasonable and justifiable to decide the issue by political principle, or by preferences for particular kinds of political or social institution, or the distribution of power. But the pretence often seems to be made that preferences and decisions are in accordance with economic expertise, when in fact there is no well-tested or corroborated

---

[1] v. C. L. Stevenson, *Ethics and Language*, 1944, Chapter VII, pp. 174 ff.

[2] Myrdal himself says at one point that it is 'the essential character of science . . . to make policy more rational . . . by clarifying the causal relations between means and aims', which seems to imply that the means-ends formula *can* be legitimately employed. v. *Value in Social Theory*, edited by P. Streeten, 1958, p. 35.

economic theory or generalization to support them, while latent
and arbitrary value-judgments are made treating political institutions
and principles as pure 'means'. The confusion is fostered by packing
all the many varieties of ends into a monistic hold-all such as 'maximum economic welfare'. It does not seem to be putting the point
right to argue that the difficulties and misuse of the means-ends
classification constitutes an *inevitable* source of value-judgments and
'value-loadedness' in the discussion of economic policies. But the
critics are, nevertheless, getting at a very real source of normative-
positive confusion in policy discussions, that is the difficulty of
stating even reasonably fully and precisely the objectives of policies.
This is the main topic of the second half of this book.

(11) SUMMARY AND CONCLUSIONS

This survey has wound to and fro through the preliminaries, processes, and boundaries of economic theorizing and its applications,
and we shall now try to summarize and review our conclusions. We
have tried to make reasonably complete this account of the different
types, sources and entry-points of value-judgments and bias in
economics. We think that the important types have been covered,
and that such as have not, could, in the main, be regarded as variants
or different formulations or combinations of the types with which
we *have* dealt.

The first distinction is between: (1) kinds of value-judgment or
'proposal' that are logically inevitable in any 'science' just as much
as in economics; and (2) value-judgments which are by no means
absolutely inevitable, but which logically have either to be postulated
or affirmed if policy recommendations are to be discussed; further,
(3) there are the questions of the sources and entry-points of subjectivity and possible bias in 'positive' statements, whether theories,
causal explanations or predictions.

As regards (1), in economics, as in all 'sciences', value-judgments
of a kind, or 'proposals', have to be made regarding (*a*) the choice
of problems to be studied, and (*b*) the choice of epistemological
criteria. But simply from a choice of problems or epistemological
criteria no value-judgments as to policy objectives or policy recommendations can ever *logically* follow. Nor can the choice of questions
make bias and dogmatism logically inevitable in the answers to
them.

(2) As regards those value-judgments which are certainly not
logically inevitable, but which may be introduced, these arise only,
or almost only, when policies, and therefore the more or less precise
objectives of policies, are being discussed. No value-judgments
inevitably have to be *asserted* even in discussions of policies, which

can always be treated in the perfectly 'positive' technical-hypothetical mood by simply *postulating* (not asserting) particular objectives, and examining to what extent different policy-measures attain them. Of course, if policy recommendations as to the objectives of policies *are* being made, then political or ethical value-judgments are inevitable. Logic and clarity require that as clear a distinction as possible be made between 'positive' theories, predictions or propositions, and political and ethical value-judgments regarding the effects or objectives of policies, if the latter are indulged in (though many authorities think they should not be).[1] Logic also requires that value-judgments regarding the objectives of policies, or policy-preferences, should be reasonably fully stated, not leaving camouflaged, for example, such political objectives as the widest possible operation of 'free' price mechanisms, on the one hand, or the maximum of 'social control' or distributive equality, on the other hand. The means-ends dichotomy, though it need not inevitably lend itself to this sort of partial camouflage, is liable to be misused in this way.

The inevitable value-judgments or 'proposals' of type (1), regarding choices of questions and criteria, come logically *before* the scientific process of analysis and testing, and might, therefore, be described as 'pre-scientific'. Value-judgments of type (2), relating to the choice of policies and policy objectives, come logically *after* the scientific process proper, and might, therefore, be described as 'post-scientific', since they arise only when theories are being 'applied', however loosely, to policies. As regards (3), subjectivity and possible bias, this operates in the scientific process itself—where no value-judgments are logically required, or, according to the rules, logically in order—by influencing the selection of 'positive' theories, explanations or predictions, which are asserted as empirically valid or unrefuted, when no adequate tests leading to a measure of consensus have been made.

The problems of bias, and the detection and neutralization of its devious workings, are more difficult than those of value-judgments. There is a strong initial drive and propensity to bias in the ideological prejudices and 'visions' with which economic problems are approached, and which often shape initial hypotheses about economic

---

[1] For a vigorous statement of the view that the 'scientist' should aim at making recommendations as to what *ought* to be done by developing methods of measuring the values of policy-objectives, see C. W. Churchman, *Prediction and Optimal Decision*, 1961. Churchman seems to be striving after something like the economist's choice-criterion of objectives or values—that people should do, or have, what they prefer. But he perceives the difficulty, as economists sometimes do not, that to serve as an adequate criterion, 'choice' must be 'adequately or fully informed choice', and that it is difficult to know what this would be when adequate or full information is not available, and even to define 'adequate' or 'full' information.

behaviour. When the scientific testing process gets started, the practicable tests are often inadequate, or too inconclusive, to promote consensus. Testing may narrow the range of hypotheses, but still leave a number of sharply conflicting competitors in the field, and, where tests fail to 'select', bias or prejudice (mostly more or less political), is free to, and often does, take over.

Though the biased 'selection' or use of persuasive value-loaded terminology and concepts has been prominent throughout much of the history of economic thought, this infringement of scientific procedure or criteria does not seem today to be more than a minor controversial nuisance *among economists*, and infringements are usually not difficult to detect and neutralize.

It is in historical evidence, causal explanations, and in predictions, particularly when a high degree of uncertainty is inevitable, as is most often the case, that selection by political bias, rather than by scientific criteria, becomes serious. Though it may not be difficult for the critical economist to detect it in the works of the more blatant propagandists and ideologues who write about economics and economic policy, it may, also, not be easy to tell just where it ends and some genuine positive insight may be beginning. When the propagandist element in one's own or other people's writings is not deliberate, the difficulties of detection may obviously be very great, especially when the evidence that would constitute an adequate test is not obtainable.

Moreover, bias may and does operate not only when policy proposals and objectives are under discussion but at the general theoretical level, for example with regard to short and long period treatment, theories of interest, and even of value, which may be shaped by ideological prejudices or political predilections for or against 'capitalism' or 'socialism', free markets or state regulation. In fact, though general theorizing only logically requires value-judgments or 'proposals' of type (1), and not those of type (2), which have either to be postulated or asserted in policy discussions, subjectivity and bias operate almost as pervasively in general theorizing as in policy discussions and decisions. Certainly, in the case of policy discussions, the pressure of prejudice is likely to be more acute, and the pretext of the need for rapid decision and action on uncertain evidence more effective. Indeed, when particular policy proposals, and the predictions involved, are being debated, flatly contradictory empirical generalizations may be asserted as valid (e.g. with regard to the presence of economies of scale in a larger European market).

Furthermore, in acting or in recommending action on uncertain predictions, a kind of value-judgment as to risk-attitudes is inevitably involved. Orthodox analysis of consumers' or policy choices in terms of certainties has encouraged too facile a separation of normative and positive. Though we are not prepared completely to agree with Churchman 'that knowledge and value are "inseparable" concepts',[1] they are intertwined much more deeply than may be realized by those who have concentrated on the choices between certainties.

Finally, the much more complex and often conflicting nature of policy objectives, discussed by economists and aimed at by governments in the last decade or two, has logically required, but has not been matched by, much more complex and precise value-judgments in the discussion of policies. For, apart from the inevitable 'preliminary' value-judgments and 'proposals' regarding choices of problems and criteria, it is policy objectives, in the broadest sense, that bias and value-judgments, latent or explicit, are mainly about. When it is reasonably, if optimistically, demanded that political value-judgments should be made clear and explicit, it is as clear and full statements, as reasonably possible, of policy-preferences, or reasonably full evaluations of different policy objectives, that are required.

[1] *Prediction and Optimal Decision*, 1961, p. 187.

PART II

POLICY OBJECTIVES

CHAPTER 3

The Objectives of Economic Policies—
An Historical Review

> 'That fabulous animal formally called "econo-
> mic policy" . . . in its current meaning of a
> haphazard collection of pressurized decisions
> remotely related to an indefinable objective.'
>
> G. A. DUNCAN
> *Economic Journal*
> December 1961, p. 811 and p. 814

> 'One can, even today, after hours of argument
> between experts, sometimes achieve an almost
> sensational effect by asking what is the precise
> objective of the policy-measures under dis-
> cussion.'
>
> E. WELTER
> in *Wirtschaftsfragen der Freien Welt*
> edited by E. von Beckerath, F. W. Meyer and
> A. Müller-Armack, 1957, p. 26

(1) INTRODUCTION

The main kind of value-judgments and subjective bias which is
relevant when we examine how far these must, or do, enter into
economics, are those expressing a favourable or unfavourable
attitude to objectives of policy, or suggesting that certain social
states or outcomes are to be desired and aimed at, or not to be desired
and aimed at. This, at any rate, seems to be much the most important
content of the evaluative, persuasive or 'ideological' statements and
assumptions with which we are concerned. An 'objective' is here
understood in a very broad sense, ranging from the vague compre-
hensiveness of the establishment or abolition of 'socialism' or
'capitalism', on the one hand, to promoting a high and stable level
of employment on the other hand, and from immediate tactical,
instrumental objectives to the highest ultimate objectives or values.
Included as 'objectives' are, of course, the maintenance of institutions and traditions. The rightness, justice and desirability of

objectives may be expressed in explicit value-judgments setting out scales of preferences, or they may be inexplicitly suggested by biased presentation of evidence and by persuasive language. It may be a counsel of perfection, or an impossibility, that economists, as is sometimes urged, should state *all* their value-premises. But in discussing policies, or in presenting policy conclusions, hypothetically or as direct recommendations, not merely disagreement but confusion is obviously likely, if policy objectives are not reasonably fully stated. It follows that as policy objectives get more ambitiously complex and comprehensive, the value-premises logically required also need to be more complex and comprehensive. To trace out the development of increasingly complex and comprehensive policy objectives is one of the main purposes of the following historical survey.

Historians of economic thought in treating of doctrines about policy, or the principles of economic policy, have concentrated largely on how far and in what respects economists have advocated the free operation of a competitive price mechanism, on the one hand, and on how wide, and what sort of, a role they have envisaged for state action and regulation, on the other hand. It would be perpetrating an error condemned in the last chapter, to say that they have rather concentrated on 'means' than 'ends'—though this is how it might sometimes tend to be described—because, of course, 'ends' and not simply 'means', are, or may be, involved or comprised in choosing between 'planning' and 'the price mechanism'. Anyhow, not so much has been attempted by way of examining historically other objectives of economic policy, the differing priorities given to various objectives, and how these have been conceived and formulated by economists of different periods and schools. Certainly, this is not an easy subject of which to give a clear and precise historical account, since policy objectives, the explicit or latent approval or disapproval of which represent the most significant kind of value-judgments in economics, are seldom at all fully, clearly and precisely stated. In fact, to find an economist who has given a full and precise statement of his postulated or recommended preference functions in respect of policy objectives, would be as or even more difficult than to find a consumer who has actually given a full and precise statement of his preference functions or preference maps, as implied by the indifference-curve diagrams, for example, to be found in textbooks and on blackboards.

Another frequent source of obscurity is whether and how far what are stated as policy 'objectives', 'ends', 'aims', 'goals', 'targets', 'desired outcomes', and so on, are meant as ultimate or simply as proximate objectives. So in surveying historically the policy objectives which economists have formulated or advocated we must expect

much haziness of detail and definition, though certain broad directions and priorities can generally be discerned. We are, of course,
concentrating on *economists'* ideas about the objectives of policies
rather than on the actual objectives of policy-makers, and we shall
not attempt to assess how far at different times the objectives advocated by economists have been shared by governments or by the
public. Though we are concerned with economists' ideas, as to
policy objectives, we are not simply concerned with economic
objectives. As we shall see, Adam Smith and especially J. S. Mill
were very concerned with political objectives. More recently,
economic 'welfarism' has brought a marked narrowing. We shall be
examining different types of policy objectives further in the next
chapter. But certain distinctions may be useful in a rapid historical
survey in picking out changes and contrasts. First, there is the distinction between *direct* objectives of policies—with which we are
primarily concerned—and *desiderata* not to be aimed at directly by
policies. Obviously a high level of employment or a high rate of
growth was a *desideratum* and, in a sense, even an indirect policy
objective from Smith to Marshall, though a high level of employment
was probably not so high on their scales of preferences as it has been
for many economists in the last two or three decades. But it obviously
was not a direct objective that should, or, for Smith, even could, be
promoted by direct government policies, but only indirectly approached by maintaining and upholding a flexible competitive price
system or its framework. It was not to be made the object of collective choices and decisions, but was best left to emerge from all the
decentralized individual choices and decisions. In fact, in classical
political economy there was little or no room for collectively chosen
or pursued objectives of policy apart from those involved in the
setting up of a competitive framework.

This brings us to a further distinction, that between policy objectives concerned with setting up and maintaining a constitutional
framework, or economic order for society, leaving the economic
process within this framework to find its own objectives; and, on the
other hand, policy objectives concerned with *desiderata* to be aimed
at directly by government policy—a high level of employment or
rate of growth. The precise frontiers between these two kinds of
objective are certainly not immediately and sharply definable—they
shade into one another and have to be weighed against one another.
But at their centres they seem sufficiently distinct for the classification to be useful. This distinction is a commonplace in German
treatises on economic policy under the categories of '*Ordnungspolitik*' and '*Prozesspolitik*'—policies concerned with the economic
order or constitutional framework, and policies concerned with
economic processes. Henry Simons's distinction between policy

objectives concerned with 'rules' and policy objectives aimed at directly by 'authorities', is a closely similar distinction.[1]

By and large, since Adam Smith, liberal economic policies have been primarily concerned with establishing and maintaining a constitutional framework in accordance with the competitive market mechanism, that is with 'rules' or with *'Ordnungspolitik'*.[2] In its more thorough-going form, economic liberalism confined policy objectives largely or entirely to the establishment and maintenance of 'rules', those, basically of Smith's 'simple system of natural liberty'. Indeed, in its most extreme form, even the establishment and maintenance of the constitutional framework was regarded as the mainly negative task of dismantling 'unnatural' state interventions, on the removal of which the 'natural' system would more or less spontaneously establish and maintain itself. 'Liberalism', T. S. Eliot has said, is 'a movement not so much defined by its end as by its starting-point'. Whether or not this is an entirely satisfactory description, it brings out that essentially 'liberal' economic policies have as their objectives the 'starting-point' of the competitive individualist framework, that is, of 'the simple system of natural liberty', or, to use a perhaps impressive and 'persuasive' modern translation, 'the free society'. A 'mixed' economy will, of course, be based on a mixture of *Ordnungspolitik* and *Prozesspolitik*. It was not really until the rise of modern macro-economic policies, in the first quarter of this century, aimed at regulating aggregate monetary processes, rather than at establishing a monetary constitution of rules and institutions, that extensive and systematic *'Prozesspolitik'* began to develop. The nineteenth-century intervention in respect of Factory Acts, and hours and conditions of labour, could be held to be concerned rather with modifying the constitution of the economy.

Ordnungspolitik will mainly, though not inevitably, have objectives that are primarily 'political' and qualitative, and only secondarily economic and quantitative, giving high or overriding priorities to such values or objectives as freedom of choice and initiative and the decentralization of power, which may be described as 'political' though they relate to economic institutions and activities and not necessarily to the political order,—(Adam Smith would probably not

---

[1] Tinbergen distinguishes between *'reforms, qualitative policy and quantitative policy'*. 'Reforms' are equivalent to changes in 'foundations', such as 'the introduction of a social security scheme'. Qualitative policy involves 'less essential aspects of social organization, such as a change in the number of taxes'. This second category of Tinbergen's seems to draw on both *'Ordnungspolitik'* and *'Prozesspolitik'*. For our limited purposes the simpler two-fold distinction, though it has its difficulties, seems the more economical. See J. Tinbergen, *Economic Policy: Principles and Design*, 1956, p. 7.

[2] See T. Pütz, *Theorie der Allgemeinen Wirtschaftspolitik und Wirtschaftslenkung*, 1948, p. 27.

so immediately and enthusiastically have favoured political freedom in the modern sense comprehending regular free elections and complete adult suffrage).

It is often very difficult to tell how far economic objectives are being advocated as ultimate or proximate, and, of course, it may be that some economists have advocated the 'political' and constitutional objectives of the maintenance of a competitive market economy for *purely* economic reasons, believing that it promoted the optimum or maximum favourable movements, in the long run and in peace time at any rate, of indices of national income, rates of growth, price-levels and employment percentages. For some economists these have perhaps been their primary, or even sole, policy objectives. If so, they would presumably have been ready immediately and totally to renounce the political-constitutional objectives embodied in the competitive individualist framework, if such abandonment could be shown, probably in fact, to allow more favourable movements in the economic indices embodying their primary economic objectives. It is very difficult to say, because it is all too easy for explicitness to be avoided by making implicitly the general assumption—which is of course a matter of 'positive', empirical, though extraordinarily complex, facts—that the political and economic objectives are complementary so that no choice is necessary. It is the main characteristic of Utopian thinking that, if only a particular Utopia is adopted, no hard choices between values and objectives are necessary, since the particular Utopia will provide *all* real *desiderata*, liberty, equality and fraternity, or freedom, social cohesion, stability economic and political, justice in distribution, the highest rate of economic growth, full employment—and if there *are* any other *desiderata* they are not really worth desiring.[1] In the communist Utopia all conflicts are, allegedly, abolished, and in the liberal Utopia they are all optimally mediated through the price mechanism. Viner has cogently analysed an example of this kind of Utopian, opportunity-costless philosophizing in his review of Hayek's *Constitution of Liberty*:

'He manages also to reach his conclusions without giving evidence that to do so he had found it necessary to labour with the weighing and measuring of competing values ... avoiding what is, in social thought, the generally unavoidable and troublesome necessity of coping with major conflicts between values ... His procedure consists of narrowing the range of final positive values, which he recognizes as entitled to consideration in the sector of political behaviour, and of finding only complementarity, instead of rivalry, among the accepted values ... He relegates to the category of

[1] Cf. H. Giersch, *Allgemeine Wirtschaftspolitik*, Grundlagen, 1960, p. 62.

instrumental values what to others are final ends or else rejects as
irrelevant to government what are or may be final values ... He
perhaps justifies the inference that if his attack on coercion for its
instrumental defects were to fail he would be willing to attack it also
as an evil in itself.'[1]

Similarly, when socialistic economists set up as a proximate
objective the nationalization of an industry or industries, they not
infrequently seem to suggest that the two sorts of ulterior objectives
which nationalization promotes are complementary and not competitive, for example the economic objective of more efficient production, and political and social objectives of a 'better' distribution
of property, and even 'freedom' as they understand it. Of course,
they *may* be advocating nationalization as a (for them, though
they should not assume for other people) purely neutral 'means',
that is, purely on economic grounds for its assumed effects on
indices of output and costs. But the other political and social
objectives of policies of public ownership also seem to be widely
maintained by their advocates; and it is seldom clear whether, if the
two sets of objectives were shown to be competitive rather than
complementary at the margin, what a socialist's subjective marginal
rates of substitution would be. An arbitrarily assumed Utopian

[1] See 'Hayek on Freedom and Control', *Southern Economic Journal*, January
1961, p. 230 and p. 234. A notable exception is H. C. Wallich, who cogently
expounds the case for freedom and 'the free economy' in non-Utopian terms,
i.e. taking account of costs: 'By claiming as we so often do, that our free economy
maximizes everything at once—the enjoyment of freedom itself, present living
standards and future progress, we render freedom a poor service. We are
implying that we are really making no sacrifice for freedom. We are getting it
cheap, almost as a by-product. The truth is otherwise. Freedom has its cost and
it is our good fortune that we are able and willing to pay it. . . . The nature of
the coin in which we may have to pay will not always be the same. It may be
efficiency, it may be immediate progress, it may be stability or equality. Gains
in all these could perhaps be had—of this too we can never be sure—at the cost
of a little freedom here and there.' *The Cost of Freedom*, 1960, p. 49 and p. 62.
Cf. also M. Oakeshott, *Rationalism in Politics*, 1962, p. 58: 'The political economy
of freedom rests upon the clear acknowledgment that what is being considered
is not "economics" (not the maximization of wealth, not productivity or the
standard of life), but *politics*, that is, the custody of a manner of living; that these
arrangements have to be paid for, are a charge upon our productive capacity;
that they are worth paying for so long as the price is not a diminution of what
we have learned to recognize as liberty.' Milton Friedman, on the other hand,
approaches rather nearer to Hayek's 'opportunity-costless' assumptions of
complementarity, without going quite so far: 'Free institutions offer a surer,
if perhaps at times a slower, route to the ends they [our fellow men] seek than the
power of the state.' The italicized phrase at least represents some qualification
of complete opportunity-costless complementarity. Of course, this qualification
might have to cover acute misery for a significant period of their lives for some
of the present population. See *Capitalism and Freedom*, 1962, p. 202. (Italics
added.)

relationship of harmony between the two sorts of objectives again enables explicit choices to be avoided.[1]

Anyhow, difficult though it may often be to get at anything approaching economists' marginal rates of substitution between policy objectives, which would embody their really significant value-judgments, and which are required for a full and clear statement of value-premises, we shall try in the following brief survey to keep in focus, where possible, their treatment of non-economic as compared with economic objectives.

(2) BEFORE SMITH

Before the Physiocrats and Adam Smith, with political economy hardly yet separated from political and moral philosophy and systematized around a theoretical framework of its own, economic objectives, or the economic aspects of policies, were hardly separated off at all sharply from the political effects and objectives of economic policies. We need not involve ourselves in the issues debated by Heckscher and Viner as to how far 'power' or 'plenty' were regarded as the main objective of economic policies by 'the mercantilists'. It is sufficient if we note that political effects and objectives, particularly in respect of national power, were often given as full and as explicit weight as more purely economic objectives in the discussion of economic policies. As Viner has put it: 'Political and religious considerations were mingled with the economic to a degree without parallel in modern economic literature.'[2]

Furthermore, as is well known, in the century before Adam Smith political economists set out a considerably wider range of economic policy objectives to be attained by direct government regulation, or manipulation of economic *processes*, than did their classical successors, whose policies were directed much more to setting up a framework for a system that would attain its own beneficent objectives. For example, as today, a favourable balance of trade and a high level of employment were advocated as direct aims of government policies. According to Steuart the government 'must continually be in action', and he described 'the object of the art of political

---

[1] Sir Isaiah Berlin (discussing Condorcet) has observed: 'In common with many thinkers of his day, he took it for granted all too easily that all good things were certainly compatible, and indeed interlocked, with each other. We need not go into the reasons for this peculiar belief which has dominated much western thought at all times.' (*Proceedings of the Aristotelian Society*, Vol. 56, 1955–56, p. 318.) Elsewhere Sir Isaiah refers to 'the natural tendency of all but a very few thinkers to believe that all the things they hold good must be intimately connected, or at least compatible, with one another' (*Two Concepts of Liberty*, 1958, p. 13: see below, Section 6 on J. S. Mill).

[2] *Studies in the Theory of International Trade*, 1937, p. 111.

I

economy' as being 'to provide food, other necessaries and employment to every one of the society'.[1] Thus the objectives of policies
were formulated more pluralistically, both in terms of economic and
political objectives, than they later came to be under the influence of
monistic, all-comprehensive, utilitarian maximization and optimiza-
tion formulae—though these latter can, of course, be found in the
writings of the earlier part of the eighteenth century.

(3) ADAM SMITH

The Wealth of Nations is generally and justifiably regarded as the
most important single step towards establishing political economy as
a separate subject. But the separation of political economy from
moral and political philosophy was far less complete in The Wealth
of Nations than often seems to be assumed today by economists who
read the book simply as a treatise on economics, and in it the
objectives of policies are conceived much more in political and/or
politico-economic terms, than purely or mainly economically. It
must be remembered that The Wealth of Nations was only one part
of a much larger plan of Smith's aimed at covering the whole range
of political, social and economic behaviour and institutions, the
organizing principle of which was the idea of the progress of society—
economic progress being the fundamental theme of The Wealth of
Nations.[2] For Smith, progress is not something which comes about
by conscious deliberate planning, or by governments laying down
aims or objectives. Progress comes about indirectly, almost as a by-
product of the development of a society the framework of which is
shaped by beneficent natural law. Smith, therefore, did not so much
set up direct objectives for government policies, such as maximum
production, high rates of growth or employment, economic stability
or a favourable balance of trade, but rather looked to the attainment
and harmonization of these objectives by setting free 'natural' forces
in the framework of 'the simple system of natural liberty'.

For Smith, then, and for the economic liberalism of which he is
the father, economic policy is predominantly 'Ordnungspolitik', that
is, policy recommendations are primarily concerned with creating
and maintaining a constitutional framework and then letting the
economy so constituted find its own objectives, and settle conflicts
between them, rather than—as with his predecessors, such as
Steuart—with direct objectives to be attained by a government
'continually in action'. Smith explicitly makes this point in his
definition of political economy which, he says, 'considered as a

[1] An Inquiry into the Principles of Political Economy, 1767, Book I, Introduction.
[2] Cf. Duncan Forbes, 'Scientific Whiggism: Adam Smith and John Millar',
Cambridge Journal, August 1954, p. 643.

branch of the science of a statesman or legislator, proposes two distinct objects: first, to provide a plentiful revenue or subsistence for the people or'—and here Smith explicitly corrects himself, in vital contrast with Steuart—'*more properly to enable them to provide such a revenue or subsistence for themselves*'.[1]

Apart from policies to set up and maintain 'the simple system of natural liberty', Smith's recommendations, as with his classical successors, to a large extent take the form of exhortations to private individuals. He sought to keep up the rate of saving and investment by preaching the unconditional virtues of private parsimony, just as his successors preached self-help and self-restraint to the worse-off. A higher rate of saving or a statutory minimum level of wages was not merely an undesirable, but an impossible objective for *direct* government policy, and 'unnatural' government policies would only obstruct their attainment. However, the precise details of the monetary framework, which would more or less automatically maintain a high and stable level of activity with a minimum of day-to-day government activity, were not clearly or fully articulated by Smith, or indeed, by his successors.

Distributive justice or policies of redistribution hardly began to come within the range of government agenda as Smith conceived it. Regard for property rights, an essential basis of 'the simple system of natural liberty', and hence for enterprise and growth, in the main precluded progressive taxation for Smith, as for the classical economists generally (though Smith did at one point allow that 'it is not very unreasonable that the rich should contribute to the public expense, not only in proportion to their revenue, but something more than in that proportion').[2] Furthermore, as Stigler has argued, Smith held, in contrast with some modern 'welfare' economists, that the utility or satisfaction people enjoyed was to a large extent independent of the level of their own income, and that it was related more to past income and the incomes of neighbours.[3] The interdependence of utilities, or 'externalities', were not for Smith rather odd or irrational exceptions to a general norm of independence, but were essential economic psychology.

Of the various harmonies Smith believed to exist in the politico-economic universe one of the most vital and significant was that between economic freedom and economic progress or growth. In his first extant treatment of this theme he said: 'Little else is required to carry a state to the highest degree of affluence from the lowest barbarism but peace, easy taxes and a tolerable administration of justice; all the rest being brought about by the natural course of

[1] *The Wealth of Nations*, Modern Library Edition, p. 397, italics added.
[2] *Op. cit.*, p. 794.
[3] G. J. Stigler, *Five Lectures on Economic Problems*, 1950, p. 6.

things.'[1] Since they are in harmony, there is no problem of choice at the margin between more or less economic freedom and more or less rapid growth. But if one could imagine Smith confronted with an inevitable conflict, and forced to choose, as some countries may be today, it seems that the 'political' objective of freedom of individual initiative would have been very difficult to dislodge from the higher positions on his scales of preference. For it was the primarily political objective of a community of self-reliant, self-disciplined, independent individuals, at least as much as quantifiable economic aims in terms of rising levels of national income, which his interest and enthusiasm inclined towards, to an extent only approached among his leading successors by John Stuart Mill. As regards Adam Smith, there is certainly much truth in the proposition that 'the desire for better men, rather than for larger national incomes, was a main theme of the classical economics'.[2] Political and moral objectives, that is, were overriding for Smith. Their assumed fortunate harmony with the objective of long-run economic growth should perhaps even be regarded as to some extent in the nature of a secondary reinforcement—though, to get the balance of emphasis right, we must not, of course, appear to be trying to deny that economic efficiency and progress were not also a major concern of Smith and the classical economists.

(4) BENTHAM

If Smith inclines more than other leading economists to natural law ideas, Bentham, of course, is the supreme representative of Utilitarianism. The contrast is important, and Bentham's formulation of the objectives of economic policies is to be fundamentally distinguished from Smith's, being much nearer to Steuart's than Smith's. The main difference is that Bentham lays down policy objectives which government can and should directly pursue, rather than confine itself to creating and maintaining a constitutional framework for individual initiative.

[1] Quoted by D. Stewart, *Memoir of Adam Smith*, 1811, p. 100. It is interesting to compare Smith's generalization with Thomas Jefferson's pronouncement in his inaugural address of 1801, when after enumerating the rich opportunities open to Americans, he went on: 'With all these blessings, what more is necessary to make us a happy and prosperous people? Still one thing more, fellow-citizens —a wise and frugal government, which shall restrain men from injuring one another, which shall leave them otherwise free to regulate their own pursuits of industry and improvement, and shall not take from the mouth of labour the bread it has earned.' Quoted by W. Letwin, *A Documentary History of American Economic Policy since 1789*, 1961, p. XV.

[2] G. J. Stigler, *op. cit.*, p. 4. Cf. also J. Viner, *Journal of Law and Economics*, October 1960, p. 60: 'It is quite probable, therefore, that Adam Smith would have rejected an extensive program of state regulation of economic enterprise even if he had believed that the wealth of nations could thereby be augmented.'

Bentham varies very slightly the formulation of his policy objectives from manuscript to manuscript, but generally settles for the following four: subsistence, security, opulence and equality.[1] These are subordinate to 'the general end or *end* paramount' which is 'the maximum of happiness with reference to the several members of the community taken together, and with reference to the whole expanse of time'. But having formally acknowledged the existence of his all-embracing monistic maximand, Bentham concentrates on his four-fold second order in the hierarchy of policy objectives. He recognizes the existence of conflicts as well as complementarity between his four objectives, but, as we have seen earlier, the resolution of conflicts, as Bentham saw it, or tried to see it, did not require value-judgments but simply what he regarded as accurate empirical observations and objective measurements of utility.

The first of Bentham's four 'objects' of economic policy, subsistence, he did not consider could be left to the free price mechanism. Like Steuart he wanted a maximum price for corn, and proposed the formation of government stocks to ensure subsistence and a secure food supply for the poor. It is true that these proposals were made in time of war. But vast price fluctuations were not then confined to war-time, and, in any case, many of the leading classical writers opposed, or would probably then have opposed, such schemes even in war-time. This first policy objective of Bentham, though he would not find it relevant today for modern Western countries, would presumably still take first place on his list for many of the poorer countries of the world.

Bentham's second objective of policy, 'security', he regarded as especially a responsibility of government. 'Security' covers defence and justice, and also the security of property and legitimate expectations in accordance with what he called 'the disappointment-preventing principle'. Indeed freedom and essential political values, as Bentham saw them the necessary basis for enterprise and growth, come under his heading of 'security'—though today 'security' and freedom might be regarded as tending to conflict.

Thirdly, comes 'abundance', which means increasing population, and wealth above the subsistence level, and this can—according to

---

[1] See, e.g. *Jeremy Bentham's Economic Writings*, edited by W. Stark, Vol. III, p. 307. Bentham's starting-point for an exposition of the principles of economic policy, the setting up of four or five objectives, or categories of politico-economic objectives, though not adopted by his classical or neo-classical successors, has been used by a number of writers in recent years (v. below, Chapter IV). Bentham's objectives are at an 'intermediate', politico-economic level, like those, for example, of Boulding, Giersch, and Dahl and Lindblom cited below; that is, they are 'above' the more instrumental, purely economic objectives, such as price-stability, but rather 'below' the 'highest' ultimate ethico-political level. See below, Part II, Chapter 2, Section 2.

Bentham, in contrast with Smith—be promoted by state policies, for example by the state investing 'forced savings' in times of unemployment. However, Bentham was hesitant as to how far this theoretical possibility could successfully be pursued in practice, though the recognition of such a theoretical possibility marks a sharp contrast with classical doctrines.

The fourth and last of the objectives Bentham lays down is 'equality', and he explicitly places it well after the first three. The promotion of equality, he emphasizes, will certainly tend to conflict with other objectives, in particular with the second objective 'security', especially security of property, and in case of conflicts equality must give way. But at any rate Bentham expressly recognizes equality as an objective, and he developed, for what it is worth, the utility argument in favour of it. Bentham therefore took an important step, to be followed rather tentatively by J. S. Mill, though certainly not by other classical economists, towards getting a 'better' distribution recognized as an objective of policy on the agenda for governments.

(5) RICARDO

Ricardo's conception of the objectives of economic policies is markedly different both from that of Smith, on the one hand, and Bentham on the other, and in some ways is much closer to that of many modern theoretical economists. Of course Ricardo, with his abstract model-building, carried the separation of political economy from political and moral philosophizing much further than Smith, abstracting economic processes both from 'frictions' within the economic system and from interferences from outside it. For the most part Ricardo seems to be focusing on *economic* processes and on policies directed towards much more exclusively *economic* objectives, and in his main writings there is little or none of Smith's eloquent stress on political and moral values. In fact, Ricardo's conception of the objectives of economic policies seems simple almost to the point of being monistic. Maximum output was for him the overriding economic objective, which was not so much subordinate to, as the expression in the field of economic policy of, the great overriding principle of utility. Ricardo, as he himself said, had his doubts removed regarding the simple and certain criterion for judging policies which 'the great principle of utility' provided, when James Mill showed him

'that instead of being a science, the practical results of which must always be uncertain, rendering it always prudent to try to remain in the state we are in, rather than venture the unknown effects of a change, legislation is essentially a science the effects of which may be computed with an extraordinary degree of certainty; and the friends of human nature cannot proceed with too much energy in beating down every obstacle which opposes the progress of human welfare . . . The ends are there, in the first place, known—they are clear and definite. What you have after that to determine is the choice of the means, and under glorious helps for directing the judgment.'[1]

The exclusion or underestimation of the uncertainty factor has been a simplificatory feature of much subsequent theorizing about economic processes and the effects of policies. The acceptance from his mentor of this simple structure shaped Ricardo's almost monistic conception of the objectives of economic policies, and of a simple pseudo-technical kind of means-end relation between policies and their objectives, a pattern which has had great influence ever since. For enlightened policy-makers, who accepted the great new criterion, conflicts of value-judgments or of objectives hardly arose, since there was a single overriding end, the means to which were not dependent on value-judgments but were laid down by the laws of the new science of political economy. The criterion, also, seemed so easy and certain in application.

According to Stigler, 'Ricardo is as much to be censured for his preoccupation with maximum output as certain modern economists for their preoccupation with equality'.[2] Certainly this preoccupation went quite a long way. In agreement with Smith, and in disagreement with Bentham, Ricardo denied the possibility that the state could or should promote investment in times of depression and held that aggregate stability should be left to, and would beneficently settle itself within, the competitive framework—though he gave rather more attention to the monetary aspects of the framework than Smith. As regards distribution, the propounding of laws about which was the main task and achievement of the new science as Ricardo conceived it, this could and should be a concern of government policy only to the very minor and inevitable extent required for levying an essential minimum of taxation; and then the objective should largely be to leave distribution after taxation as near as possible to distribution before taxation. As Shoup has noted, 'equity issues in taxation appear now and again in Ricardo's writings and speeches. . . . But he makes no co-ordinated assault on the problem of justice in distribution of the tax burden'—in contrast with J. S. Mill.[3] There was no question for Ricardo of laying down subsistence for all as a prime objective of policy, as there was for Steuart and

[1] See Mill's letters in *D. Ricardo, Works and Correspondence*, edited by Sraffa, Vol. VII, pp. 210–11, p. 228 and p. 234.
[2] *Five Lectures on Economic Problems*, 1950, p. 10.
[3] C. S. Shoup, *Ricardo on Taxation*, 1960, p. 249.

Bentham. Of course Ricardo wanted to see a rise in the living-standards of the people, but in his view this could only be approached by setting free natural competitive forces and by preaching self-help to the poor, not by government policies of redistribution.

(6) J. S. MILL

The most important feature and emphasis of Mill's conception of policy objectives and politico-economic goals is the comparatively low order of preference he attaches to increasing wealth or production, or national income per head. The following points are all, to a large extent, variations on this theme.

First, there is the emphasis Mill places on political, social and moral values and policy objectives, as contrasted with more narrowly economic ones. In doing so he is implementing the programme he set himself at the start of his *Principles* of returning to the scope and treatment of Adam Smith in *The Wealth of Nations*:

'The most characteristic quality of that work ... is that it invariably associates the principles with their applications. This of itself implies a much wider range of ideas and of topics than are included in Political Economy, considered as a branch of abstract speculation. For practical purposes, Political Economy is inseparably intertwined with many other branches of Social Philosophy. Except on matters of mere detail, there are perhaps no practical questions, even among those which approach nearest to the character of purely economical questions, which admit of being decided on economical premises alone. And it is because Adam Smith never loses sight of this truth; because, in his applications of Political Economy, he perpetually appeals to other and often far larger considerations than pure Political Economy affords—that he gives that well-grounded feeling of command over the principles of the subject for purposes of practice. . . .'[1]

Mill would certainly not have approved of judging policies simply in terms of 'economic welfare'. It is a feature of Mill's treatment of policy objectives in the *Principles* not simply that he often appeals to 'far larger considerations than pure Political Economy', but that he gives such great weight to political and moral objectives as contrasted with narrowly economic objectives.

Secondly, there is Mill's advocacy of distribution as a possible and legitimate policy objective, which he launched by his distinction between the laws of production as 'physical truths', about which there is nothing 'optional or arbitrary', and the laws of distribution,

[1] *Principles of Political Economy*, ed. W. J. Ashley, p. XXVII.

which depended on 'the laws and customs of society' and 'the opinions and feelings of the ruling portion of the community' and which 'are very different in different ages and countries and might be still more different, if mankind so chose'.[1] Certainly his concern with what Cairnes called 'the great Malthusian difficulty' excluded any possibilities of very drastic redistribution. But Mill's emphasis cleared the way and gave a lead to those in subsequent decades, when 'the great Malthusian difficulty' had lifted in Britain, to put forward re-distribution as a major objective of economic policies. Though opposed to progressive income-taxation Mill advocated severely progressive inheritance duties, and his discussion of public finance, as Shoup says, is pervaded by 'a consuming interest in equity, an interest not to be found in Ricardo'.[2] He did not, however, make use of Bentham's 'utility' arguments for equality, or attempt to treat distribution as a purely economic problem of the efficient allocation of resources so as to maximize social utility or welfare. He based himself simply on what he called 'the general principles of justice'.[3]

Thirdly, Mill's emphasis on political and moral values and objectives, as against economic ones, is illustrated in his rather ambivalent treatment of competition. Its role in promoting economic growth is rather grudgingly and temporarily admitted in his remark that 'while minds are coarse they require coarse stimuli'.[4] As regards the efficient satisfaction of wants through the system of competitive individualism, though certainly opposed to paternalism, Mill is hardly enthusiastic: 'The proposition that the consumer is a competent judge of the commodity, can be admitted only with numerous abatements and exceptions'.[5] It is largely for the sake of the freedom of the individual and individual initiative that Mill argues in favour of competition, that is, because of the political dangers in over-centralizing power—which are 'no less important in a democratic than in any other government'[6]—and for the sake of the beneficent effects of spreading initiative and responsibility and of 'the cultivation of the active faculties by exercise, diffused through the whole community, in itself one of the most valuable of national possessions.'[7]

---

[1] *Op. cit.*, p. 200.

[2] C. S. Shoup, *Ricardo on Taxation*, 1960, p. 258.

[3] *Principles of Political Economy*, ed. W. J. Ashley, p. 804.

[4] *Op. cit.*, p. 749.

[5] *Op. cit.*, p. 953.

[6] *Op. cit.*, p. 945.

[7] *Op. cit.*, p. 949. Sir Isaiah Berlin (*Two Concepts of Liberty*, 1958, p. 13) argues that Mill confused two distinct notions which historically may sometimes go together but often have not: on the one hand, the minimum of coercion and interference, and, on the other hand, men of fearless, original, non-conforming,

Nor was aggregate stability of much urgency for Mill as an economic objective. As a recent study concludes: 'The elimination or mitigation of the commercial cycle was not a leading problem for Mill. . . . For his neglect of depression as a social problem . . . the belief that depression was very brief and that the normal state of affairs was a state of full employment was certainly most important'.[1] But it might be added that Mill argues that as the stationary state grew nearer a more active role for government in warding off depression might become possible and desirable.[2]

Finally, a striking and characteristic theme of Mill's with regard to policy objectives, is the comparatively low degree of preference he gives to the growth of output. Certainly, to a considerable extent Mill's lack of enthusiasm for economic growth simply held so long as one assumed that Malthusian conditions, or absence of population restraint by the poor, made it impossible to raise their living standards, that is, while growth simply increased the comforts of the middle and upper classes and the numbers of the poor at a subsistence level. All the same, one can imagine Mill scrutinizing pretty critically contemporary enthusiasm for more ambitious 'growth' targets. He concedes that 'for the safety of national independence' a country must not fall too far behind in production, though actual warfare he regarded as 'now usually confined, in almost every country, to those distant and outlying possessions at which it comes into contact with savages'.[3]

Mill's conception of the main long-run directions and objectives of economic policy has a breadth and passion absent from more modern concentration on real-income-per-head and 'welfare' criteria. It is presented most fully and most eloquently in his discussion of the stationary state. Though this passage has often been

truth-loving character. Sir Isaiah claims that 'the evidence of history tends to show . . . that integrity, love of truth and fiery individualism grow at least as often in severely disciplined communities among, for example, the puritan Calvinists of Scotland or New England, or under military discipline, as in more tolerant or indifferent societies. . . . If his two goals proved incompatible, Mill would be faced with a cruel dilemma.' Sir Isaiah Berlin notes: 'This is but another illustration of the natural tendency of all but a very few thinkers to believe that all the things they hold good must be intimately connected, or at least compatible, with one another.' We have called attention above to Adam Smith's attractive harmony assumption regarding the goals of freedom and rapid economic growth and to even more far-reaching assumptions of harmony, complementarity and 'opportunity-costlessness' by contemporaries (see Sections 1 and 2 of this chapter).

[1] R. G. Link, *English Theories of Economic Fluctuations 1815–1848*, 1959, pp. 168 and 179.

[2] *Principles of Political Economy*, W. J. Ashley's edition, 1909, Book IV, Chapter 5.

[3] Quoted by M. St J. Packe, *Life of John Stuart Mill*, 1954, p. 303.

quoted, some extensive extracts seem justified since it is one of the most remarkable in economic literature relevant to the subject of this chapter. Incidentally, it indicates how keenly aware Mill was of the limitations of the assumption of independent utilities, long before the age of subtopia, mass motoring and the transistor radio:

'I cannot, therefore, regard the stationary state of capital and wealth with the unaffected aversion so generally manifested towards it by political economists of the old school. I am inclined to believe that it would be, on the whole, a very considerable improvement on our present condition. I confess I am not charmed with the ideal of life held out by those who think that the normal state of human beings is that of struggling to get on; that the trampling, crushing, elbowing and treading-on each other's heels, which form the existing type of social life, are the most desirable lot of human kind, or anything but the disagreeable symptoms of one of the phases of industrial progress. . . .

'That the energies of mankind should be kept in employment by the struggle for riches, as they were formerly by the struggle of war, until the better minds succeed in educating the others into better things, is undoubtedly more desirable than that they should rust and stagnate. While minds are coarse they require coarse stimuli, and let them have them. In the meantime, those who do not accept the very early stage of human improvement as its ultimate type, may be excused for being comparatively indifferent to the kind of economical progress which excites the congratulations of ordinary politicians; the mere increase of production and accumulation. For the safety of national independence it is essential that a country should not fall much behind its neighbours in these things. But in themselves they are of little importance, so long as either the increase of population or anything else prevents the mass of the people from reaping any part of the benefit of them. . . . It is only in the backward countries of the world that increased production is still an important object: in those most advanced, what is economically needed is a better distribution, of which one indispensable means is a stricter restraint on population.

'There is room in the world, no doubt, and even in old countries, for a great increase of population, supposing the arts of life to go on improving, and capital to increase. But even if innocuous, I confess I see very little reason for desiring it. The density of population necessary to enable mankind to obtain, in the greatest degree, all the advantages both of co-operation and of social intercourse, has, in all the most populous countries, been attained. A population may be too crowded, though all be amply supplied with food and raiment. It is not good for man to be kept perforce at all times in the presence of his species. A world from which solitude is extirpated is a very poor ideal. Solitude, in the sense of being often alone, is essential to any depth of meditation or of character; and solitude in the presence of natural beauty and grandeur, is the cradle of thoughts and aspirations which are not only good for the individual, but which society could ill do without. Nor is there much satisfaction in contemplating the world with nothing left to the spontaneous activity of nature; with every rood of land brought into cultivation, which is capable of growing food for human beings; every flowery waste or natural pasture ploughed up, all quadrupeds or birds which are not domesticated for man's use exterminated as his rivals for foods, every hedgerow or superfluous tree rooted out, and scarcely a place left where a wild shrub or flower could grow without being eradicated as a weed in the name of improved agriculture. If the earth must lose that great portion of its pleasantness which it owes to things that the unlimited increase of wealth and population would extirpate from it, for the mere purpose of enabling it to support a larger, but not a better or a happier population, I sincerely hope, for the sake of posterity, that they will be content to be stationary, long before necessity compels them to it.'[1]

(7) MARGINAL UTILITY AND DISTRIBUTION

The emergence of the marginal utility concept after 1871 was accompanied by an increased attention to the problem of distribution and to the possibilities of redistribution as an aim of policy, foreshadowed by J. S. Mill's emphasis on the role of social conventions in determining distribution and its 'laws'. With the melting away of the classical 'laws', and, in Britain, of 'the great Malthusian difficulty', redistribution became an open problem and a possible objective of policy in a way it had never been under the classical régime. When, after about 1890, the marginal productivity theory became the widely accepted orthodoxy, it never attained to the same restrictive authority as the classical 'laws'. At the same time the introduction of the utility concept directed attention to the *use*, or allocation of income, and hence its distribution nationally or socially, while also leading to the re-emergence of Bentham's theorem, derived from the principle of diminishing utility, as to how an equal distribution of wealth, *ceteris paribus*, maximizes 'social utility'. In fact, the theory of distribution became mainly an optimum-allocation theorem of the neo-classical pattern. Moreover, the utility concept most generally adopted involved the simplifying assumption that an individual's utility is dependent only on the individual's own current income—a simplification which Smith, Senior, and J. S. Mill, for

[1] *Principles of Political Economy*, Book IV, Chapter VI, Section 2.

example, would probably not have accepted as a general basis for policies.

The theory of economic policy thus took on a second major dimension, as recognized by Sidgwick in his Principles (1883), where he lays down that 'political economy considered as an art' has two dimensions or objectives; that of 'making the proportion of produce to population a maximum' being coupled with that 'of rightly distributing produce among members of the community, whether on any principle of Equity or Justice, or on the economic principle of making the whole produce as useful as possible'.[1]

But perhaps the most important and direct practical consequences for policy of the development of marginal utility analysis and of the principle of diminishing utility were those for taxation policy. Here the fairly firm classical insistence on proportionality came to be supplanted by the interpretation (or adaptation) of 'equal sacrifice' in terms of 'minimum sacrifice', which was described by Edgeworth (1897) as 'the direct emanation of pure utilitarianism' and 'the sovereign principle of taxation'.[2] The new principle was held to point clearly in the direction of, and to justify, progressiveness rather than proportionality. Whether this development should be described as the emergence into greater importance of the relatively new objective of distributive justice, or simply as a reinterpretation of the old concept of 'equality of sacrifice' in taxation, we need not explore further.

(8) MARSHALL

The increased emphasis on distribution and on the use, or optimum 'distributional' allocation, of wealth and resources, as contrasted with the extreme Ricardian emphasis on the maximum 'productional' allocation, was expressed by Marshall as follows:

'The spirit of the age induces a closer attention to the question whether our increasing wealth may not be made to go further than it does in promoting the general well-being; and this again compels us to examine how far the exchange value of any elements of wealth, whether in collective or individual use, represents accurately the addition which it makes to happiness and well-being.'[3]

'Happiness' and 'well-being', rather than production or economic welfare, were Marshall's expressions for the ultimate social maximand, and he did not try to separate off sharply the economic aspects or causes of happiness and well-being in the formulation of

[1] *Principles of Political Economy*, 1883, p. 403.
[2] F. Y. Edgeworth, *Papers relating to Political Economy*, 1925, Vol. II, p. 107.
[3] *Principles of Economics*, 8th Ed., p. 85.

economic policies. Certainly his keen regard for professional expertise and for its limited range of competence, an increased awareness of which characterized the development of economics as a specialized academic discipline around the turn of the century, led him to mark off distinctly issues 'within the scope of scientific treatment . . . by the methods of economics',[1] from political and ethical issues. But it seems that, following the tradition of his classical predecessors, Smith and J. S. Mill, he would have rejected, as misleadingly over-simplified, exclusive concentration on the economic effects of policies and the economic causes of welfare, in isolation from non-economic causes and effects. 'The economist like everyone else must concern himself with the ultimate aims of man,' has become one of Marshall's most celebrated dicta, and in discussing systems of import duties he wrote: 'The indirect are often much more important than the direct effects; in some of them the economic element predominates, and in others the ethical and political. It is impossible to discuss fiscal policy without reference to all these elements.'[2] Some modern 'welfare' economists have not shrunk from this 'impossibility'.

The problem of povery in Britain, or 'the social question' of his time, was the great stimulus behind Marshall's life-work. As he said to the Royal Commission on the Aged Poor (1893): 'I think I should perhaps say that I have devoted myself for the last twenty-five years to the problem of poverty, and that very little of my work has been devoted to any inquiry which does not bear on that.'[3] But he became increasingly impressed, as is apparent in *Industry and Trade*, for example, by the clash of objectives involved between attempts to counter poverty immediately and directly by 'improving' distribution, and the maintenance of the high rate of growth necessary to maintain Britain's place in the world.[4] As regards stability of employment, though he considered its 'inconstancy' a great evil, he thought it was one which was exaggerated and was not increasing.[5]

---

[1] *Industry and Trade*, 1919, p. 676, see above, Chapter 1, Section 5.

[2] *Official Papers*, by Alfred Marshall, 1926, p. 367.

[3] *Op. cit.*, p. 205.

[4] Marshall's concern with growth and progress is hardly typical of his contemporary neo-classicals. Generally they believed in Adam Smith's assumption of harmony between the economic freedoms and 'growth'. Cf. J. Buttrick, in *Theories of Economic Growth*, edited by B. Hoselitz, 1960, p. 160: 'The neo-classicists felt that "growth" would in the main take care of itself if an appropriate socio-political environment were provided. Furthermore, they believed that free competition, conceived of as a regulatory device used in conjunction with supplementary government controls, would assure such an environment. . . . We now tend to feel that at essential points these assertions rested on an act of faith.'

[5] *Official Papers*, by Alfred Marshall, 1926, p. 92, and *Principles of Economics*, 8th Ed., 1920, p. 687.

(9) THE RISE OF MODERN WELFARE ANALYSIS

In the heyday of neo-classical theory, between, say, 1890 and 1914, economic analysis was mainly 'micro-economic', concerned with the relative prices of goods, services or factors of production, and with the effects of particular taxes and subsidies, within a social framework (with public expenditure less, or not much more, than 10 per cent of national income) such as that of Victorian and Edwardian Britain. This was the 'stable general culture' which Pigou explicitly assumes in 'Western Europe',[1] and which could much more easily be taken as 'given' than in subsequent decades in Britain or elsewhere. It was out of this neo-classical, 'micro-economic' analysis of allocation formulae, productional and distributional, that modern welfare economics developed, with production and distribution as its two dimensions, or policy objectives, or criteria. The attempt was launched, under the strong but considerably 'lagged' influence of Utilitarian philosophizing, to formulate a precise economic objective or criterion for economic policies, which would narrowly delimit— and even, on some views, more or less abolish—political and ethical value-judgments in applying theory to policy. The change from 'Political Economy' to 'Economics', the latter related to policy through the criterion of 'economic welfare',was part of the development of the subject as an increasingly 'academic' discipline, 'independent' of politics. The consumer and the firm were assumed to maximize utility and profits respectively, and, by pure deduction, formulae could be obtained regarding the allocation of their resources. The attempt was therefore correspondingly made to arrive at conclusions as to the economically 'right' or optimum allocation of resources, in production and distribution, by society, by pure deduction from the assumed objective of maximum 'social utility' or 'economic welfare', and thus to fix the analysis of economic policies in a simple monistic framework. Only a single ultimate value-judgment, that 'social utility' or 'economic welfare' *ought* to be maximized, seemed necessary, and it was assumed that an effective criterion as to what were 'increases' or 'decreases' in these entities was available. If it had to be admitted that maximizing 'economic welfare' might conflict with political or other objectives, or 'other aspects of welfare', the sweeping assumption was introduced, of which Pigou seems to have been the main originator, that a relation of harmony or complementarity generally obtained—though admittedly not 'rigidly'—between changes in 'economic' and 'other kinds' of welfare. Thus changes in economic welfare would generally be in the same direction as, or would not generally run counter to,

---

[1] *Economics of Welfare*, 3rd Ed., 1929, p. 21.

concomitant changes in the 'other kinds of welfare'.[1] Alternatively, it was simply urged that the economist must 'stick to his last' and concentrate on the effects of policies on 'economic welfare'.[2]

The contrast with the treatment of the objectives of economic policies by Smith, Senior, J. S. Mill, and probably also Marshall, was considerable. One aspect of this contrast was the very different nature of the arguments for competition which were now advanced. What were claimed to be non-political (or almost non-political) formulae, regarding the efficiency of the allocation of resources under perfect competition, were now given first place, while generalizations regarding competition as a stimulus to progress, or the explicit appeal to political and moral values or objectives, such as the freedom of the individual and the decentralization of power, on which Mill had placed so much emphasis, took second place or disappeared altogether.

(10) THE RISE OF 'MACRO'-POLICIES—A LONG REVOLUTION

We have seen that modern 'welfare' analysis had as its points of departure, and retained as its essential foundations, 'micro-economic' price theory, either of the general or partial equilibrium type. Also, it defined economic welfare in two-dimensional terms as dependent simply on the size of the national product and its distribution. In this respect the treatment, from the second edition onwards, in Pigou's *Economics of Welfare* follows the two-dimensional treatment of the principles of economic policy adopted by Sidgwick, and also Léon Walras, and suggested by J. S. Mill in his distinction between the laws of production and distribution (though Mill by no means confined his appraisal of policies to these two economic dimensions). But for a fleeting period—1912 to 1924 to be precise—Pigou had included a third main dimension in economic welfare, which appeared in, and was indeed the starting-point of *Wealth and Welfare* (1912), and which figured on equal terms with production and distribution in the first edition of *The Economics of Welfare* (1920), only to be

[1] See the classic (though surely most un-classical) discussion by Pigou, *op. cit.*, Chapter I.

[2] v. D. H. Robertson, 'On Sticking to One's Last', *Economic Journal*, 1949, p. 506, who questioned whether 'the old view that the economist as such is concerned only with certain parts or aspects—the more material parts or aspects —of human welfare is really out of date'. He went on to argue that the 'Victorian' concept of 'Economic Welfare as an Objective of Policy' had been reprieved and rehabilitated by the New Welfare Economics against 'Georgian' criticisms. Here we only want to venture an historical comment. The 'old view' is certainly not as old as Smith, J. S. Mill or even, we would suggest, as Marshall. It is not so much Victorian as Edwardian or Georgian, probably the best date that could be given for its birth being 1912, when Pigou's *Wealth and Welfare* was published.

withdrawn, for separate treatment elsewhere, from the second edition (1924).

As its preface makes clear, Pigou's *Wealth and Welfare* grew out of a concern with the causes of fluctuations in unemployment that is, with what might be called the macro-stability problem, and in its successor (the first edition of the Economics of Welfare) 'the relation of economic welfare to the national dividend' is a three-dimensional one depending on the volume of the latter, its distribution and its variability.[1] 'The economic welfare,' Pigou asserts, 'of a group of individuals is likely to be larger the more evenly the consumption of the representative or average member is distributed through time,' and he lays it down as 'a main proposition' that 'any cause which diminishes the variability of the national dividend, provided that it neither diminishes its volume nor injures its distribution, will, in general, increase economic welfare'.[2] The conclusion is drawn that 'there is ground for philanthropic or governmental action designed to make the earnings of labour more stable, even though such action involves a certain amount of direct cost'.[3] There follows an examination of the causes of trade cycles and of the possibilities of counter-cyclical monetary policies, including a favourable verdict on Irving Fisher's plan for stabilizing the purchasing power of money. Thus, for a fleeting period, the economics of 'welfare' had, for its English originator, a third dimension, which was both macro-economic and inter-temporal. It seems a pity that this third dimension dropped out. Much over-simplification of the problems and objectives of economic policy, tending to obscure inevitable clashes of objectives, might have been avoided. The problem would have had to be faced of the precise significant criteria for an increase or diminution in the variability of the national dividend. As it was, *micro*-economic welfare analysis of production and distribution was developed on the basis of ignoring 'that some resources are generally unemployed against the will of the owners'.[4] At the same time *macro*-economic counter-cyclical and employment policies were not related to 'welfare' analysis and criteria (although paradoxically, *Wealth and Welfare* had been inspired by just those problems). In fact it has never been precisely clear how far 'welfare' criteria and techniques were to be confined to micro-economic policy issues, and in discussing real-world policy issues the 'micro' and 'macro' distinction is often not easy to draw.

Just at the time when 'welfare' analysis was being refined and developed to fit the principles of economic policy into the simplified

[1] *Economics of Welfare*, 1st Ed., 1920, p. 42.
[2] *Op. cit.*, p. 65 and p. 67.
[3] *Op. cit.*, p. 878.
[4] *Op. cit.*, 3rd Ed., 1929, p. 129.

K

Procrustean framework of micro-economic maxima and optimal criteria,—with a view to eliminating or simplifying the value-judgments underlying economic policy recommendations,—a new explicit interest and emphasis on 'macro-economic' 'aggregate' policies and objectives was developing. Johan Åkerman boldly proclaims 1914 to be the date of 'the great divide' from which 'macro' plans and 'macro' policies can be dated.[1] Over the next few decades it became more and more widely held that new, explicit, collectively-made choices of objectives, with central government policies to implement them, should supplement the results of individual choices and automatic monetary rules, with regard, successively, to price stability, the level of employment, and, finally, the rate of growth. There would be objections to *any* precise date that could be suggested as marking the definite emergence and acceptance of macro-economic policies and policy objectives in the monetary, counter-cyclical or employment fields. But 1914 or 1929 would seem to be the least objectionable single dates which could be named—certainly one well before 1936. The rise in public expenditure as a percentage of national income had been a partially associated development.

Discussions of price-stability as a possible and desirable objective of monetary policy could be traced back many decades, and tentative suggestions regarding counter-cyclical and employment policies were being made before 1914. On the other hand, it was only after 1929 that the development of macro-policies and aggregate policy objectives really got under way in one country after another, with the levels of prices and employment becoming explicit objectives of policies in place of such traditional, and, from a short-term point of view, almost unfunctional criteria as maintaining the gold standard and balancing the budget. Under the pre-1914 gold standard, it has been said, 'monetary policy was in principle no policy at all', and though this may be something of an epigrammatic exaggeration, it is certain that almost the sole aim of monetary policy was simply the maintenance of the monetary standard.[2] Such an objective would

---

[1] Cf. J. Åkerman, *Theory of Industrialism*, 1960, p. 244: 'We can then rest assured that macro-plans could not and did not belong to economic policy and theory in the industrial countries previous to 1914. . . . The great divide in this respect is not to be found in 1928 (the beginning of the first five-year plan of the Soviet Union), nor in 1931 (the new economic principles of British economic policy), nor in 1933 (the American New Deal and also the German Hitler-régime) but in 1914.' On the other hand, Sir Roy Harrod holds that 'it was in 1922–23 that the great change occurred that divides the modern world from the old', that is when the Federal Reserve System launched out on the path of 'managed money' by ignoring the size of its gold reserve in its credit policy (*Policy against Inflation*, 1958, p. 33). Anyhow, one aspect of this long revolution is well summed up in Hicks's phrase 'the nationalization of money'.

[2] See G. Myrdal, *Beyond the Welfare State*, 1960, p. 17. Also A. I. Bloomfield, *Monetary Policy under the International Gold Standard, 1880–1914*, 1959, pp. 23–4:

now be widely regarded as a 'fetish'. But this may be to look at it from a much more short-term point of view than the nineteenth-century advocates of the gold standard. From their more long-term point of view, such an aim, perhaps quite wrongly, but not entirely irrationally, represents the best 'means', or monetary-constitutional framework, to growth, stability and other genuine 'ends', particularly certain forms of freedom.

After the First World War orthodox policies were directed at returning to the limited objectives of pre-1914 'normalcy'. When in Britain in the nineteen-twenties Keynes raised questions of 'alternative aims in monetary policy', such as devaluation *versus* deflation and stability of prices *versus* stability of exchanges, this was regarded as risqué and unsound in orthodox policy-making circles.[1] Nor, even, was the examination of new objectives for monetary policy taken very far in the report of the Macmillan Committee (1931). The development of ideas regarding the objectives of monetary policy over the last half-century is summarized in the report of the Radcliffe Committee (1959):

'Great as have been the changes in economic circumstances, changes in opinions have, during the last three decades, been even more profound. As part and parcel of this reshaping of ideas, not only have the objectives of Government economic policy become more complex but the degree of priority which is to be attached to any one in relation to the others varies from time to time with changes in economic circumstances . . .

'The beginning of this development is barely discernible in the

'Although official pronouncements in published, or oral form, before 1914 as to the objectives and criteria of central banking policy were relatively few and usually lacking precision, it is of course undeniable that the dominant and over-riding objective of monetary policy in the various gold standard countries was to maintain the convertibility of the national currency directly or indirectly into gold at the legal parity. . . . The view, so widely recognized and accepted in recent decades, of central banking policy as a means of facilitating the achievement and maintenance of reasonable stability in the level of economic activity and of prices was scarcely thought about before 1914, and certainly not accepted as a formal objective of policy.' As an example of academic textbook views there is the pronouncement of W. S. Jevons, no timid thinker on fundamentals: 'The only method of regulating the *amount* of the currency is to leave it at perfect freedom to regulate itself . . . to attempt to regulate its quantity is the last thing which a statesman should do.' *Money*, 23rd Ed., 1910, p. 334 (1st Ed., 1875).

[1] Cf. J. M. Keynes, *A Tract on Monetary Reform*, 1923, and the comment on such questions by Sir Harry Goschen, Chairman of the National Provincial Bank (1924), quoted by Keynes in *Essays in Persuasion*, 1931, p. 222. 'I cannot help thinking that there has been lately far too much irresponsible discussion as to the comparative advantages of Inflation and Deflation. Discussions of this kind can only breed suspicion in the minds of our neighbours as to whether we shall adopt either of these courses, and, if so, which. I think we had better let matters take their natural course.'

Report of the Macmillan Committee. Before 1914 the maintenance of convertibility at a fixed gold value of the pound was sufficient definition of the duty of the Bank of England: this carried with it, according to contemporary thought, sufficient guarantee of the purchasing power of the pound. . . . At the same time "scarcely anyone" according to the Macmillan Committee "considered that the price level could or ought to be the care and pre-occupation, far less a main objective of policy" of a central bank. The Macmillan Committee itself found it impossible to maintain quite the old simplicity, but did not depart from it. . . . When it came to elaborate the major objectives of monetary policy—"the maintenance of the parity of the foreign exchanges without unnecessary disturbance to domestic business, the avoidance of the credit cycle, and the stability of the price level"—it still placed foreign exchange stability first. Only later did it explicitly state as an objective "stability of output and employment at a high level", though this was no doubt implicit in its earlier phrase "the avoidance of the credit cycle". Most significantly, it took for granted the broad consistency of these objectives.'[1]

The great depression made, in most countries, during the ensuing decade of the nineteen-thirties, the reduction of unemployment *the* great direct overriding problem or *desideratum*, as it had been also in Britain, to some extent, in the nineteen-twenties as well. Raising the level of employment was a policy objective which, for a considerable way, was not only compatible with, but helpful or even essential for other objectives, for example with more rapid economic growth—though this was not, of course, prominent as an explicit aim at the time—with stability of prices, insofar as this might mean raising them from unduly depressed levels, and with 'better' distribution. A position of heavy unemployment has some parallels with a Pareto non-optimum position not only in that more of one good can be produced, without less being produced of any other, but that at least as regards the main macro-economic objectives it may be possible to improve one index without worsening others. However, this will not hold for the whole range of objectives, including 'constitutional' objectives, or the maintenance of traditional institutions. Employment policies were *not* at that time compatible with such traditional aims and ideals of classical British 'Ordnungspolitik' as a balanced budget, free trade and the gold standard. However, in the debates at the time the issues do not seem to have been set out in terms of an explicit clash of objectives and therefore of value-judgments. It is rather that conflicting value-judgments and objectives seem to have

[1] Report of the Committee on the Working of the Monetary System, Cmnd. 827, 1959, p. 17. See also the comments of Lord Franks, *Some Reflections on Monetary Policy*, 1960, pp. 7–12.

been considerably mixed up with conflicts of positive diagnosis (or sometimes pseudo-positive diagnosis) and of empirical generalization and prediction. The term 'Keynesian Revolution' is used, often rather undiscriminatingly, to cover developments, on the one hand, in pure analysis or empirical theories, and, on the other hand, changes in the widely advocated norms and objectives of economic policies. Of course, historically they are all closely inter-related, but clarity and agreement have been difficult to attain while the different kinds of issue have not been distinguished sufficiently.

Anyhow, there is clearly much truth in the following summary: 'The Great Depression made the cure of unemployment the great social problem—to an extent that has largely faded from our minds today. Full employment emerged as a single dominating economic objective and thus assumed a role similar to that of maximum accumulation in the vision of the Classical Economists. For a few years after the publication of the *General Theory*, it seemed as though policies could be approved or rejected solely by reference to their effect on aggregate demand—in the same way as a Ricardian could appeal to the effect of proposed measures on profits.'[1]

Thus for nearly four decades, from 1914 to about 1950, to a very large extent in Britain and to a significant if lesser extent in other countries, the objectives for economic policies were dominated by crises of one sort or another, war and post-war inflation part of the time, and severe unemployment, depression and deflation for much of the rest of the time. In crises, though conflicts of aim and value-judgment of course remain, they tend to a considerable extent to be simplified and mitigated. Of course such conflicts were very sharp in the thirties. All the same, pretty well all shades of opinion would, as the decade wore on, have held that the reduction of unemployment should have had the highest priority among economic policy objectives. As Myrdal has acutely noted:

'The more "normal" conditions are, the greater is the number of conflicting programmes. In a crisis—economic, social or political—there really is an approximation to "interest harmony" in society because interests have, for the time being, been taken away from long-range objectives and concentrated upon one, mutually shared, short-range objective. In a depression both employers and employees can be shown to have a common interest in economic expansion, raising the volume of credit, demand, prices, production, employ-

[1] A. Smithies, *Economics and Public Policy*, Brookings Lectures 1954, 1955, p. 12. Cf. also P. Samuelson, in *Income Stabilization for a Developing Democracy*, edited by M. F. Millikan, 1953, p. 547: 'I think it no exaggeration to say that for a dozen or more years following 1930 economists were obsessed with the problem of full employment.'

ment and wage-earnings. In war the common interest rising above other goals is to win victory. In a crisis the problem for practical research is, therefore, relatively simple.'[1]

With economics and economic policies reconverted, by about 1950, to a condition of peace-time full-employment unprecedented in Britain for nearly forty years, it was necessary, for the elucidation of the choices between alternative policies, that clashes in objectives be faced, and, where recommendations were being made, for explicit value-judgments to be set out. In Britain 'a high and stable level of employment' had been explicitly laid down as an agreed aim of government policy. In 1956 this was followed by an explicit pledge 'to foster conditions in which the nation can, if it so wills, realize its full potentialities for growth in terms of production and living standards'. As the Radcliffe report comments: 'As a broad objective of policy this, like employment, is not wholly new. . . . But it is newly explicit as an objective of Governments, and particularly it is new as a justification for positive measures in the broad field of financial policy.'[2] Economic growth is certainly an objective the pursuit of which might have much more profound and comprehensive consequences for the role of government in the economy, and hence for certain fundamental political values and objectives, even than the goal of full employment. More and more ambitious objectives and combinations of objectives, with higher criteria and standards of performance, have been widely advocated and expected, while the possibility of conflicts and the need for explicit choices and value-judgments have often not been adequately faced. The Radcliffe report indeed concludes that 'as the objectives of policy have become more explicit and more elaborate, the possibilities of conflict have loomed larger',[3] and it has been noted by a leading authority on planning, that 'much wishful thinking has taken place regarding the harmony which is supposed to exist between the different objectives'.[4] Clashes of objectives have indeed been the more acute just because of the very 'success' with which in some directions, aggregate 'macro'-economic policies have been carried out—for example, in maintaining a high level of employment. Of course the existence of such clashes of broad objectives and values as Progress and Security, Growth and Stability, and Freedom and Justice, have long been recognized in general terms. But from the early nineteen-fifties onwards such clashes have been much more immediately, acutely and practically involved in the choices of current policies, without always

---

[1] G. Myrdal, *Value in Social Theory*, edited by P. Streeten, 1958, p. 159n.
[2] Report of the Committee on the Working of the Monetary System, Cmnd. 827, 1959, p. 19.
[3] *Op. cit.*, p. 19.
[4] v. R. Frisch, *Generalities in Planning*, 1957, p. 11.

obtaining the clear and explicit recognition and formulation necessary if these choices of policies were to be elucidated. But, after all, peace-time full-employment had been till the 1950s a condition almost unknown for quite a long time in Britain, and rare and fleeting in other countries, and meanwhile the scope and objectives of policies had been completely transformed by a long revolution. The need for much more elaborate and explicit value-judgments, if confused disagreement was not to descend on the discussion of economic policies, was something new and to a considerable extent unprecedented. Moreover, not only were the economic objectives of economic policies becoming more complex and conflicting, but the neglect of the political effects and objectives of the more comprehensive economic policies was becoming increasingly questionable, and was perhaps a latent source of fundamental disagreement over policy measures.

(11) POLITICAL AND SOCIAL EFFECTS AND OBJECTIVES OF ECONOMIC POLICIES

The economic welfarist 'presumption', as Pigou called it, 'that qualitative conclusions about the effect of an economic cause upon economic welfare will hold good also of the effect on total welfare', has, tacitly or explicitly, obtained very wide acceptance among economists. Pigou, however, as we have noted, only claimed validity for this presumption 'among nations with a stable general culture, like those inhabiting Western Europe'[1] (at the period presumably when *The Economics of Welfare* was written). A further condition, not always explicitly stated but perhaps tacitly implied, was that only the effects on economic and other sorts of welfare of '*micro*'-policies, that is policies concerned with individual taxes and subsidies, or particular industries and markets, were being 'presumed', and that aggregate, '*macro*'-policies with more widespread effects, pervading and perhaps shaping the whole economy, were not envisaged, or, at any rate, not included in the analysis. Indeed a broadly high and stable level of employment seems to be assumed throughout Pigou's *Economics of Welfare*, brought about, it appears, by the self-adjusting mechanism of a competitive economy rather than by direct policy. However, economists more recently seem widely to have adopted Pigou's 'presumption' even with regard to the effects of policies aimed at the control of chronic inflation, and at high levels of employment and growth. It hardly needs arguing that policies of this scope, the main preoccupations of economists in the last decade or more, certainly may have important effects on political and social

[1] *Economics of Welfare*, 3rd Ed., 1929, pp. 20–1. As already noted, D. H. Robertson reasserts this hypothesis as one on which 'we can reasonably plan our studies' without mentioning Pigou's reservation as to 'stable general culture' and Western Europe. *Lectures on Economic Principles*, Vol. I, 1957, p. 18.

values, objectives or institutions. Different policies aimed at combining 'full' employment, price stability and more rapid economic growth, obviously have considerable effects on the whole politico-economic constitution of society, the nature and extent of freedom, and the distribution, centralization and decentralization, not only of income, but of power.

It has several times been pointed out how the modern problem of chronic inflation is, to an important extent, a sociological problem. Moreover, foreign political objectives have in the last decade or two become of increasing importance for decisions about economic policies, and in fact are sometimes invoked as the main ground for raising the rate of growth at home and for the reshaping of the economy which it might be held to entail. 'The subordination of economic interests to foreign political goals,' it has been said, 'has been one of the outstanding national policy developments of this generation.'[1] One may consider this subordination quite wrong and the goals it implies valueless or worse, but that, of course, requires a value-judgment about political objectives which should be made explicit.

It is, however, with regard to policies aimed at promoting growth, and especially at the rapid growth of economically less developed countries, on which economists have focused so much attention in the last decade, that political and social objectives are obviously of major importance, and which it is obviously sheer philistinism to neglect. Here, Pigou's explicit limiting assumption regarding the negligibility of the political and social effects of economic policies only holding 'among nations with a stable general culture, like those inhabiting Western Europe'—at the relevant period—has to be stressed. It is the whole life of a community which is being acted upon when policies for rapid economic growth are enacted.[2] The point has been very strongly put by Bensusan-Butt:

'The ultimate fruits of civilization are slow growths that need a stable environment, and ... the economic motive running loose in circumstances that permit or compel violent economic change must wreck this environment. Save to the extent that rapid progress may today often serve, and in the past served more often still, to relieve real poverty, there is surely not even a presumption that it also promotes the other ends of social welfare. Name a society whose

---

[1] R. F. Mikesell, *Papers and Proceedings of the American Economic Association*, 1959, 1960, p. 258. See also J. Viner, *International Trade and Economic Development*, p. 5: 'It is today always necessary, therefore, as it was not for the English classical economists, to be perfectly clear whether we are considering a problem of, say, commercial policy from a national or from a cosmopolitan point of view.'

[2] 'We are talking about transforming whole societies.' Eugene R. Black, 'The Age of Economic Development', *Economic Journal*, June 1960, p. 266.

economic advance delights its statisticians and you name one in which the good qualities of its earlier life are decaying and in which no new civilization has emerged. That good will come from this evil is a possibility, but the economist cannot honestly pretend to know that it is more.'[1]

Again, one may strongly disapprove of the kind of values expressed in this quotation with regard to social institutions and environments, but we repeat that an explicit political value-judgment is, in any case, required. We are not concerned here to express support for one value-judgment rather than another, but simply that *some* value-judgments are involved, and that the need for these cannot simply be dismissed by assuming that the political and social effects of economic policies can be assumed to be in complementary harmony with economic effects, or a particular economic effect. The value-judgments logically required in discussing economic policies are as wide ranging as the effects, or possible effects, of those policies, and, with regard to growth policies this is very wide.

A more general attack, from a position which he claims to be 'different from that which seems to be occupied by many economists', has been launched by Hicks against Pigou's widely accepted assumption that the political and social effects of economic policies can be neglected, and that value-judgments regarding political and social values and objectives are hardly required in the discussion of economic policies. 'Welfarists,' Hicks claims, 'even those who limit their concept of economic welfare to the Production and Distribution of the Social Dividend, have become, almost unconsciously and unintentionally, something like the dominant school of economic thought.' What Hicks finds to be 'the characteristic feature of economic welfarism' is 'that it finds the *ends* of economic life *within* economics'. He emphasizes the 'artificiality' of the assumptions of welfare analysis and points out how policy problems are cut down to the size of the technique by simplifications which 'beat reality into

[1] D. M. Bensusan-Butt, *On Economic Growth*, 1960, p. 213. Cf. also J. L. Sadie, 'The Social Anthropology of Economic Underdevelopment', *Economic Journal*, June 1960, p. 302: 'Economic development of an underdeveloped people by themselves is not compatible with the maintenance of their traditional customs and mores. A break with the latter is a pre-requisite to economic progress. What is needed is a revolution in the totality of social, cultural and religious institutions and habits, and thus in their psychological attitude, their philosophy and way of life. What is, therefore, required amounts in reality to social disorganization. Unhappiness and discontentment in the sense of wanting more than is obtainable at any moment is to be generated. The suffering and dislocation that may be caused in the process may be objectionable but it appears to be the price that has to be paid for economic development; the condition of economic progress.' This analysis may apply also, of course, to raising rapidly the rate of growth in a comparatively developed country.

a form which makes it tractable to economic analysis'. Hicks takes his main example of the inadequacy of welfare analysis not from the treatment of aggregate 'macro'-policy issues, but rather that of anti-monopoly policy based on the *micro*-economic price theory out of which welfare theorems were developed. He concludes that the economist is allowed and even encouraged to hold that if he

'has shown that a particular course of action is to be recommended, *for economic reasons*, he has done his job. I would now say that if he limits his function in that manner, he does not rise to his responsibilities. It is impossible to make 'economic' proposals that do not have 'non-economic' aspects, as the Welfarist would call them; when the economist makes a recommendation, he is responsible for it in the round; all aspects of that recommendation, whether he chooses to label them economic or not, are his concern.'[1]

We are not here going to pursue the question of the right concerns or responsibilities of the economist. Let us simply note that the wheel has turned, if not exactly full circle, at any rate most of the way. Senior (1836) held that the economist should not 'add one syllable of advice', because advice on policy should take into account a wide range of non-economic considerations.[2] Hicks (1958) may wish to add one (or more) syllables of advice, but condemns, like Senior, the giving of some kind of purely economic advice, on purely economic criteria, which he describes as having become the practice of 'something like the dominant school of economic thought'.

In the nineteenth century the classical economists were often fiercely criticized by social philosophers, such as Carlyle and Ruskin, for propagating a narrow and sordid materialism. As against J. S. Mill, outstandingly, and others as well, such a charge could be

---

[1] J. R. Hicks, *Essays in World Economics*, 1959, pp. VIII–XI. On the subject of anti-monopoly policy J. Wiseman has stressed the 'confusions' due to 'the unwillingness of economists to think about their problems in relation to more than one policy aim at once', and 'the difficulties created for the policy-maker by the narrowness of the economists' approach to policy questions. . . . Economists have made little attempt at consistent examination of problems in relation to aims other than choice, and have given even less time to discussion of policy questions in contexts requiring consideration of more than one policy aim at once. Indeed, when faced with a problem involving plurality of aims, their inclination has frequently been to seek ways round it, in order to make "scientifically pure" statements about choice, rather than to accept the need for a wider cast of the net.' (*Economic Journal*, September 1960, pp. 458–60.)

[2] For another statement of this perhaps rather platitudinous, but nevertheless dangerously neglected point, see *The Significance and Basic Postulates of Economic Theory*, 1938, p. 165: 'Only advice and policy which is based on an estimate of the political, sociological and economic effects *together* of a policy or measure can be sensibly acted on.'

shown to be unfair. We have seen above how Senior, Cairnes, Sidgwick and J. N. Keynes all strongly urged how dangerous and misleading it could be to set up purely or narrowly economic criteria
and policy objectives.[1] The criticisms of Carlyle and Ruskin were
carried on, in the first quarter of this century, by J. A. Hobson,
Graham Wallas and W. A. Robson.[2] The kind of point which Hicks
and Bensusan-Butt are making, though far from being basically new,
has quite recently—like that regarding clashes of policy objectives—
taken on a much sharper and explicit relevance with the setting up
of unlimited or maximum percentage increases in indices of income-
per-head as major, and perhaps over-riding, policy objectives. Today
it is economists themselves who are making the charge of 'materialism'—or, at any rate, a rather similar charge—against their own
colleagues.[3] The gravamen of the charge should not so much be that
the majority of economists are completely devoted to exclusively
materialist goals but rather that they are inevitably tempted to focus
on measurable, quantitative objectives rather than qualitative non-
measurable ones, and measurable goals inevitably tend to be somewhat materialistically conceived. As is well known, qualitative
elements, even of the simplest material kind, largely elude indices of
production or consumption. On top of this, the largely tacit adoption of Pigou's assumption of 'welfare harmony' encourages the
conclusion that if policies are shown to be beneficial according to an
economic welfare criterion, they will generally be totally beneficial,
since 'other aspects of welfare' will either be unaffected, or will move
in the same direction as 'economic welfare'. Pigou's assumption
probably did not stem from any emphatic or conscious inclination

---

[1] *Senior* held that it was 'neither advisable nor perhaps practical to use as
the sole, or even the principal guides in the actual conduct of affairs', purely
economic principles or criteria. *Cairnes*, in discussing policy conclusions, stressed
political and social 'consequences so weighty as to turn the scale against purely
economic solutions' of policy issues. *Sidgwick* did not regard distribution questions *simply* as questions of quantities or degrees of economic welfare, but held
that they enter 'into the most fundamental controversies as to the ultimate basis
and end of the political union'. *J. N. Keynes* emphasized that 'purely economic
data rarely by themselves suffice for the complete solution of practical problems'.
See Part I, Chapter 2, Sections 2 and 3.

[2] See J. A. Hobson, *Work and Health*, 1914, p. 29 et passim; G. Wallas, *The
Great Society*, 1914, Chapter XIII; and W. A. Robson, *The Relation of Wealth
to Welfare*, 1924, Chapter I: 'With the progressive development during the past
hundred and fifty years of the old political economy into the modern subject of
economics, the whole tendency has been for economic discussion to become in
the first place increasingly preoccupied with the more easily measurable facts of
human nature and lamentably anxious to avoid those presenting greater difficulty' (p. 19).

[3] Cf. A. Smithies, *Economics and Public Policy*, Brookings Lectures 1954, 1955,
p. 10: 'The attitude fostered by the Pigouvian welfare economics is one of crass
materialism.'

either towards materialism or towards Utopianism, but rather from the Marshallian, partial, one-at-a-time method of analysis based on an assumption of *ceteris paribus* (the *ceteris* in this case being other aspects of welfare). Such an assumption seemed also to justify academic economists in making policy recommendations while not trespassing outside their specialist discipline. Nevertheless, the assumption promotes what has been called 'the fallacy of the unexplored remainder',[1] along with its materialist and Utopian implications.

Recent anti-materialist, or anti-'measurabilist', criticism finds most thorough-going expression in a concern for the preservation of the non-materialist values and cultural institutions of 'under-developed' countries in the process of industrializing themselves. E. F. Schumacher has written:

'Present-day economics, while claiming to be ethically neutral, in fact, propagates a philosophy of unlimited expansionism, without any regard to the true and genuine needs of man, which are limited.

'It is this that gives the Western way of life that destructive and paralysing effect upon the so-called "under-developed" countries which has been rightly called the "withering touch". To recognize this fatal weakness does not mean underestimating the stupendous achievements of the West. . . . The West can indeed help the others, as the rich can always help the poor. But it is not an easy matter, expressible in terms of money alone. It demands a deep respect for the indigenous culture of those that are to be helped—may be even a deeper respect than is possessed by many of them themselves.'[2]

We happen to believe that there is a challenge here which should at least be taken seriously. But that is not the point we are now concerned with. We are here simply concerned to emphasize that if a latent 'abstract materialist' or 'measurabilist' bias is to be avoided in the discussion of economic policies, explicitly argued assumptions about the non-economic effects and objectives of policies must be set out. In the discussion of economic policies for 'under-developed'

---

[1] 'To reach final conclusions upon the basis of consideration of a single value, or of a very limited set of values, is liable to result in what has been called "the fallacy of the unexplored remainder".' J. Viner, 'Hayek on Freedom and Coercion', *Southern Economic Journal*, January 1961, p. 230.

[2] E. F. Schumacher, *Roots of Economic Growth*, 1962, p. 13. Cf. also p. 30: 'The neglect of non-economic realities seems to me to be the principal barrier to worthwhile progress in the very field of economic development with which we are concerned. The science of economics becomes the more exclusively quantitative (and thus a pure abstraction) the more rigorously it is developed. This may be useful for narrowly circumscribed tasks of analysis within a given and stable setting; but it is of extremely limited applicability and generally misleading when the task is one of changing the setting itself.'

countries the importance of the political and social effects of economic policies, and the need for choices between politico-social and economic objectives, and for explicit value-premisses expressing these choices, are particularly obvious. But these effects, choices and value-premisses are also present, if rather less obviously and fundamentally, in the discussion of economic policies in comparatively developed economies, and the failure to make them explicit can equally lead to argumentative confusion, latent bias, and a failure to elucidate the choice of policies.

CHAPTER 4

The Formulation of Policy Objectives and Policy Preferences

'Those of us who are economic theorists are only too familiar with models which assume a single goal, treated as if it were endowed with a single characteristic varying only in quantity or degree, such as "economic welfare", "prosperity", "utility" or "equilibrium". Such models are indeed the major part of our professional inventory. The legislator, on the other hand, is, or should be, always conscious that he is repeatedly facing the necessity of choosing between extensive combinations of objectives, all of which clamour for consideration.'

J. VINER
(*International Trade and Economic Development*, 1953, p. 2)

'In so far as economic doctrines have an influence on the choice of objectives for national policy, on the whole it is obscurantist rather than helpful. . . . The very fallacies that economics is supposed to guard against, economists are the first to fall into.'

J. ROBINSON
(*Economic Philosophy*, 1962, p. 130)

'Progress rests . . . with the clarity of our conception of our ends, and with the realism of their choice.'

K. R. POPPER
(*The Open Society*, 4th Ed., 1962, Vol. II, p. 280)

'We cannot reason ourselves out of our basic irrationality. All we can do is to learn the art of being irrational in a reasonable way.'

A. HUXLEY
(*Island*, 1962, p. 171)

(1) 'WELFARE' ANALYSIS AND POLICY OBJECTIVES

The formal treatment of the principles of economic policy has been dealt with in the branch of the subject known as 'welfare economics'. The single objective of policy on which 'welfare' economists, especially pure theorists, have concentrated, has been formulated as a maximum or optimum of 'welfare', or 'economic welfare'. This amounts to a monistic, or, at most, dualistic formulation, with 'maximum welfare' as the sole over-riding objective or criterion, depending on two doubtfully separable subordinates, the size and the distribution of the national dividend. 'Other aspects of welfare'— than 'economic welfare'—are generally assumed to be unaffected, or at any rate not unfavourably affected, by changes in 'economic welfare'. The 'other aspects' are then largely left out of account.

We are not attempting here another critical analysis of welfare economics, going again over the questions of interdependence, compensation, 'second-best' policies and so on, which have been so expertly and extensively treated in recent years.[1] Nor are we concerned with the ways in which 'welfare' theory—like most theories especially when first propounded—has been exploited politically.[2] 'Welfare Economics' is a term with a vague and extensive coverage, sometimes, apparently, meaning any application of price theory to policy. We are not concerned with a target as broad as that. Of course, also, it can be useful to work out the logical implications of precise criteria—such as the choice criterion—or to analyse the effects of policies in terms of such criteria, provided the conclusions are not tendentiously interpreted, or upheld as complete and generally valid guides to policy. Certainly, also, if 'welfare' analysis has been politically misused in some directions, in others it has been used critically to deflate Utopian simplications, liberalist and socialist. We only wish to attempt a few more general comments on the adequacy of the monistic conception of the objectives of economic policies, and the over-simplification of the value-judgments logically involved, which has often been fostered by 'welfare economics'.

There does seem to have been, at least until recently, something fundamentally circle-squaring in the alleged primary purpose of welfare economics of 'trying to set up standards of judgment by which events and policies can be judged as "economically desirable",' or, 'to formulate propositions by which we may rank, on the scale of better or worse, alternative economic situations open to society';[3]

---

[1] See E. J. Mishan, 'A Survey of Welfare Economics 1939–1959' (*Economic Journal*, June 1960, pp. 197 ff.), who appends a bibliography of 250 items.

[2] 'The theory has been persistently used, by all sides, as a political weapon.' I. M. D. Little, *A Critique of Welfare Economics*, 2nd Ed., 1957, p. 273.

[3] See K. E. Boulding, in *Survey of Contemporary Economics*, Vol. II, edited by B. F. Haley, 1952, p. 3; and E. J. Mishan, *op. cit.*, p. 199.

and to do this within the confines, apparently, of only such value-judgments, if any, as are universally or generally acceptable, or as part of 'a positive science of what is and tends to be, not a normative science of what ought to be'.[1] It is from this basic claim, or attempt, of welfare economics, or the attitude it represents or fosters, that so much confusion has resulted for the discussion of policies, in that choice is rather eliminated than elucidated.

Welfare economics shares a common utilitarian intellectual parentage and common family features with, and is a kind of elaboration of, the theory of consumers' behaviour—though each has a non-Utilitarian 'Paretian' variant. Both are purely or almost purely deductive, starting from some very comprehensive generalization, the one positive, the other (presumably) normative, and attempting to extract significant conclusions by logico-mathematical analysis.[2]

In some respects the community welfare-maximization principle is much vaguer and more detached from reality than the utility-maximizing principle or postulate for the individual consumer. This is with regard to the definition of the would-be, or should be, maximizing unit. For though there may be vaguenesses in the exact definition of the composition or time-horizon of the 'household' whose utility is assumed to be maximized, these are not likely to be the subject of the crucial initial disagreements which are certain to arise when the attempt is made to define, for the purpose of a particular policy application, the local and temporal characteristics of the 'community' whose welfare is to be maximized. Even if some illumination can be derived from the principle that 'the community's'

---

[1] A. C. Pigou, *Economics of Welfare*, 3rd Ed., 1929, p. 5. Cf. T. D. Weldon, *The Vocabulary of Politics*, 1953, p. 150: 'The demand for "objective" standards in politics and in morals is simply a demand for a criterion which will enable us to grade people and institutions with the same sort of certainty and confidence as that with which, with very minor qualifications, we can grade physical bodies in terms of size and weight. We would like to appraise actions and constitutions as "good", "not so good" and "bad", with the same simplicity and the same approximation to certainty and infallibility as that which we achieve in grading men as "more than 6 feet tall" and "6 feet tall or less". Ideally we aim at the complete certainty and infallibility we have in the case of "seven is greater than six and six is greater than five".

'At this point, however, we must stop and ask "Does this demand make any sense? What does it mean to talk about a criterion of this kind, and are those who cry for it looking for something which they might have but have not got and would be of value to them if they had it? Or are they looking for something which it is nonsense to ask for at all?" '

[2] It should be pointed out that Pigou's *Economics of Welfare* was, to a very large extent, a critical case-by-case review of current policies. But that aspect of the book was soon largely forgotten and it was simply the structure of the analysis, and basic assumptions, to which subsequent discussion has mainly been devoted.

welfare is to be maximized, the question, of course, remains as to which 'community'—some national unit, a group of associated countries, 'western', 'eastern', 'commonwealth' or otherwise, the whole world, or some kind of weighted index? And with what time-horizon, or weighting of different generations? Of course, for the purposes of arbitrary abstract model-building, the definition of 'the community' can be left blank. But the basic method of welfare analysis, indeed the whole object of the exercise, is to start from a norm or criterion which commands very wide general assent, and logically to deduce conclusions for policies from it. If the analysis is ever to be applied the blank has to be filled in, and at once the general assent to the proposal to maximize 'the community's' welfare will evaporate. The whole question is begged of what Dahl and Lindblom have called 'appropriate inclusion',[1] which requires complex choices or value-judgments with regard to 'weighting' which might vary for each goal, objective or 'aspect of welfare'. There is no reason for supposing that these value-judgments with regard to 'appropriate inclusion', in local and temporal terms, would ever command general assent in any practical application of 'welfare' analysis to the maximization of 'welfare' in any particular case.

But if, in this way, the community welfare-maximization principle or objective is vaguer than the individual or household utility-maximization principle, it has a similar tenuousness or emptiness, in the one case of refutable empirical content, and in the other of deniable normative content. The individual 'positive' generalization tends to be almost, or sometimes, reducible and reduced to 'whatever the consumer maximizes, he maximizes', and the normative community principle, almost or sometimes, to 'whatever the community should maximize, it should maximize'. The very wide seemingly uncontroversial policy objective of welfare-maximization is meant to reduce value-judgments and policy-choices to a minimum, in the same way that the hypothesis about consumers' behaviour, however it is precisely formulated, is apt to have its empirical refutable content reduced to a minimum. Not that bits of content do not get read into or assumed in the normative welfare-maximization principle; but as soon as they are, they immediately render the principle controversial,—e.g. when 'the community' is defined in a

---

[1] *Politics, Economics and Welfare*, 1953, p. 51: 'In setting forth goals to serve as criteria for appraising different politico-economic techniques, we have so far deliberately begged one vital question. We have advocated the goal of freedom for ourselves "and others", but we have not defined what "others" we had in mind. We have made a case for political and subjective equality "with others". What others? We want security for "others" as well as ourselves; progress for others. Who are these others? The human race? People who agree with us? Americans? Members of the Western democracies? . . . The answer would vary with the particular goals involved.'

L

particular way, or when it is assumed that a policy generally affects 'other aspects of welfare' in the same direction as 'economic welfare'. But the essence of the method of welfare analysis is to start from *un*controversial value-judgments.[1]

Moreover, ruling out as almost or absolutely inconceivable that a position of *less* 'welfare' might be chosen for a community, rather than more, amounts to ruling out the *choice* of policies in any significant sense. 'Deciding' on a policy ('decision' is probably a misnomer here) means simply registering by expert analysis that one policy produces more 'welfare' than another (or more 'economic welfare', leaving 'other aspects' not unfavourably affected). For the analysis of consumers' behaviour and that of 'welfare' economics share the basic simplification of the neglect of uncertainty, and 'welfare' economics, for some of its conclusions at any rate, also requires the assumption of some kind of 'perfect knowledge', or omniscience, both on the part of the individual units in forecasting their own wants, and on the part of the observing economist, or policy-maker, or adviser.[2] Just as from earlier versions, at any rate, of the pure theory of consumers' behaviour there emerged a utility-maximizing automaton rather than a person engaged in choice and decision, so pure welfare analysis eliminates the need for policy 'choices' and decisions in any significant sense, replacing them by welfare calculations or computations, on the assumption that alternative policies can be shown to produce, with certainty, different quantities or degrees of 'welfare', since all the indifference-curves and possibility-lines are given, with complete certainty and precision.[3] For example, when the compensation principle was introduced, it often seemed to be assumed that the right quantity of compensation could be known with certainty, as though consumers' indifference-curves were perfectly known and agreed. Alternatively, it is apparently left to any allegedly injured individual to state, after a policy change, what compensation he is to have if he is to feel at least equally well-off, which sounds like allowing all plaintiffs to fix

[1] Cf. J. de V. Graaff, *Theoretical Welfare Economics*, 1957, pp. 167–8: 'The purpose of theoretical welfare economics . . . is largely to see that *specific* injunctions can be deduced from *general* premises—that is, from premises that are widely accepted. The injunctions must be fairly specific if they are to be of any interest—it would not help much to be told that the price of coal should lie somewhere between zero and plus infinity. And the premises must command wide acceptance, for otherwise the injunctions they entail would hardly be worth deducing. . . . It does not seem to be realized how *detailed* the agreement on ends must be if a consistent theory of welfare economics is to be erected.'

[2] Cf. J. M. Buchanan, 'Positive Economics, Welfare Economics and Political Economy', *The Journal of Law and Economics*, October 1959, p. 126; and J. de V. Graaff, *Theoretical Welfare Economics*, 1957, p. 13.

[3] Cf. T. W. Hutchison, *The Significance and Basic Postulates of Economic Theory*, 1938, reprinted 1960, p. 88, and pp. 109–14.

their own damages, which, of course, they might often put at a figure higher than the prospective gains of the parties who are to benefit (though any estimates of these gains would also be highly uncertain or expectational). Just as the analysis of the consumer reduces his choices to automatic mechanical determination, so 'welfare' analysis seems to aim at the complete reduction of policy-choices to pure calculation. Shackle has eloquently criticized the orthodox analysis of choice, and his criticism, *mutatis mutandis*, applies as cogently, or even more so, to 'welfare' analysis as it does to the theory of the consumer or the firm:

'In economics of the accepted, Western maximizing kinds we are confronted with a basic contradiction: men are choosers; they choose the best, each for himself; what is the best can always be known to each person, either by merely consulting his own tastes or by applying the techniques of engineering or, where knowledge lacks a *simple* precision, by applying statistical techniques which turn ignorance of the particular into knowledge of the aggregate. Thus that action which will attain 'the best' can always be discovered, its prior discovery is part of that policy of rational action which is attributed by economics to the Economic Man in his modern sophisticated form; and all men in some degree approximate to this, or would wish to. And so we have man in this situation: what is "the best" for him is known to him uniquely and for certain; how to attain it is dictated by circumstances, and can be inferred from them. What, then, is left for him to do in the way of *choosing*? Where is there room for his judgment? . . .

'Conventional economics is not about choice, but about acting according to necessity. Economic man obeys the *dictates* of reason, follows the *logic of choice*. To call this conduct choice is surely a misuse of words, when we suppose that to him the ends amongst which he can select, and the criteria of selection, are given, and the means to each end are known. . . . Choice in such a theory is empty, and conventional economics should abandon the word.'[1]

[1] G. L. S. Shackle, *Decision Order and Time in Human Affairs*, 1961, p. 272. Shackle's fundamental criticism was an important, though much evaded, theme in Keynes's attack on what he called 'classical economics'. The following applies fairly precisely to the 'welfare' analyst's approach to economic policy: 'I accuse the classical economic theory of being itself one of those pretty, polite techniques which try to deal with the present by abstracting from the fact that we know very little about the future. I daresay that a classical economist would readily admit this. But, even so, I think he has overlooked the precise nature of the difference which his abstraction makes between theory and practice, and the character of the fallacies into which he is likely to be led. . . . The orthodox theory assumes that we have a knowledge of the future of a kind quite different from that which we actually possess. This false realization follows the lines of the Benthamite calculus. The hypothesis of a calculable future leads to a wrong

We are not concerned to deny that welfare analysis might have some use as a purely propaideutic abstraction, or that there can be any useful applications for some of its concepts (e.g. private and social products, externalities, etc.). But the ambitions and claims of 'welfarists' have often gone, and still go, much further: they attempt, or claim, to pronounce economic events, conditions or policies, better or worse, or economically desirable or undesirable. It might be argued—though I think mistakenly—that welfare analysis cannot have done much practical harm because it seldom emerges from the 'transparent' omniscient models of textbook and blackboard geometry into explicit application to real-world policy-making. As Leibenstein has recently pointed out: 'Welfare economics is an apparatus of thought for dealing with the choice of economic policies. Strangely enough, at a time when there is a great deal of intervention by democratic governments in the economic life of the community there is almost no use of this particular apparatus.'[1]

Leibenstein goes on to suggest that this may be because the criterion of the Pareto optimum seems to deny majority rule in that it 'gives a veto power to anyone opposed to a change'. It seems doubtful whether the Pareto criterion has, in fact, explicitly been much used in this sense, which would surely be politically completely paralysing, though it may, nevertheless, have had a latent, inhibiting effect. On the other hand, if it is argued 'that all contemporary welfare economics says is that where universal consent does not exist, then welfare economists simply are unable to declare whether there has been an increase in welfare in the cases in which some people feel better off and others feel worse off', then, certainly, the conclusion seems to follow—and this seems to put it in rather moderate terms—that 'in most cases welfare economics is irrelevant.'[2] In fact, analysis in Pareto-optimum terms seems confined to situations not restricted by scarcity in a relevant politico-economic sense, that is to situations in which more can be had of one *desideratum* (A's welfare) without diminishing some other *desideratum* (B's welfare).

interpretation of the principles of behaviour which the need for action compels us to adopt.' *The New Economics*, edited by Seymour Harris, 1947, p. 186 and p. 192.

[1] *Economic Journal*, June 1962, p. 299.

[2] *Op. cit*, p. 311. Cf. also R. A. Dahl and C. E. Lindblom, *Politics, Economics and Welfare*, 1953, p. 47. Cf. also P. J. D. Wiles, *The Political Economy of Communism*, 1962, pp. 91-2: 'The attention of the best theoretical minds has thus been shifted . . . from the essentially *practical* problem of the allocation of scarce resources to that of identifying an unambiguous increase in the welfare of all persons. . . . This kind of question, I submit, is scholastic and without practical application in economics or politics. . . . The study of the extremely few cases in which they [value-judgments] need not be made is certainly not worth the intellectual gifts that have recently been lavished upon it.'

In its Paretian form welfare analysis may have inhibiting effects in favour of the *status quo*. In any case, excessive claims for welfare economics have fostered the illusion of policies without politics, or that significant policy-recommendations can be made without controversial value-judgments (i.e. other than that it is better to have more wants satisfied rather than less). In its fuller-blooded 'Utilitarian' form, the effects of welfare analysis may tend not so much to paralyse policy recommendations as to obscure policy-choices by leaving essential value-judgments latent and policy objectives not sufficiently fully and precisely stated.

We are not concerned here with charges of a materialistic 'measurabilism', or of a kind of abstract materialism, in concentrating on maximizing the rate of increase of a particular index of real income per head. Nor need we stress the possible totalitarian implications of any rigidly monistic conception of the objectives of the community, or the idea of its political arrangements as a utility- or welfare-maximizing mechanism.[1] The point to be made is rather that the monistic, welfare-maximizing formulation of policy objectives obscures clashes of objectives and the need for choices and valuations: 'The introduction of such a supreme value as "general welfare" would blunt awareness and understanding of the complex of problems arising from the connections between the different objectives.'[2]

The nature of this kind of monistic framework for the discussion of economic policies has been well summed up by Viner:

'Economic theory tends, probably out of methodological if not psychological compulsions, to conduct welfare analysis in terms of single objectives, assumed to represent simple and homogeneous quantities of welfare—stuff such as "gain", "benefit", "development", "income" and so forth. Economic theory tends to accept the limitations imposed by a law of parsimony of social goals as well as by a law of parsimony of causes.

'In the actual course of policy-making in the real world, however, the monistic concepts that economic theory uses in its welfare analysis seem always to be catch-all labels for complex package[s]

---

[1] Cf. K. R. Popper, *The Open Society and its Enemies*, 4th Ed., 1962, Vol. II, p. 396: 'Monolithic social ends would mean the death of freedom.' See also G. Myrdal, *The Political Element in the Development of Economic Theory*, translated by P. Streeten, 1953, p. 54. The classic statement of this point is Acton's: 'Whenever a single definite object is made the supreme end of the State, be it the advantage of a class, the safety or the power of the country, the greatest happiness of the greatest number, or the support of any speculative idea, the State becomes for the time inevitably absolute.' *Essays on Freedom and Power*, Meridian Books, 1955, p. 159.

[2] W. A. Jöhr and H. W. Singer, *The Role of the Economist as Adviser*, 1955, p. 116.

of objectives that the policy-maker in practice is forced to separate out and to weigh against each other when they conflict with each other.'[1]

If the task of the economist is primarily to elucidate the choice of policies and to focus attention on the need to choose, and on the consequences and costs of different choices in terms of alternatives, the formulation of the objectives of policy in the manner of welfare analysis is liable to be seriously misleading, if it is not simply inhibiting. As Max Weber insisted: 'The social sciences . . . are the least fitted to presume to save the individual the difficulty of making a choice, and they should therefore not create the impression that they can do so.'[2]

Analytical economists have long ago—or at least since Walras and Marshall—replaced simple monistic cause-and-effect relationships by comprehensive interdependence formulae. But though policy objectives can be regarded as a translation into the teleological mood of the 'effects' of 'causes', the complexity of the repercussions of a policy change through a general interdependent system is monistically packaged into an 'effect' on 'economic welfare', though this always involves aggregating or packing together heterogeneous entities, different goods in the hands of different people.[3] There is a striking contrast between the recognition of complex interdependence in general equilibrium analysis and the monistic oversimplification with which the 'effects' of policies are presented in 'welfare' analysis.

The more thorough-going type of 'welfarist' believes that it is possible to pronounce significantly and objectively that one policy will produce more 'economic welfare' than another. This encourages him to present as objective conclusions about matters of fact, what are actually highly value-loaded subjective judgments. For example, a policy based on price-stability as an overriding objective, as compared with a policy aimed at, or allowing, some significant rise in the price level, will lead to a different distribution of income and also of power, and will encourage and discourage different kinds of social institutions. In fact, the two different policies might eventually lead to different kinds of society organized in different ways. Complex value-judgments, and long-term and perhaps highly uncertain predictions, are mixed together in statements favouring price-

[1] J. Viner, *Economics and Public Policy*, Brookings Lectures 1954, 1955, p. 121.
[2] Max Weber on *The Methodology of the Social Sciences*, translated and edited by E. A. Shils and H. A. Finch, 1949, p. 19.
[3] As Alf Ross puts it, policy proposals almost always involve 'the integration of multiple considerations' and this 'integration' logically requires extra-scientific valuations. See *On Law and Justice*, 1958, Chapter 14, quoted by F. Forte, *Economia del Benessere, Verifica Empirica, Linguaggio*, Studia Ghisleriana, 1961, p. 379n.

stability on the one hand, or rising prices on the other, as objectives of policy. But for the 'welfarist' this is just a 'positive' question of different quantities or degrees of 'welfare'. No subjective choices are involved other than the preference of objectively more, to objectively less 'welfare'. Though his predictions may inevitably be highly uncertain, the economic expert can—the 'welfarist' suggests—pronounce one prospect as one of greater welfare than another by reason of objective expertise, without any involvement in choosing between conflicting political values. We are therefore apt to find the more thorough-going kind of 'welfare' economist putting forward policy recommendations—for example with regard to price stability as an objective of policy—with the 'air of presenting some kind of objective truth, to which all persons of good sense would spontaneously assent, if only they knew enough about it', in the confident assured tone of . . . 'sensible men presenting objective conclusions about an ascertainable body of fact'.[1] Of course, there is nothing whatsoever wrong in holding or expressing, in a discussion of economic policies, a definite political point of view explicitly stated as such. But it is extremely damaging and dangerous to put forward political value-judgments as objective economic expertise. Instead of seeking to squeeze out or submerge the area of ethical-political choice and decision by means of 'welfarist' expertise, and instead of performing inexplicitly and arbitrarily the integration of the multiple considerations involved, should not the economist rather aim at elucidating choice by dragging to the surface and high-lighting the inevitable normative questions?

This inexplicitness of economic 'welfarism' is liable also to encourage another weakness to which democratic governments are inevitably prone. This is a reluctance to face the fact of conflicting interests, and the temptation to fend off awkward political choices and decisions by trying to get experts to produce 'objective' answers. National Councils, Commissions and Committees may have, of course, an important or indispensable role in elucidating the choices and opportunity costs of alternative policies. On the other hand such bodies *can* act more or less as executive agents of government, seeking to fulfil the norms and objectives approved by the political authority, to whom they may have suggested, or elaborated more precisely, these objectives in the first place. But if the illusion is propagated that political decisions and choices between conflicting norms can somehow be conjured away by welfare-economic expertise, the only result sooner or later is likely to be public confusion and disillusion regarding the application and applicability of economic knowledge to public policy.

[1] See the *Observer*, February 23, 1958, p. 12, discussing the First Report of the Council on Prices, Productivity and Incomes.

Policy Objectives

Source: Number of Objectives								Notes
R. A. Dahl and C. E. Lindblom (*Politics, Economics and Welfare*, 1953, pp. 28–54): (7)	Freedom:	Rationality:	Democracy:	Subjective equality:	Security:	Progress:	Appropriate inclusion	'Seven basic ends for social action' . . . or 'instrumental goals'—as contrasted with 'the prime goals' of survival, love, power, etc.
H. Giersch (*Allgemeine Wirtschaftspolitik*, Grundlagen, 1960, p. 68): (5)	Freedom:	Peace:	Justice:	Security:	Welfare			'The most important social-political objectives...in [German] alphabetical order.'
K. Boulding (*Principles of Economic Policy* 1958, p. 19): (4)	Economic progress:	Economic stabilization:	Economic freedom:	Economic justice:				'Major objectives of economic policy.' . . . 'Useful system of classification which leaves surprisingly few loose ends.'
J. Tinbergen (*Economic Policy: Principles and Design*, 1956, pp. 15–17): (5)	Maintenance of international peace:	Maximum real expenditure per capita with 'full' employment and monetary equilibrium:	Improvement of distribution of real income or expenditure over social groups and countries:	Emancipation of certain underprivileged groups:	As much personal freedom as compatible with the other aims			'The aims of economic policy in modern times' . . .'an "average" of existing preferences.'
J. Tinbergen (*op. cit.*, pp. 207–8): (7)	Production per capita:	Social justice:	Cultural development:	Freedom:	Stability:	International peace:	Social peace	'Elements of welfare' . . . 'an invitation to the reader to choose this form of summarizing his own appraisal of the means of economic policy considered.'

Source: Number of Objectives	Policy Objectives							Notes
A. Smithies ('Economic Welfare and Policy', in *Economics and Public Policy*, Brookings Lectures 1954, 1955, p. 14): (6)	Continued economic growth:	High and stable employment:	Reasonable stability of the price level:	Equitable distribution of income and social security:	Allocation of resources through the market mechanism:	Conservation of cultural and material resources		'I suggest that leaving aside its international policy, the economic policy of an advanced industrial economy, particularly that of the United States, should achieve a compromise among these objectives.'
Committee on the Working of the Monetary System (Cmnd. 827, 1959, pp. 22–3): (5)	A high and stable level of employment:	Reasonable stability of the internal purchasing power of money:	Steady economic growth and improvement in the standard of living;	Some contribution implying a margin in the balance of payments, to the economic development of the outside world:	A strengthening of London's international reserves, implying further margin in the balance of payments			'The objectives in pursuit of which monetary measures may be used.'
The Commission on Money and Credit (1961, pp. 9–12): (7)	An adequate rate of economic growth:	Sustained high levels of production and employment:	Reasonable stability of prices:	Adequate national security:	Harmonious international economic relations, and contributions to economic development abroad:	Desirable degree of economic freedom and reliance on the market mechanism and strengthening of competition:	Equitable distribution of opportunity and income	'An adequate rate of economic growth, sustained high levels of production and employment, and reasonable stability of prices are clearly the three objectives of central concern for monetary, credit, and fiscal policies. These three goals, however, must be sought in the context of other important national objectives which necessarily impose constraints on their pursuit.'

Such are the consequences of the 'welfarist' attitude to economic policies, and of the attempt it implies to reduce policy objectives to a single, or to one or two, 'catch-all' concepts. It is bound to lead to imprecise and inexplicit value-judgments and hence confused disagreement. Instead of promoting the necessary discussion of alternative or conflicting goals and values, and the elucidation of policy-choices, it obscures and confuses. Moreover the mistake is encouraged that values or objectives are beyond discussion. As Dahl and Lindblom observe: 'Economic theory has tended to postulate a highly restricted set of goals and reality situations within which maximizing takes place. . . . If conclusions based on this arbitrary world were translated and accepted policy makers would often be less rather than more able to make intelligent policy decisions.'[1]

(2) THE PLURALIST FORMULATION OF POLICY OBJECTIVES

If the elucidation rather than the elimination of value-judgments and of the choice of policies is to be attempted, the monistic 'welfare' hold-all must be unpacked, and a range of possibly—and often actually—conflicting or competing alternatives must be recognized and set out. Though their authors do not always explicitly argue for the rejection of 'welfarist' analysis and criteria, there have been attempts in a number of recent writings to break away from a monistic treatment of the objectives and criteria of policies, and to start from a manageable set of some four to eight objectives in a manner which is reminiscent of the little-known treatment of Bentham. Some of these formulations are at a rather 'higher', more abstract politico-ethical level, like those of Dahl and Lindblom and Giersch. Others are at a 'lower', more specifically economic and instrumental level, such as the Radcliffe Committee's formulation of the objectives of monetary policy. Indeed, the setting out of three or four, at least partially or at some levels conflicting objectives—such as employment, growth and price stability—has become a commonplace in discussions of macro-economic policy problems.[2]

Roughly speaking at an intermediate level, between, or combining, the 'higher' political and the 'lower' economic-instrumental level, are those of Boulding and Tinbergen (the pioneer of a systematic approach to economic policy on these lines). We have drawn up a

[1] *Politics, Economics and Welfare*, 1953, p. 81.
[2] For an illuminating discussion of sets of policy objectives see D. S. Watson, *Economic Policy*, 1960, pp. 94 ff. In his editorial introduction to this book, Carl Kaysen writes (p. XII): 'The basic axiom of public policy in economics as in other fields is: "No policy without politics"; by facing it directly, rather than trying to push it beyond the boundaries of economic discussion, Professor Watson makes a great step forward from the traditional treatment.'

selected list of some recent leading examples of sets of economic policy objectives.

Of those we list, that of the Radcliffe Committee is the only set which omits *any* political heading, or, for example, any reference to 'freedom' or 'justice'. Certainly the Radcliffe list is not strictly of 'objectives of economic policy', but simply of 'objectives in pursuit of which monetary measures may be used'. But the Radcliffe treatment seems to be somewhat in the 'welfarist' tradition of Pigou in disregarding 'the non-economic aspects of welfare', on the assumption that these are not affected, or only affected favourably, by the fulfilment of the objectives of monetary policy as set out. However, immediately after listing its five objectives the Radcliffe Report does refer to 'the continuous and orderly life of society' as limiting a government's pursuit of these five objectives, and to the danger of 'the immoderate pursuit of one or several of these ends' placing 'an intolerable strain on the body politic'.[1] Whether or not one shares the point of view of the liberal critics who complained that 'no room among the objectives is found for freedom',[2] the point is valid that, in the actual five-fold list, objectives were not being fully stated, or that value-judgments were left latent which, for the elucidation of policy-choices, would better have been made explicit. Moreover, to imply, as the Radcliffe Committee might be taken as implying, that the choice between monetary policy and fiscal policy, or controls, is simply one of neutral 'means', is to make latently a political value-judgment, a quite legitimate one if explicitly stated as such, but a controversial one, by no means universally shared. The procedure of the American 'Commission on Money and Credit' in explicitly stating political objectives (e.g. 'freedom'), or giving a political dimension to economic objectives ('harmonious international relations'), elucidates important choices more explicitly than introducing 'the body politic', and 'the continuous and orderly life of society', as afterthoughts—whether or not one shares the precise kind of value-judgments the American Commission suggests. For the two sorts of objectives, political and economic, have often, at the margin, to be chosen between and weighed against one another. It may be helpful, up to a point, to try to separate objectives relating to the constitution or framework of the economy, from those relating to the processes of the economy, or to distinguish between 'constitutional principles' and other policy objectives. But policy proposals and choices have, above all, to be weighed up comprehensively. Each kind of predicted effect of a policy has to be weighed against the other kinds of effect, however politico-ethical and qualitative the one may be, and however 'purely economic', 'material-

[1] Committee on the Working of the Monetary System, Cmnd. 827, 1959, p. 23.
[2] Cf. *Not Unanimous*, edited by A. Seldon, 1960, p. 104.

ist' or quantitative the other. This remains necessary however much one may wish to give absolute overriding priority to a certain basic framework of political-constitutional objectives, values or institutions.[1]

The question might arise as to whether some concept of 'welfare' is essential, comprising what it is that each of a set of objectives contributes to, or is an element of. Tinbergen describes his set of objectives or aims as 'elements of welfare' or 'the elements entering into the policy-maker's welfare function'.[2] If, however, one holds that the theory of consumers' choice can and should dispense with a utility concept, then it would seem possible for a theory of policy or social choice to dispense with a 'welfare' concept—though it hardly seems worth pursuing this question further. Certainly it is highly desirable that it should be clear which objectives are ultimate and which are wholly or partly instrumental to 'higher' objectives, and, in this case, to set out what these 'higher' objectives are and how, positively, they are promoted by the 'lower' instrumental objectives. But to blanket the 'higher' objectives under the monistic,

---

[1] An exactly parallel point was made with great force by Wicksteed (and also by Robbins in *The Nature and Significance of Economic Science*) as to the inseparability of 'material' and 'non-material' goods in the rational allocation of resources. Wicksteed was, of course, concerned with the individual consumer, but the same point applies to the principles of public policy and the following classic passage can easily be translated into the terms of the latter: 'In our private administration of resources we are concerned both with things that are and things that are not in the circle of exchange, and the principle of distribution of resources is identical in both cases. The independent student who is apportioning his time and energy between pursuing his own line of research and keeping abreast of the literature of his subject is forming estimates of differential significance and is equating them to each other just as directly as the housewife who is hesitating between two stalls in the market. And when we are considering whether we will live in the country or the town, we may find, on examination, that we are carefully equating increments and decrements of such apparently heterogeneous indulgences as those associated with fresh eggs and friendship. Or, more generally, the inner care of our life problems and the gratification of all our ultimate desires (which are indeed inextricably interlaced with our command of exchangeable things, but are the ends to which the others are means) obey the same all-permeating law. Virtue, wisdom, sagacity, prudence, success, imply different schemes of values, but they all submit to the law formulated by Aristotle with reference to virtue, and analysed by modern writers with reference to business, for they all consist in combining factors κατ' ὀρθὸν λόγον, *in the right proportion*, as fixed by that distribution of resources which establishes the equilibrium of their differential significances in securing the object contemplated, whether that object be tranquillity of mind, the indulgence of an overmastering passion or affection, the command of things and services in the circle of exchange, or a combination of all these, or any other conceivable factors of life.' *The Common Sense of Political Economy* and selected papers and reviews, Vol. II, 1933, p. 776.

[2] Cf. J. Tinbergen, *Economic Policy: Principles and Design*, 1956, pp. 11–18 and 206–9.

catch-all term 'welfare', far from assisting, simply sidetracks, this elucidation of the relations between 'lower' and 'higher' objectives. At least, sets of objectives like those we have listed would begin to bring out the possibilities and actualities of competing objectives, and of conflicts that have to be faced. Thus they would help to counter Utopianism and 'the fallacy of the unexplored remainder'. They bring to the explicit surface at least an outline of the kind of choices and value-judgments which have to be made, and they at least suggest what may have to be forgone, or that something desirable may have to be forgone, if one particular objective is given over-riding priority. But obviously much ambiguity about such sets of objectives remains. One way in which they could be formulated or interpreted is simply as taxonomies of the effects or objectives of policies, that is as classifications, or empty boxes, to be filled in with desired or actual quantitative or qualitative targets, as contrasted with actual realized achievements. This is not exactly how any of the sets of objectives included in our selection seem to be regarded by their authors. Though the content is often highly vague and elastic, they are not set up as explicitly empty boxes. But taken simply as taxonomies they would represent useful ways of formulating the 'algebraic' headings, which people with differing values and objectives could fill up in different ways, particularly, for example, the more politico-ethical headings, such as distributive justice and 'economic freedom' (Boulding), or 'the allocation of resources through the market mechanism' (Smithies), to which some might want to give a nil, or negative, target definition. In this sense a set of such headings, conceived simply as a taxonomy, would be devoid of value-judgments and serve as a framework or a check-list for grouping together policy objectives and value-judgments in a manageable form. To some extent this is suggested by Tinbergen's description of his headings as 'an invitation to the reader to choose this form of summarizing his own appraisal'[1] of policies, and also by Boulding's account of his set as a 'useful system of classification'.[2] As a suggested taxonomy, a set of objectives should be manageable but comprehensive. There should be includable under one heading or another every kind of effect, objective or desideratum, especially if it might compete or conflict with any of those included. Though the terminology in which such taxonomies were drawn up might be more or less persuasive, a pure taxonomy, as such, being empty of value-judgments, might be inconvenient or liable to misinterpretation, but could not logically contradict an alternative taxonomy. In fact the sets of objectives we have listed do not seem to be meant as pure taxonomies, but, to some extent, as expressing rather imprecise

[1] *Economic Policy: Principles and Design*, 1956, p. 207.
[2] *Principles of Economic Policy*, 1958, p. 19.

value-judgments. Though drawn up for differing purposes by economists from four different countries there is quite a range of coincidence and compatibility. But the significance of such broad, vague agreement between the various sets of headings does not reach very far.

In fact, though the pluralistic formulation of sets of objectives is, as compared with 'welfarist' monism, at least a start towards the elucidation of policy-choices, it is still only a fairly crude beginning towards bringing explicitly to the surface the value-judgments which must underlie the choice of policies. It is rather like an attempt to arrive at an adequate account of a consumer's tastes, or his value-judgments underlying his choices, by making a list of headings like 'Food', 'Clothing', 'Housing', 'Entertainments', and so on, as is made in the classifications of consumption-spending in tables of National Expenditure, filling in some of the headings fairly precisely, for example with a total of calories, while adding 'a high level of', or such adjectives as 'reasonable', or 'adequate', to other headings and particularly to the unquantifiable headings. Some of the objectives are stated in 'maximum' terms, without any indication as to what prices, in terms of other objectives forgone, might have to be paid as the level attained rises. The common practice of stating single objectives in 'maximum' or 'minimum' terms, when their pursuit may conflict with other objectives, is liable to be extremely vague, and to cloak or foster Utopian illusions as to the compatibility of different objectives.

Whether expressed in maximum, minimum or 'satisficing'[1] terms, as precise points or as ranges, it will often be essential for clarity and explicitness to give *some* indication of the kind of time-horizon envisaged for objectives. This seems particularly important for some of the principal economic objectives such as more rapid growth and price stability, and also, for example, with regard to redistributive policies and their effects through time on the supply of effort and innovation.

For example, if different orderings of policy-preferences, or contrasting marginal rates of substitution, as between price-stability and more rapid economic growth, are not simply to pass one another by as more or less vague emotional expressions, but are to get to grips with one another in an attempt to separate and clarify the normative and positive issues, and so to elucidate policy-choices, then some reference to time-horizons will often be relevant or indeed necessary. One side may be arguing, positively, that insistence on strict price-stability will inevitably involve a cost in terms of economic growth which, normatively, they consider ought not to be paid. But, on the other side, the advocates of strict price-stability, though also

[1] The word is H. A. Simon's: see *American Economic Review*, June 1959, p. 262.

normatively concerned with their conceptions of distributive justice and other social or political values, also often seem to assert or imply, positively, that price-stability is conducive to *long*-run growth They may well admit, positively—it might be difficult not to do so— that in a shorter (perhaps only very short) run, a higher rate of growth *could* be brought about if some significant rise in prices was allowed. But they would insist, also positively, that in the longer run the erosion of incentives and institutions resulting from a lasting and significant abandonment of price-stability would prove fatal or harmful to growth. The normative and positive elements in the conflicting viewpoints may well be turning, to an important extent, on different time-horizons. Of course, the longer the run to which positive generalizations or predictions refer, the more difficult they are to test and to reach any kind of consensus on, in cases of disagreement. But it will be impossible to elucidate the positive differences as to possibility functions, and keep them separate from the normative differences over preference functions, and thus help towards elucidating the choice of policies, unless some attempt is made to indicate the time-horizons involved where these are differing, as they often seem to do.

Price-stability is clearly a mainly, or entirely, instrumental goal or *extrinsic* value, rather than one of the 'higher' ultimate or intrinsic goals or values. To a greater or lesser extent this is the case with most or all of the more narrowly economic objectives, at any rate for people whose values are not highly materialist or 'measurabilist'.[1] To clarify values and objectives which are often in part extrinsic or instrumental, and to elucidate the preference functions involved, 'vertical' relationships must be explored as well as their 'horizontal' relationships in terms of conflict and complementarity.[2] Some attempt is therefore necessary to indicate how more narrowly economic objectives, such as price-stability, full employment and more rapid growth—in so far as these are not simply intrinsic values aimed at for their own sakes—are conducive to the higher, more purely intrinsic values of 'a good society'. But the 'higher' one goes in the hierarchy of values the vaguer and more comprehensive they become,

[1] It is sometimes argued that economic growth is not necessarily a narrowly materialist policy objective, because it simply represents expanding choices and *can* be taken out in more artists, writers, musicians, teachers, clergy and more books, pictures, concert halls and churches. This is certainly, if rather hypothetically, true. But measures of real income-per-head cannot, of course, take account of quality, whether, say, a new £1 million building is a revolting eyesore ruining a whole district for generations, or an inspiring addition to the cultural heritage. For some, this will be the all-important question, not simply that there has been a £1 million addition to investment. Ultimate or 'highest' objectives are essentially non-measurable.

[2] A thorough attempt to set out a hierarchy of policy objectives is made by D. S. Watson (*Economic Policy*, 1960, pp. 106–8).

the less technical-economic and the more speculative and politico-ethical. They become increasingly untestable and non-measurable the more purely intrinsic they are, and positive analysis and prediction about them inevitably gives away to value-judgments. As Wicksteed put it: 'The rule seems to hold that the higher and more ideal your purpose, the greater your difficulty in gaining any assurance that you have accomplished it.'[1] But the positive relationship of wholly or partially instrumental goals or extrinsic values to the 'higher' or more intrinsic values which they promote, must be explored in terms of positive generalizations and predictions, particularly if the more instrumental goals such as the economic objectives of more rapid growth, price-stability and so on, are in conflict. It is then particularly relevant how far each objective, or a marginal increment therein, conduces to 'higher' political and social values, and it is very desirable to attempt to ascertain more precisely—so far as this is possible—what these higher values and objectives are (and should be), if policy choices are really to be elucidated.

We referred earlier, when discussing 'means' and 'ends', to some of the complexities in relationships between values, goals or objectives, and how one and the same objective can be both instrumental or extrinsic, and, at the same time, also intrinsic.[2] One frequent case in which value-judgments are left vague and inexplicit is that where the extrinsic-instrumental elements for which a goal or objective— e.g. price-stability—is valued, are not clearly distinguished from the intrinsic elements, and where it is not clearly set out just what the higher intrinsic values are to which the extrinsic contribute and just how they are promoted by them.

Two conclusions can be drawn. First, it is clear that the interweaving of extrinsic or instrumental objectives with ultimate intrinsic objectives or ends, implies an interweaving—though not an inseparable or inextricable one—of positive analysis and predictions with value-judgments and normative statements of objectives. Secondly, it is already clear that the admirable proposal that value-judgments should be stated clearly and explicitly is one of great complexity, though there are further important complexities still to be elaborated. But, at least, working with a manageable but comprehensive set of objectives such as those we have discussed, is likely to stimulate much fuller and more precise statements of values and objectives, acting as a check-list or reminder as to the multifarious effects and objectives of policies which have to be taken into account, instead of obscuring the whole problem, as does monistic welfarism. As such

[1] *The Common Sense of Political Economy*, 1933, Vol. II, p. 676, quoted by W. A. Robson, *The Relation of Wealth to Welfare*, 1924, p. 135.
[2] See the illuminating analysis of C. L. Stevenson, *Ethics and Language*, 1944, Chapter VIII.

it can form a starting-point for an attack on ideological Utopian assumptions—liberalist, socialist or otherwise—as to the harmony and compatibility of their policy objectives and on the notions of 'opportunity-costless' policies which they foster. Discussions of policies, starting from such a list of objectives, would be less likely to fall into 'the fallacy of the unexplored remainder' and would be more inclined to deal explicitly with all, or all the main, different effects of policies.

(3) FROM POLICY OBJECTIVES TO PREFERENCE FUNCTIONS

For purposes of abstract analysis it can be, and is, assumed that all the value-judgments involved in policy recommendations can be comprised in a social welfare function in which 'all possible configurations of the social system are arranged in order of value'[1] or which provides an ordering of 'social states'. At the top of this order there would be for utilitarians a state which corresponded to what Edgeworth described, in his utilitarian way, as 'the greatest possible sum total of pleasure summed through all time and all sentience'.[2] An indication of the content of a 'social state' has been given by Arrow:

'The most precise definition of a social state would be a complete description of the amount of each type of commodity in the hands of each individual, the amount of labour to be supplied by each individual, the amount of each productive resource invested in each type of productive activity, and the amounts of various types of collective activity, such as municipal services, diplomacy and its continuation by other means, and the erection of statues to famous men. It is assumed that each individual in the community has a definite ordering of all conceivable social states, in terms of their desirability to him.'[3]

Such an account, though it is one of the fullest available, hardly does more than broadly indicate the economic political and social complexities involved—an indicative wave of the hand at an entire universe. But when one is free to make intellectually Utopian assumptions there are no difficulties: one just writes down the capital letter 'W'.

No doubt a dictator might convince himself that he could draw up a reasonably adequate and consistent ordering. But, in fact, even the most confident dictator would have a very arduous task, even

---

[1] I. M. D. Little, *A Critique of Welfare Economics*, 2nd Ed., 1957, p. 117.
[2] *Mathematical Physics*, 1881, p. VII.
[3] K. J. Arrow, *Social Choice and Individual Values*, 1951, p. 17.

M

with the largest and most efficient posse of economic advisers to help him, in getting down a reasonably consistent ordering. Indeed, a 'superman', as Little suggests, would indeed be required, not simply in terms of power, but in self-knowledge and analysis. If, on the other hand, 'W' is to be, in some way or other, democratically and individualistically arrived at, the task gets much more problematic (for example, with regard to transport policies and choices between road and rail and the possibilities in terms of taxes and subsidies, congestion and amenities). Moreover, when time-horizons, uncertainty and risk- or uncertainty-attitudes are introduced, as in any realistic policy analysis or ordering of policy choices they must be, further vast dimensions are added to the difficulties.

If one recognizes the fantastic complexity of setting out even a reasonably adequate, precise and consistent ordering of social states, in conditions of uncertainty, and with adequate attention to time-horizons, the purpose of the 'pluralist' sets of objectives will appear in the help they may give in the realistic tasks of getting *some* coherent content into 'W', and of seeing that at least it brings out explicitly the main types of value-judgments involved in practical policy recommendations. Moreover, the intellectual Utopianism of trying to start, or imagining that one is starting, from an adequate, precise and consistent 'W', fosters the further Utopianism involved in conceiving practical policy-making as merely taking the top-ranking 'social state'—say, that corresponding to 'the greatest possible sum total of pleasure summed through all time and over all sentience'—and then moving one's system straight to it by a comparative-static transformation, as simple as moving one's chalk along an indifference-curve on a blackboard.

In fact, starting from 'pluralist' sets of objectives may stimulate the exploration of policy in empirical, piece-meal or 'incremental' terms[1] from the starting-point of actual conditions, and bring out the costs of each improvement in the fulfilment of one objective, in terms of the forgoing of others. That is, it would be useful to elicit, where it is practically possible, preference functions, at least roughly indicative of marginal rates of substitution.

Like consumers or housewives, 'policy-makers base their acts consciously or unconsciously on preferences'.[2] We are not concerned here with the political process by which policy-preferences and preference—,or social—,welfare functions are, or should be, arrived at, or with whence they are ultimately to be derived by the economist, or with questions of political constitution-making or voting procedures. The economist may take a view as to what he *thinks* these

[1] See 'Policy Analysis', by C. E. Lindblom, *American Economic Review*, June 1958, p. 302.

[2] J. Tinbergen, *Economic Policy: Principles and Design*, 1956, p. 11.

preferences are for the community he is concerned with, or he may regard some elected representative as entitled to formulate them, at any rate in some areas. In any case, formulations of preference functions are bound to be highly presumptive and uncertain, and this will particularly be the case with predictions or assumptions as to their stability over a period.

As Tinbergen says regarding preferences between different policy objectives: 'In most cases such knowledge has so far not been collected explicitly.' But a certain scepticism seems permissible when he adds that 'it certainly would not be difficult to do so, with, for example, the help of interviews', that is, 'to construct indifference curves of policy-makers with regard to, say, employment, balance of payments surplus, price rises and so on'.[1] Though quantifiable two-dimensional preference functions might be elicited over a certain range in a reasonably precise and consistent form, the relevant multi-dimensional answers, which included essential qualitative political objectives, would certainly be complex and difficult to formulate. All the same, it must be emphasized that, however difficult it may be to obtain a full range of precise and consistent indifference curves, or preference functions, the 'rational' application of systematic economic knowledge to policy must depend on making the best attempts possible. To the extent that these attempts are inadequate or incomplete, to that extent the application of economic knowledge to policy is 'irrationally' or, at any rate, inadequately based, and one is simply launching policies with no clear and precise ideas of the objectives one is arriving at or trying to arrive at. Therefore, one of the first necessary tasks in elucidating the choice of policies is to elicit, as precisely as possible, whether from a minister or from the public, the answers on which preference functions can be drawn up. One authority has even claimed that he has 'known cases where the main achievement of an economist, but not a negligible one, has been simply to let a minister think aloud about his problems and bring to the surface his real motives and his judgments on social and economic policy; the economist can carry out the function of a psychotherapist'.[2]

The essential pre-requisite in this psychotherapeutic process of getting preference functions stated as fully and precisely as possible, is to break down any Utopian traces of 'the natural tendency of all but a very few thinkers to believe that all the things they hold good must be intimately connected, or at least compatible, with one another'[3]—combined with a disregard of all other values. This

---

[1] *Op. cit.*, p. 17.
[2] D. Seers, 'Why Visiting Economists Fail', *Journal of Political Economy*, August 1962, p. 338.
[3] Isaiah Berlin, *Two Concepts of Liberty*, 1958, p. 13n. See above, Part II,

180 *'Positive' Economics and Policy Objectives*

simply means forcing recognition that choice 'positively' is, or may be, necessary. It has to be elicited from the political authority what precisely it is prepared to forgo in terms of other objectives in order to get more of one particular objective. If more of one *desideratum* can be had without giving up something of another *desideratum*, then no really controversial policy issue arises, since the policy objectives are not all scarce.

The eliciting of preference functions must, of course, be accompanied by the attempt to formulate or predict possibility functions or opportunity lines. The fact that the possibility functions are not known at all certainly or precisely makes the eliciting of preference functions much more difficult and complicated. It is not, as in the textbook analysis of consumers' behaviour, simply a question of which point on a given opportunity or budget line, known with certainty, the consumer chooses. On the other hand, the analysis of consumers' behaviour, not wildly unrealistically, assumes that opportunity lines, or possibility functions, are known with certainty. It is more or less the main task of any applied, 'fruit-bearing', positive economics to try to estimate possibility functions for policies. But, obviously, these can often only be guessed at with the utmost tentativeness and uncertainty, while sometimes all that could candidly be asserted would be that one guess would be as good, or almost as good, as another. With regard to some pairs of objectives, for example, price-stability and levels of employment, tentative predictions have recently been attempted. But with regard to other pairs, for example, the central neo-classical pair, or the two original components or dimensions of the concept of 'economic welfare', production and distribution, or the maximum size of the national income, as against its just, equitable or more equal distribution, very little can be said. Predictions as to how much a more equal distribution through progressive taxation will decrease the future size of the national income, or its growth, are so imprecise, uncertain and subjective that they often hardly express more than the political preconceptions of those pronouncing on the subject. It is too easy to believe what one wants to believe, with any serious testing so difficult, practically, to achieve.[1]

Chapter 3, Section 6. However, some economists proclaim that, if economic knowledge was fully deployed, the main economic goals would be compatible: 'Even with present knowledge, a team of economists selected, let us say, by the membership of the Royal Economic Society—and provided with unlimited *legal* powers—could maintain full employment without inflation; could produce a close approximation to an optimum allocation of resources and a fair approximation to an optimal rate of economic progress; and it could improve the income distribution at the same time.' B. Higgins, *What do Economists Know?* 1951, p. 28.

[1] Cf. The following sceptical pronouncement on the theory of public finance: 'The theory is not used simply because it is useless. There are very few definite

It seems uncertain just how far there is diminishing social utility or welfare from the more intensive fulfilment of the various objectives of policies.[1] But there are clearly, over certain relevant ranges, increasing opportunity costs—in terms of forgoing other objectives —of fulfilling one particular objective more intensively. At lower levels of fulfilment objectives may be compatible or complementary. But opportunity costs often seem to rise sharply at the higher levels. It is the last 1 per cent or so on the employment level, an extra 1 or 2 per cent on aggregate output, or keeping the rise in the price level below 1 or 2 per cent, which in each case seems to impair the fulfilment of one, or both, of the other objectives; while, if it may be claimed that two, or even all three, of these might be realized at very high levels, then it often seems that it would be at the cost of jeopardizing what many would consider vital political values or objectives, such as some kinds of freedom or distributive justice.

Moreover, to some extent the more intensive pursuit of certain objectives will involve an increasing drain on scarce resources of administrative and intelligence or research talent, which are then not available for the higher attainment of other valued objectives. At any rate, this may probably often hold for less developed countries:

'What is very often overlooked, particularly by those of the left, is that instruments of policy are also subject to boundary conditions, and that these conditions are rigorous in underdeveloped areas because of weakness in administration. To attempt strict import controls, for example, may only increase smuggling or corruption and demoralize the whole public service, reducing its total capacity to administer an economic programme. Even if such limits do not hamper particular policies, they may restrict the combinations of policies that can be followed in various fields. Typically, there are two or three really good and selfless top administrators, and a score or so of capable young men, and these cannot be deployed on all fronts at the same time. It may be possible to tighten up income tax collection, *or* reorganize education, *or* operate import quotas, *or* reform land tenure, *or* set up a statistical office, *or* nationalize the railways; one may even be able to do two or three of these things at the same time. But any economic programme that implies doing them all simultaneously may prove to be just as unrealistic as one

propositions: an income tax may raise or lower the supply of effort, the substitution of death duties for a tax on investment income may raise or lower saving, replacing a direct by an indirect tax may or may not improve resource allocation—and so on and so forth.' R. Turvey, *Economic Journal*, March 1961, p. 150.

[1] Dahl and Lindblom hold without qualification that 'goals are subject to diminishing marginal utility'. *Politics, Economics and Welfare*, 1953, p. 81.

that requires, for example, more imports than can possibly be financed.'[1]

Of course, in this respect, the difference between less and more 'developed' countries will only be one of degree as regards the supply and distribution of the requisite administrative ability and the mores of the public.[2]

When we draw, therefore, some summary comparisons between the pure logic of choice as applied to individual consumers, and its possible application to public policy-choices, the main difference is the much higher degree of uncertainty, and possible incompleteness, that must be attached to preference and possibility functions, or to indifference curves and possibility lines, in the case of public policy-choices.[3] This implies that a pure theory of choice in terms of certainties, while at least within the realm of an interesting approximation as regards consumers and households, is scarcely so with regard to policy-choices. This is because, first, there is no reasonably ascertainable concept corresponding to the consumer's fixed income, which, though it may not always be known to him with certainty, can generally be assumed to be known approximately without too fantastic a degree of unrealism. Similarly, relative prices and opportunity costs can generally be assumed to be known by consumers with a reasonably high degree of certainty, whereas in many important respects—without some Utopian leap-forward in knowledge—they will continue to remain deeply uncertain with regard to vital policy alternatives (e.g. the incentive effects on production of direct taxation). Opportunity costs, also, will always be highly complex, made up of a range of heterogeneous effects or 'multiple considerations'. It can simply be asserted, somewhat tentatively, that, very roughly, as compared with the principles of diminishing marginal utility and diminishing marginal rates of substitution for consumers, marginal increments in the fulfilment of one policy objective will often tend to entail higher and higher opportunity costs in terms of other objectives (particularly, perhaps, political objectives and values) as well as in terms of scarce administrative resources.

[1] D. Seers, 'Why Visiting Economists Fail', *Journal of Political Economy*, August 1962, p. 331. It is obviously misleading to defend a proposal to introduce, say, a compulsory saving scheme, or currency controls, in a politically immature country, by arguing that a similar scheme has given no political or administrative trouble in Britain.

[2] One Oxford economist has stated that the British Civil Service, particularly since the Second World War, has been seriously lacking in the ability to administer economic policies efficiently, while he claims that, if it was reformed in the way he proposed, far more ambitious and complex policies could be successfully carried out. See T. Balogh's contribution to *The Establishment*, edited by H. Thomas, paperback edition, 1962, pp. 72 ff.

[3] Cf. H. Theil, *Economic Forecasts and Policy*, 2nd Ed., 1961, pp. 377 ff.

As regards the precision, certainty and stability of policy preferences, as compared with individual consumers' preferences, it might be that a clear-headed dictator, aided by an efficient team of psychotherapist economic advisers, could set out a fuller, clearer, more precise and more stable set of preference functions, or ordering of social states, than the textbook housewife. But if one is concerned with democratic preference-functions, intended to represent in some way what the members of the community really want, or would want if they had reasonably full and clear knowledge of all the alternatives, then any ascertainable preference functions seem likely to be shrouded with profound uncertainty, imprecision and perhaps instability.[1]

(4) CALCULATION AND 'ART' IN POLICY DECISIONS

The problems of choosing or deciding on a policy, or on what to do, can be approached by resolving them into answering, and relating the answers to, two questions, the positive-scientific-technical question 'What *can* be done?' and the ethical-political-evaluative question 'What *should* be done?'[2] The textbook theory of consumers' choice and the 'welfare' analysis built on it assume that the answers to these two questions are given with certainty by possibility and preference functions. This reduces the problem as a whole to a purely technical one in the sense that it is soluble simply by calculation—logical, mathematical or geometrical—from data which are available with certainty. In this analysis consumers' 'choices' or 'decisions'—if they should be so described—are given simply by calculations. Policy problems *could* be (and sometimes are) formulated in the same simplified way as purely calculable maximizing allocation problems, concerned with certainties.[3] But the resulting formulae not merely tend to be pretty empty boxes, but practically unfillable boxes. They would represent in one sense of that ambiguous adjective a (or the) extreme 'rationalist' attitude to policy, a kind of 'Surrationalism'.[4]

---

[1] Any kind of 'choice criterion' seems to need or imply an assumption of, in some sense, adequate knowledge, or reasonable possible freedom from ignorance. Anyhow, the concept of 'an expansion of choice' which has been offered as a definition of an increase in welfare, seems to depend on an assumption of complete knowledge. A narrowing of his range of choice might make someone better off if the narrower choice could be exercised with more knowledge of the alternatives.

[2] Cf. H. Albert, *Ökonomische Ideologie und Politische Theorie*, 1954, p. 15.

[3] Cf. H. Theil, *Economic Forecasts and Policy*, 2nd Ed., 1961, p. 377.

[4] For Popper the adjective 'rationalist' has strongly favourable overtones, meaning roughly 'open to criticism and discussion', the opposite of dogmatism and obscurantism. For Oakeshott 'rationalist' has strongly unfavourable overtones signifying 'crudely oversimplificatory', or attempting to reduce to calculation the inherently incalculable. We are using the word rather in Oakeshott's sense. (Perhaps 'reasonable' might be a better, or, at any rate, distinctive, adjec-

It is the diffuseness and imprecision of the objectives of policies, and the inevitably high degree of uncertainty as to the ramifications of their effects, which make it dangerously misleading to try to represent policy problems *simply* as calculations, and to evade or underestimate the role of uncertainty-attitudes and judgment.

The choice of policies might be, broadly, for example, between a 'bolder' policy promising a higher rate of growth with a greater risk of serious inflation, or a 'safer' policy promising less rapid growth with a smaller risk of inflation. Though, of course, it would, or could, be very oversimplificatory to base a policy-choice simply on a two-dimensional preference function, in terms simply of rates of growth and rates of inflation, assuming all other objectives to be negligible or unaffected, it would be possible for two economists to draw up their indifference curves, or preference functions, at least as an abstract exercise, in terms of *certain* outcomes with regard to the two objectives only of growth rates and price stability. But even if their preference functions happened to coincide as regards the choice between certainties, the two economists might disagree on a policy-decision which had to take account of the uncertainties of the real world, because one had a much stronger uncertainty-aversion than the other. But an economist favouring, say, a 'safer' policy would have to be highly accomplished at self-analysis to be able to tell precisely whether he differed from a 'bolder' colleague because he started from (1) different normative preferences as between growth-rates and price-stability, in terms of certainties; (2) different positive predictions as to the probable effects of different 'growth' policies on the price level; (3) different degrees of uncertainty-preference or aversion. To elicit preferences under uncertainty from political authorities would indeed be difficult even for an accomplished economic psychotherapist.

Because preference functions are so complex and unquantifiable that they are difficult to state at all completely, and because possibility functions are shrouded in such uncertainty, and the effects of

tive for Popper's concept, but unfortunately there is no euphonious abstract noun to correspond.) On the connection between 'rationalism', in Oakeshott's sense, and the assumption of certainty see his *Rationalism in Politics*, 1962, p. 11: 'The heart of the matter is the pre-occupation of the Rationalist with certainty. Technique and certainty are, for him, inseparably joined because certain knowledge is, for him, knowledge which does not require to look beyond itself for certainty; knowledge, that is, which not only ends with certainty but begins with certainty and is certain throughout. And this is precisely what technical knowledge appears to be. It seems to be a self-complete sort of knowledge because it seems to range between an identifiable initial point (where it breaks in upon sheer ignorance) and an identifiable terminal point, where it is complete. . . . It has the aspect of knowledge that can be contained wholly between the two covers of a book, whose application is, as nearly as possible, purely technical, and which does not assume a knowledge not itself provided in the technique.'

policies are so uncertain in their repercussions and ramifications, the purely technical presentation of policy-recommendations (which is possible, given or postulating the norms or objectives, within the rules of scientific procedure) has in practice to be supplemented by what may be called 'art'. The nineteenth-century term 'the art of political economy', now obsolete, very aptly described an important component in policy-making. This has got squeezed out, with misleading and harmful consequences, by a narrowly defined positive economics supplemented by 'welfare' analysis, with both usually, or often, based on the simplified logic of choice between certainties. But 'the art of political economy', though it was not very clearly and explicitly explained by nineteenth-century writers, at least suggests the elements of judgment, guesswork, feel and hunch, involved in practical estimates of possibility functions, and the subjectiveness of the inevitable probability 'guess-timates' required in real policy recommendations. It stresses 'connoisseurship' rather than technique. It also suggests the possible elements of normative bias involved in interpreting imprecisely and incompletely formulated preference functions, and in the subjective risk—or uncertainty—aversions and preferences which are an inevitable element in real choices between policies. Moreover, an essential characteristic of 'the art of political economy' was that it had to draw on other fields or sciences than that of economics. It is all the more necessary to emphasize this element of 'art' when such a preponderance of attention and such an overriding preference is given, in the discussion of economic policies, to particular measurable economic indices, such as real income per head. We must emphasize, however, that introducing or reintroducing the concept of the art of political economy, or calling attention to the inevitable and vital role played by the subjective elements contained in that concept, need not and should not encourage the blurring of the definition of the science of economics or of the demarcation line between it and the art of political economy and value-judgments generally.

In the field of economics and the social sciences, policies or policy ambitions so far outrun critically tested or widely agreed hypotheses on which to base them, that a choice between conflicting highly uncertain hypotheses, with their varying evidence, has to be made. No one would dream of building a bridge, putting a new aircraft in service, or a new vaccine in public use, on the basis of hypotheses of anything approaching the degree of uncertainty on which economic policy-makers have to rely with regard to *their* hypotheses, though the health and nutrition of whole populations may sometimes be involved. The question inevitably arises as to the essential limits of scientific activity, pure and applied, where no reasonable consensus exists as to which of a number of conflicting uncertain hypotheses

N

would stand up to critical significant testing, if, practically, this could be, and was, carried out. An economist may feel that there is a reasonable amount of evidence for his hypothesis, or he may frankly admit that he believes in it simply on the basis of 'hunch' or guess-work, and that there is little evidence available. He may, and presumably will, try to weigh up or appraise the evidence, or to indicate a subjective measure of probability (perhaps by actually investing his own money). But the essence of the situation is that other economists may not agree with his subjective probability estimate or his particular uncertainty-attitude, and that he will be making a kind of value-judgment in advocating policies based on his particular estimates and attitudes.

With regard to reasonably certain prognoses, it is comparatively easy to draw a line between the function of the 'positive' expert and the responsibilities of the political authority (Minister, Government, or electorate), and doubtless in such Utopian conditions this frontier line would come to be quite regularly observed, if or in so far as policy-choices were between policies with reasonably certain outcomes. But a solution of the problem of this frontier-line in respect simply of choices between more or less certainties is obviously an over-simplification which—like many economic models—leaves out the difficulties of the real-world problem. The economic expert can set out all the evidence for a hypothesis, or all the information on which alternative progress could be based. He will have to do this for a whole set of prognoses as to the effects of different policies, including a prognosis as to the outcome if no new policy-intervention is undertaken. He can point out that some alternatives seem 'riskier' than others, though in the realistic sort of case we are concerned with only quite subjective indications of numerical probabilities would be possible. But the amount of information may be so extensive and complex that it cannot be appreciated in full by a political authority without the latter himself becoming a full-time expert.[1] The interpretation of the available information in terms of the support of one prognosis rather than another requires a whole background of expertise. To paraphrase the information in an intelligence summary, so that the political authority can make his own assessment of the uncertainties and decide in terms of his own risk-preferences and risk-aversions, presents the inevitable problem of the selection, 'weighting', or possible distorting bias, in a summary.

Whether or not one says that the choice of policies in conditions of uncertainty, in addition, of course, to the inevitable choice of norms or objectives, involves a further 'normative' element, it surely involves a 'subjective' element which leaves the possibility of normative bias of one kind or another wide open. The scientific process

[1] Cf. H. Theil, *Economic Forecasts and Policy*, 2nd Ed., 1961, p. 415.

eliminates subjectivity and achieves an 'objective' validity for scientific propositions by critical testing, which, in turn, promotes an expert consensus (which, in turn, is tentative and always subject to revision). But the essence of the position is that different experts employing the same generally accepted techniques and criteria (which, to some extent, entitles them to be described as 'experts'), and with the same information available or obtainable, may well make different prognoses, only testable *ex post* and perhaps with great doubt and difficulty then.[1] As we have seen, some economists have proposed a prohibition on all prognosis by economists as essentially 'unscientific'.[2] We certainly would not try to suggest imposing prohibitions or vetoes on intellectual activities of this kind. But the inevitable subjectivity and openness to normative bias of economic prognoses, and the lack of that expert consensus about them which is the meaning and basis of scientific 'objectivity', should be clearly brought out.

The line of division between the functions of the scientific expert and the responsibilities of the political decision-maker, or client, is comparatively easy to draw in conditions of certainty. Perhaps because models in which uncertainty is assumed away have played, and continue to play, such a prominent role in economics, the real problems of this division of roles and duties often do not seem to have been fully faced.[3]

---

[1] As J. de V. Graaff puts it (*Theoretical Welfare Economics*, 1957, p. 119): 'There are, in fact, three distinct stages at which interpersonal comparisons are required—or three separate reasons why men fail to agree on the desirability of a particular event:

'(i) They may evaluate differently the contribution any one man's well-being makes to social well-being—that is, they may have different W's [social welfare functions].

'(ii) Even if they have identical W's, they may disagree on the probable consequences of the event, or on the order of likelihood of those consequences— either because their own estimates of the situation differ or because they evaluate differently the reliability of the estimates of others.

'(iii) Even if they agree on the probable consequences and their ordering, they may disagree on the "proper" way to allow for the uncertainty involved—on whether to prepare for the worst or gamble on the best.'

[2] See above, Part I, Chapter 2, Section 8.

[3] A new and important contribution to the problems of policy choices discussed in this chapter, which has unfortunately come too late to be taken into account here, is *A Strategy of Decision* by D. Braybrooke and C. E. Lindblom, 1963.

CONCLUSION

> 'Ultimately, analysis and evaluation must be
> brought together; for the former is of use
> only so far as it gives discipline to the latter.
> But they must not be forced together pre-
> maturely. They must carefully be distinguished
> before they can profitably be combined.'
>
> C. L. STEVENSON
> *Ethics and Language*, 1944, p. 222

> 'Belief in the authority of objective truth is in-
> dispensable for a free society based on mutual
> respect.'
>
> K. R. POPPER
> *Conjectures and Refutations*, 1963, p. 375

We started by noting certain apparently flatly opposed general statements about values in economics and social theory, and also how 'discussion in general in this field is obscured by a reluctance of many writers who insist that valuations somehow seep into social analysis to state clearly where precisely this seepage occurs'.[1] In other words there seemed to be too many vague and contradictory generalities in this area. What was necessary was to examine and assess particular points of 'seepage', or alleged 'seepage', whether inevitable, actual, or possible.

By way of conclusion and summary we are trying to ascend very briefly to a more general and comprehensive plane. But the risk is undoubtedly acute that at this level nothing but obviously question-able generalizations, on the one hand, or platitudes, on the other, will be discovered—though there may be, perhaps, disregarded platitudes which it is not useless to repeat. Ours, however, are not the kind of questions as to which tidily wrapped up general conclusions can be expected.

One fundamental distinction often relevant when attempting a more general comprehensive view of our questions is that between, on the one hand, logical or methodological questions or proposals, concerned with statements and theories, and distinctions between

[1] P. Streeten, Introduction to *Value in Social Theory*, by G. Myrdal, 1958, p. XXXVII.

them, and, on the other hand, questions or proposals concerned with professional ethics, or with the functions, duties and spheres of 'scientists', economists 'as such', experts, advisers, and University teachers who write, say, to *The Times*. We shall mention how, though on two different planes, the two sorts of question impinge upon one another. In the main we have been concerned with the former, logical-methodological questions regarding statements and theories. But, although we would shrink in horror from attempting to lay down the law on questions of professional ethics, we can hardly avoid, in conclusion, facing explicitly some questions of this kind, and expressing about them views—for what they are worth—which have to some extent been implicit in parts of our previous discussions. At any rate, much of the following six concluding paragraphs will be concerned with such questions of professional ethics and duties.

1. First let us glance briefly back at our historical account of the normative-positive distinction and of the controversies about it. We found that the view that economics can be, should be, and—it often seemed to be claimed—mainly is conducted as a positive science, concerned only with what is, and not immediately with what ought to be, can be regarded as almost the orthodox view, though never universally accepted. We find this justifiable, as a programme which is on the whole practicable and desirable. But it seems unduly complacent to hold that such a programme has actually yet been realized at a consistently and satisfactorily high level, approaching most of the natural sciences. Also, this programme has too often been advocated with a facile disregard of the nature of the difficulties, some of which have increased in complexity in recent decades owing to more comprehensive policy ambitions.

On the other hand, the sceptics and critics, though sometimes concerned with serious problems of ambiguity and interpretation, generally seem to be far too indiscriminate and imprecise. It is suggested, sometimes with an air of vaguely impressive profundity, that various kinds of valuations, or 'value-loadedness', are deeply embedded and all-pervasive, without it being made clear just where and what their sources and points of entry are, and how far they can be and should be shut off. On the whole, when they are systematically examined, not *very* much of importance seems to be left of the critics' and sceptics' position, or various positions, so far as these can be pinned down, though certainly in so far as they have helped to inculcate a livelier critical awareness with regard to basic assumptions their protests have been valuable.

2. It seems that it ought not to be difficult to agree that in so far as a clear distinction betcen normative and positive statements *can* be maintained, it *should* be maintained. Certainly commitment to the value-premisses and criteria of a 'scientific' discipline entails a

commitment to clarity of communication, including, or even especially, clear distinctions between normative and positive statements, or normative and positive (or descriptive and evaluative) elements in statements. If more than trivial ambiguities arise, then, 'scientifically', there is a commitment to try to remove them. But in spite of the proclamation, for a century or more, of the methodological programme of a scientific 'positive' economics, and in spite of claims as to its fulfilment, we may be making an over-optimistic assumption as to the constancy and completeness of this commitment. Keynes once stated that 'Marshall was too anxious to do good' (a dictum which could arguably be applied to the author of *Essays in Persuasion*). 'Doing good' as an economist implies getting 'good' policies adopted. 'Having influence', which is another way of describing economists' 'anxieties', means getting the policies which you approve adopted. This—if you don't happen to be a thorough-going dictator —requires persuasion of non-economists, unversed in the finer normative-positive distinctions in economic terminology. Effective persuasion often requires, or at least in the short run can often be powerfully assisted by blurring, and not emphasizing, the distinction between normative and positive (as, of course, so many advertisers with their parade of 'scientific'-sounding formulae are well aware). Separating out distinctly the positive scientific elements from the moral and normative will simply weaken the persuasiveness— possibly calling attention to the fact that one element is much more questionable than the other.

Sometimes it seems that those who most emphatically proclaim the programme of scientific positive economics are the most eagerly committed to 'doing good', or wielding influence, by persuasion, often on behalf of a political philosophy as much as any more narrowly economic *desiderata*; and it is difficult to believe that in the clash of commitments effective persuasion and the blurring of the normative-positive distinction does not often win out against the scientific commitment to its scrupulous observance. Nor does the clash of commitments arise only when policies are being discussed. It can and does go right back to the advocacy of fundamental theories of value, interest, or the inflationary process, when there may be a powerful ethical drive to persuade that a whole social or economic order is wrong or right.

When Keynes wrote of Marshall being 'too anxious to do good', he was envisaging, of course, the higher, or greater, or longer-run 'good' which Marshall might have 'done'. We venture to agree with the hypothesis suggested here that the greater, higher, longer-run good can be promoted by a firmer readiness on the part of economists regularly to put scientific criteria, including the promotion of clarity, before short-run persuasion and influence. But perhaps eradicating the hidden persuader requires a harder and deeper commitment than has been realized. It is not fulfilled by proffering a fervent and persuasive advocacy of, say, free trade, in which at the crucial point the normative-evaluative and positive-descriptive elements are ambiguously merged, followed by the pronouncement: 'As an economist I am concerned with what is and not with what ought to be, and I do not pronounce value-judgments'.

However, while calling attention to this ambiguity, at the root of the economist's commitment, between normative-positive clarity and effective persuasion and influence, we must go on to assume that the orthodox 'scientific' programme for a positive economics is to be taken at its face-value, and that it is, therefore, fundamentally agreed that the normative-positive distinction *should* be clearly maintained as far as it *can* be—even at the cost, sometimes, of effective persuasion.

3. But, of course, there cannot be any commitment or obligation to perform the impossible. The argument of the sceptics and critics of the 'orthodox' programme for a 'positive', 'scientific' economics is usually not—at any rate explicitly and on the surface—that this programme is *undesirable*, but that it is *impossible*, or even inconceivable of realization.

In some philosophical circles in recent years it seems to have been argued that the normative-positive distinction *cannot* be clearly drawn, at least in a number of significant areas, and that persuasive language and concepts blur the distinction between normative and positive, producing 'many economic statements, which appear at first sight to be merely descriptive' but which 'have value implications'.[1] This persuasiveness is essentially a question of ambiguity, and whatever may be the position in some branches of philosophy, or with regard to everyday language, there seems to be no reason if the scientific commitment to clarity is accepted, why ambiguities must persist, or why this commitment should be impossible to fulfil in economics, any more than it has been in the natural sciences. Starting from everyday speech, some terms—particularly if such an unfortunate one as 'welfare' is persisted with—will require analytical neutralizing. But even the ambiguities in this term 'welfare' are probably not going to give economists *very* much more trouble. They certainly *need* not, and if it continues to be used it may soon go the way of such originally, in 'everyday' terms, highly persuasive words as 'natural', 'productive', 'value', 'goods' and 'services', and be given and taken, in scientific contexts, with quite clearly recognized descriptive neutrality. Of course, errors in logic, and the pseudo-deduction of 'ought' from 'is', will continue to be perpetrated. But there is no reason why these should not yield to the critical processes

[1] I. M. D. Little, *A Critique of Welfare Economics*, 2nd Ed., p. 275.

of scientific procedure, like other mistakes in logic and mathematics. Of course, also, 'welfare' and other such terms may continue to be ambiguous or persuasive in 'everyday' usages, in contexts where disciplined criteria do not apply, and where persuasiveness, by whatever means, is relevant. But if and when significant failures arise in normative-positive clarity—and they certainly do occur, though less than they used to—then there are obvious means, such as the testability principle, for reducing them.

Here again, however, a question seems permissible about some economists' fundamental commitment. In discussing economic policies, some economists have described an objective—say socialism, a free market, or full employment—as 'impossible', when all that they can be justified in saying is that on their scale of preferences the objective is not worth their estimate of the costs. Similarly here, some of the arguments for the 'impossibility' of maintaining normative-positive distinctions may be expressive rather of an unwillingness to face the costs of forgoing persuasion and influence, which a strict commitment to the distinction requires. If the pretext of the impossibility of some absolute ideal clarity and purity in normative-positive distinctions—whatever that would mean—is invoked by ideologues for blurring and disregarding the distinction at will, then a dictum of R. H. Tawney's seems appropriate: 'It is like using the impossibility of absolute cleanliness as a pretext for rolling in a manure heap.'[1]

4. But the desirability and practicability of maintaining a clear distinction between normative and positive statements is, of course, separable from the doctrine that certain people, practitioners of a 'science', 'scientific' economists, or economists 'as such', should not simply confine themselves to statements that are reasonably unambiguous as between normative and positive, but are obliged also to confine themselves solely to positive statements, and to avoid all normative and evaluative ones, even when all reasonable clarity is maintained. On the one hand it is a question of a proposal regarding the recognition and description of a logical or methodological demarcation line between statements and theories, and, on the other hand, it is a question of some kind of professional obligation.

Though they are on different planes, the connection between the two questions is certainly close. In that normative-evaluative statements and theories are not in the relevant sense empirically testable and refutable, they cannot—following Popper's demarcation proposal—acquire 'scientific status' (not, of course, that all non-normative statements and theories can acquire it).[2] Therefore, the conclusion is suggested that scientists should confine their pronounce-

[1] *Equality*, 3rd Ed., 1952, p. 47.
[2] K. R. Popper, *The Logic of Scientific Discovery*, 1959, p. 37 and p. 278.

ments solely to testable statements and theories and not pronounce on or discuss normative-evaluative statements. But the conclusion does not inevitably follow. It *can*, and perhaps should, be proposed and held that 'scientists' should maintain clearly the distinction or demarcation but not necessarily confine themselves entirely to testable statements and theories.

Nevertheless, this doctrine or proposal of the avoidance by 'scientists' of all normative statements and theories has been respectably argued, particularly with regard to the duties of university teachers. Certainly there are, in any case, the inevitable normative-evaluative value-premises, or proposals, regarding choices of questions and of criteria for scientific study. But, apart from this pre-scientific range, it can be argued that normative-evaluative statements and theories should be excluded from 'science'. When policies are discussed, objectives can simply be postulated and not recommended or evaluated by the economist, who can confine himself to examining the possibilities of their attainment and to elucidating choice, without indulging in persuasion. But this doctrine may well be impracticable, and even undesirable, for example, for those working explicitly as 'economic advisers' (and, in any case, it is not clear that 'advising' should exclude persuasion, or be confined to elucidating the choice of policies without influencing it). Anyhow, there is the authority of Marshall, already quoted, for the broader doctrine that the economist, while aiming at a clear distinction between normative-evaluative and positive-empirical, should not confine himself solely to the latter:

'Economic studies are not to be limited to matters which are amenable to strictly scientific treatment. But those conclusions, whether in detail or in general, which are based on individual judgments as to the relative desirability of different social aims, or as to matters of fact which lie beyond the scope of any individual's special studies, should be clearly distinguished from those which claim to have been reached by scientific method.'[1]

5. A still more difficult problem in professional ethics is that of biased subjectivity regarding positive empirical 'matters of fact'. This is suggested by the second clause in the above dictum of Marshall, regarding clearly distinguishing from conclusions 'which claim to have been reached by scientific method', statements about 'matters of fact which lie beyond the scope of any individual's special studies'; or, one should add, 'matters of fact' *within* the scope of an individual's special studies—however this is delimited—as to which there are no statements or theories which have been tested or adequately tested,

---

[1] *Industry and Trade*, 4th Ed., 19 23, p. 676.

and as to which there is no scientific consensus. This includes many or most forecasts, and, for example, confident assertions on the one hand that progressive taxes considerably blunt incentives, or that economies of scale would be significant in a larger market, and, on the other hand, that they are, or do, not. Such assertions on matters of fact are sometimes pretty well as subjective as assertions that equalitarian policies are good or bad, though, of course, one is a 'positive' statement and the other a value-judgment. Of course, matters of fact are in principle testable and value-judgments are not (in the same sense, at any rate). But nothing like conclusive tests may have been made of what are asserted as 'matters of fact'.

Sometimes a way out is suggested by means of a distinction between the freedom and desirability of economists arguing strongly *among themselves* for their statements and theories, behind closed doors so to speak, while not employing them, without due reservations, in public policy debates. Such a distinction may be possible for, say, medical scientists, but it hardly seems workable, or to work, for economists. In the preface to the *General Theory* Keynes claimed to be addressing 'my fellow economists . . . whom I must first convince . . . not the general public':

'At this stage of the argument the general public, though welcome at the debate, are only eavesdroppers at an attempt by an economist to bring to an issue the deep divergences of opinion between fellow economists which have for the time being almost destroyed the practical influence of economic theory, and will, until they are resolved, continue to do so.'[1]

But, of course, almost inevitably, at no time was persuasion abated in the public field over current policies, that is, persuasion involving acceptance or rejection of Keynes's theories. Policies cannot possibly wait on the achievement of adequate testing and consensus regarding economists' theories, and, in fact, any new theory, with any conceivable bearing on current policies, tends to be promptly exploited politically, long before any adequate testing has been achieved. There seems, therefore, to be an important question of professional ethics not simply with regard to the maintenance of clarity between normative-evaluative and positive-empirical statements, but with regard to indicating the evidence, the extent and results of testing, and the degree of consensus, regarding positive-empirical statements and theories.

Lord Acton once proclaimed that: 'In the Moral Sciences Prejudice is Dishonesty'.[2] It is easy to object to this statement as naïve

---

[1] *The General Theory of Employment, Interest and Money*, p. VI.
[2] *Essays on Freedom and Power*, Meridian Books, 1955, p. 339.

and to point out that neither in, nor outside, the Moral Sciences, can every kind of prejudice, or everything that might reasonably be called 'prejudice', conceivably be avoided, and that 'Dishonesty' must therefore be a kind of inevitable original sin, a conclusion which many practitioners of the moral sciences would find rather unacceptable. There must, in any case, be the kind of 'prejudices', or value-premises or proposals, in favour of studying some questions rather than others, and in accordance with particular disciplined criteria. But surely Acton, though stating it with a certain aphoristic exaggeration, was attempting a worthy value-judgment or proposal regarding scientific or professional ethics. It has been argued that it is 'naïve' to suppose 'that scientific objectivity rests on the mental or psychological attitude of the individual scientist, on his training, care, and scientific detachment'[1] (or, it might be added, on his freedom from 'prejudice'). Certainly, as a sole source or basis for scientific objectivity, this would be completely unreliable. But the self-critical and therefore detached attitude of the individual 'scientist' has a useful and perhaps essential part to play, unless one believes 'holistically'—as Popper would put it—in the power of social processes, working themselves out apart from and above individuals. While he may give his untested or inadequately tested hypotheses an argumentative run for their money, up to a point, beyond this certain point caution and a self-critical confession of ignorance perhaps becomes more obligatory for the scientist. At any rate this is what some authorities hold:

'Would not economists' views command greater respect, and more truly educate the public in the issues involved, if they laid greater stress on the difficulty of coming to conclusions of general and universal validity, rather than ranged themselves in opposing schools, each, like medieval theologians in disputation, being quite certain that they have the answer.'[2]

6. As regards normative-evaluative statements, in addition to the value-premises or proposals as to questions for study and epistemological criteria, which may be regarded as pre-, meta-, or extra-scientific, at the other end of the scientific process, so to speak, value-judgments must be either postulated or asserted for any kind of policy recommendations. Some nineteenth-century utilitarians—and some economists, apparently, who seem, at least to some extent, to have followed them—have held that such value-judgments can somehow be derived from a science of ethics or of 'welfare'. More recently the attempt has persisted to simplify the necessary value-

[1] K. R. Popper, *The Poverty of Historicism*, paperback edition, 1961, p. 155.
[2] E. Devons, *Essays in Economics*, 1961, p. 44.

judgments, or reduce them to one or two simple widely-agreed principles, such as, for example, that more 'welfare' is better than less—which has often fatally confused the discussion of policies.

The statement of policy objectives must, to be adequate, be co-extensive with the full ramifying, significant effects, direct or indirect, of policies. For most realistic controversial policy-measures, these indirect ramifying effects may be very extensive. Not only have more ambitious 'macro-economic' policy-measures wider economic effects, not only are they aimed at a wider range of often conflicting economic objectives, they also have wider social and political effects. Therefore, the statement of value-judgments or objectives has to be much more complex and comprehensive than is often allowed for. Moreover, the complexity is multiplied further by the need to take account of uncertainty and to state uncertainty-attitudes, which the simplified logic of choice in terms of certainties has neglected. If policy objectives are not fully stated, either when they are simply being postulated or when they are being actually recommended, then the effects of a policy are not being fully accounted for, and not merely disagreement but normative-positive confusion may well ensue; as, for example, if a policy with the objective of promoting greater price-stability is discussed and it has effects on the rate of growth, or on distribution, or the political framework of the economy, which are not taken account of and as to which no explicit value-judgments are made. Moreover, there may be a temptation to evade the complexity of the task by tendentiously assuming a harmony between desired objectives which renders choice unnecessary since a higher fulfilment of one objective can be attained without the sacrificing of another objective. When value-judgments regarding policy objectives are clearly stated as such, and reasonably fully and precisely set out, the discussion can then proceed, of the positive empirical issues, and the nature of any disagreement will be much easier to discern.

Finally, political and constitutional principles, particularly the principles and values of an enlightened democracy, call for the maintenance of as clear a distinction as possible, in the discussion of policies, between preference functions or choice questions, on the one hand, and, on the other hand, possibility functions or 'information' questions; that is, between the choosing of objectives, which rests broadly and ultimately with the electorate, and, on the other hand, questions of how, and how far, the chosen objectives can be attained. Democratic theory seems to require that the role of the 'expert', economic or otherwise, be as clearly defined and limited as possible, and that his function should, as nearly as possible, be confined to elucidating and interpreting choices, rather than proclaiming them or aying them down. It has been said, obviously with some force, that t is difficult enough for economists themselves to keep this distinction clear, and that it is quite impossible, and quite vain to hope, that it can be kept clear in public political debate:

'Issues of economic policy are necessarily issues of politics. Even in theory it is difficult to distinguish between the economic and political aspects of a problem. Once the problem gets into the public arena, economics and politics are inextricably interwoven. . . . Even if the economist tries to distinguish between the economic and political elements in his argument, the public is unlikely to recognize the distinction. To the public an economist is an economist, and most people are not usually able, even if they were willing, to distinguish the political from the economic. Nor does the economist always try to help. . . . The need to distinguish between the economic and political element in any prescription is emphasized in academic economics, but when economists debate in public they frequently ignore this distinction.'[1]

Certainly, if the economist does not 'try to help', the distinction will never get over. But surely this is just the 'help' that an academic economist, if concerned with setting standards of public debate, ought primarily, and before all else to *try* to give. Unless to *some* extent this distinction is clear the choice of policies can hardly be elucidated. *Some* measure of clarity in respect of this distinction is fundamental for any 'rational' or reasonable discussion, and everything possible should be done to 'help' rather than to hinder clarity if one believes in government by reasonable discussion. But certainly, for those more interested in persuasive power it will be more effective to avoid or confuse the distinction.[2]

[1] E. Devons, *Essays in Economics*, 1961, p. 34 and p. 43.

[2] 'The first and most important point to be observed in every address to any Passion, Sentiment, Feeling etc. is, that it should not be introduced as such and plainly avowed, otherwise the effect will be in great measure lost.' R. Whately, *Rhetoric*, 2nd Edition, 1851, p. 49.

A SELECT BIBLIOGRAPHY

ALBERT, H.: *Ökonomische Ideologie und politische Theorie*, 1954.
— 'Das Werturteilsproblem im Lichte der logischen Analyse', *Zeitschrift für die gesamte Staatswissenschaft*, 1956, p. 410.
— 'Wissenschaft und Politik', in *Probleme der Wissenschaftstheorie, Festschrift für Victor Kraft*, 1960, p. 201.
ARCHIBALD, G. C.: 'Welfare Economics, Ethics and Essentialism', *Economica*, November 1959.
BERLIN, I.: *Two Concepts of Liberty*, 1958.
BOULDING, K.: *The Principles of Economic Policy*, 1958.
CHURCHMAN, C. W.: *Prediction and Optimal Decision*, 1961.
DAHL, R. A., and LINDBLOM, C. E.: *Politics, Economics and Welfare*, 1953.
DEVONS, E.: *Essays in Economics*, 1961, especially essays 1 and 2.
FRANK, P. G. (Ed.): *The Validation of Scientific Theories*, 1961, especially the contributions by P. G. Frank, C. W. Churchman and R. Rudner, pp. 13–35.
FRIEDMAN, M.: *Essays in Positive Economics*, 1953, especially Part I.
GIERSCH, H.: *Allgemeine Wirtschaftspolitik, Grundlagen*, 1960.
GRAAFF, J. DE V.: *Theoretical Welfare Economics*, 1957.
HALL, R. L.: 'Reflections on the Practical Application of Economics', *Economic Journal*, December 1959, p. 639.
LITTLE, I. M. D.: *A Critique of Welfare Economics*, Second Edition, 1957, especially Chapter V.
LUTZ, F. A.: 'Politische Überzeugungen und nationalökonomische Theorie', *Ordo*, Band IX, 1957.
MERING, O. VON: 'Social Ideals and Economic Theory', *Kyklos*, Vol. IV, 1950, pp. 172 ff.
MILLIKAN, M. F.: 'Inquiry and Policy: The Relation of Knowledge to Action' in *The Human Meaning of the Social Sciences*, edited by D. Lerner, paperback edition, 1959, p. 158.
MYRDAL, G.: *The Political Element in the Development of Economic Theory*, 1953.
— *Value in Social Theory*, edited by P. Streeten, 1958.
OAKESHOTT, M.: *Rationalism in Politics*, 1962.
OLIVER, H. M.: *A Critique of Socio-Economic Goals*, 1954.
PASSMORE, J. A.: 'Can the Social Sciences be Value Free?' in *Readings in the Philosophy of Science*, edited by H. Feigl and M. Brodbeck, 1953, p. 674.
POPPER, K. R.: *Conjectures and Refutations*, 1963, especially Chapters 10, 11, 16 and 18.
— *The Logic of Scientific Discovery*, 1959, especially Chapters 1–4.
— *The Open Society and its Enemies*, Fourth Edition, 1962, especially Chapters 23, 24 and 25.
— *The Poverty of Historicism*, paperback edition, 1961.

SAMUELSON, P.: *Problems of the American Economy*, The Stamp Memorial Lecture, 1961, 1962.

— 'What Economists Know' in *The Human Meaning of the Social Sciences*, edited by D. Lerner, paperback edition, 1959, p. 183.

SCHUMACHER, E. F.: *Roots of Economic Growth*, 1962.

SCHUMPETER, J. A.: *History of Economic Analysis*, 1954, especially Part I, Chapter 4, p. 33.

— 'Science and Ideology', *American Economic Review*, March 1949.

SMITHIES, A.: 'Economic Welfare and Policy' in *Economics and Public Policy*, Brookings Lectures 1954, 1955, p. 1.

STEVENSON, C. L.: *Ethics and Language*, 1944.

STIGLER, G. J.: 'The Economists and Equality' in *Five Lectures on Economic Problems*, 1950, p. 1.

— *The Goals of Economic Policy*, Henry Simons Lecture, 1958.

STREETEN, P.: 'Introduction' to *Value in Social Theory*, by G. Myrdal, 1958, p. IX.

THEIL, H.: *Economic Forecasts and Policy*, Second Edition, 1961.

TINBERGEN, J.: *Economic Policy: Principles and Design*, 1956.

VINER, J.: 'International Trade Theory and its Present Day Relevance' in *Economics and Public Policy*, Brookings Lectures 1954, 1955, p. 100.

— 'The Short View and the Long in Economic Policy' in *The Long View and the Short*, 1958, p. 103.

— 'Hayek on Freedom and Coercion', *Southern Economic Journal*, January 1961, p. 230.

WATSON, D. S.: *Economic Policy, Business and Government*, with an introduction by C. Kaysen, 1960, especially Chapters, 1, 2 and 5.

WEBER, M.: *Gesammelte Aufsätze zur Wissenschaftslehre*, 1922, especially 'Die "Objektivität" sozialwissenschaftlicher und soziapolitischer Erkenntnis', and 'Der Sinn der "Wertfreiheit" der soziologischen und ökonomischen Wissenschaften' (see the translations by E. A. Shils and H. A. Finch in *The Methodology of the Social Sciences*, 1949).

INDEX